The Cosmopolitan Imagin

CW01025250

Gerard Delanty provides a comprehensive assessment of the idea of cosmopolitanism in social and political thought which links cosmopolitan theory with critical social theory. He argues that cosmopolitanism has a critical dimension which offers a solution to one of the weaknesses in the critical theory tradition: failure to respond to the challenges of globalization and intercultural communication. Critical cosmopolitanism, he proposes, is an approach that is not only relevant to social scientific analysis but is also normatively grounded in a critical attitude. Delanty's argument for a critical, sociologically oriented cosmopolitanism aims to avoid, on the one hand, purely normative conceptions of cosmopolitanism and, on the other, approaches that reduce cosmopolitanism to the empirical expression of diversity. He attempts also to take cosmopolitan theory beyond the largely Western context with which it has generally been associated, claiming that cosmopolitan analysis must now take into account non-Western expressions of cosmopolitanism.

GERARD DELANTY is Professor of Sociology and Social and Political Thought at the University of Sussex.

The Cosmopolitan Imagination

The Renewal of Critical Social Theory

GERARD DELANTY

![Cambridge crest] **CAMBRIDGE**
UNIVERSITY PRESS

CAMBRIDGE UNIVERSITY PRESS
Cambridge, New York, Melbourne, Madrid, Cape Town, Singapore, São Paulo, Delhi

Cambridge University Press
The Edinburgh Building, Cambridge CB2 8RU, UK

Published in the United States of America by Cambridge University Press, New York

www.cambridge.org
Information on this title: www.cambridge.org/9780521695459

First published 2009

Printed in the United Kingdom at the University Press, Cambridge

A catalogue record for this publication is available from the British Library

ISBN 978-0-521-87373-4 hardback
ISBN 978-0-521-69545-9 paperback

For Tristan

Contents

Preface and acknowledgements

My intention in this book is to set out an argument for the contemporary relevance of cosmopolitanism for social science. More specifically my aim is to demonstrate the empirical and normative significance of cosmopolitanism for critical social theory. I have termed my approach critical cosmopolitanism to emphasize a dimension of cosmopolitanism that is not normally discussed in the now extensive literature on cosmopolitanism, namely the capacity for self-problematization and new ways of seeing the world that result when diverse peoples experience common problems. Against culturally oriented approaches, I see such problems as not cultural but social and economic and have significant political implications, which require a new kind of imagination – a cosmopolitan as opposed to national or market based ones – to address. The argument of this book is that such an imagination is present in the ways in which societies today, as in the past, have responded to the experience of globality.

In many ways this book is an expanded and re-worked version of an article on the idea of critical cosmopolitanism I published in 2006 in a special issue of the *British Journal of Sociology* on cosmopolitan sociology, edited by Ulrich Beck and Natan Sznaider, 'The Cosmopolitan Imagination: Critical Cosmopolitanism and Social Theory', *British Journal of Sociology* 57 (1): 25–47. Chapter 2 is a much extended and re-worked version of that article.

In the chapters that follow I have attempted to relate cosmopolitanism to debates in a wide variety of cultural and political issues relating to the consequences of globalization for contemporary societies. Europe is the specific concern of Chapters 8 and 9 where I am seeking to locate European issues in the context of what I have been calling for some time 'post-Westernization'. As is argued in Chapter 7 on modernity and global history, the true significance of cosmopolitanism is that it offers a critical approach to global issues and a way of looking at modernity beyond the limits of Eurocentrism.

Chapter 6 is a revised version of a chapter 'Dilemmas of secularism: Europe, religion and the problem of pluralism' in *Migration, Belonging and Exclusion in Europe*, edited by G. Delanty, P. Jones and R. Wodak, Liverpool University Press, 2008. It is included here with permission for the perspective it offers on post-secular society.

My ideas on cosmopolitanism have benefited from discussion with Ulrich Beck, Paul Blokker, Baogang He, David Inglis, Chris Rumford, Monica Sassatelli, Bo Strath and Shijun Tong, and from presentations at numerous conferences over the past six years. I am grateful to Piet Strydom for suggestions on linking cosmopolitanism to critical social theory.

A visiting appointment at Deakin University, Melbourne, in 2006 offered an excellent environment to develop some of the ideas that lay behind this book and to write the first draft.

Introduction

It is now widely accepted that one of the most significant developments in the present time is the enhanced momentum of globalization. Global forces have become more and more visible and take a huge variety of forms, from economic and technological to cultural and political. Globalization has brought about a tremendous transformation of social relations and it is no longer possible to think of nation-states, capitalism, the environment, citizenship, borders, consumption and communication in the same way. Virtually the entire span of human experience is in one way or the other influenced by globalization, by which I mean the overwhelming interconnectivity of the world. Yet the huge significance of globalization has some limits when it comes to social and political theory. There have been major works written on globalization as a societal condition and there has been increased recognition of the significance of transnational politics for political community. However, theories of globalization do not provide an interpretation of the social world that extends the methodological horizon of social analysis beyond a critique of some of the prevailing assumptions of modern social science. Manuel Castells's three-volume work on the information age, perhaps the most comprehensive analysis of globalization, explicitly avoided the elaboration of a normative theoretical framework and remained on an empirical level of analysis (Castells 1996, 1997, 1998). Globalization is a problem to be understood and explained, but it has not produced a significant philosophical or methodological framework. For the greater part, recognition of globalization as a reality has been incorporated into social and political analysis without leading to a significant shift in social and political theory.[1] Consideration of

---

[1] An exception in globalization theory is the work of Roland Robertson, who introduced a notion of globalization as world unicity in the sense of an awareness of the globally interconnected nature of the world (Robertson 1992). In this account, globalization is most notably present in local contexts rather than in supranational spaces.

moral and political problems such as rights and justice has of course been greatly influenced by the wider context of globalization, the rise of 'anti-globalization' movements and normative transnationalism. This critical and normative perspective on globalization opens up a range of theoretical and philosophical questions that are of great importance for a critical social and political theory.

The argument put forward in this book is that the normative significance of globalization rather consists of a different kind of reality beyond the condition of globalization as such and necessitates a new kind of imagination, which can be called the cosmopolitan imagination. The normative and methodological implications of globalization can be more readily assessed from the more conceptionally and philosophically nuanced position of cosmopolitan theory, which while admittedly a diffuse field is one that offers a more far-reaching level of analysis than is suggested by the notion of globalization. Cosmopolitanism offers a promising way to link the analysis of globalization to developments in social and political theory. It is also a fruitful way to continue the cultural turn in social science, for the cultural dimensions of globalization resonate with new conceptions of cultural cosmopolitanism. As an approach to current times, cosmopolitanism offers both a critical-normative standpoint and an empirical-analytical account of social trends. While the normative literature has been the most developed and based on a long history of political philosophy, the social scientific literature has been steadily growing in recent years. This book aims specifically to advance the social scientific approach to cosmopolitanism and to propose a broad framework for a cosmopolitan critical social theory.

Cosmopolitanism offers critical social theory with a means to adjust to new challenges. It offers a solution to one of the weaknesses in the critical theory tradition of both the Frankfurt School and Habermas's social theory, namely a failure to respond to the challenges of globalization and move beyond a preoccupation with an exclusively Western range of issues.[2] The idea of a critical cosmopolitanism is relevant to the renewal of critical theory in its traditional concern with the critique of social reality and the search for immanent transcendence, a concept that lies at the core of critical theory.[3] It also opens a route out of the

---

[2] See also Freundlieb (2000) and Mendieta (2007).
[3] I am grateful to Piet Strydom for drawing my attention to the centrality of the concept of immanence transcendence for critical theory.

critique of domination and a general notion of emancipation that has so far constrained critical theory. In addition, it offers a promising approach to connect normative philosophical analysis with empirical sociological inquiry. The cosmopolitan imagination offers critical social theory a normative foundation that makes possible new ways of seeing the world. Such forms of world disclosure have become an unavoidable part of social reality today in terms of people's experiences, identities, solidarities and values. These dimensions represent the foundations for a new conception of immanent transcendence; it is one that lies at the heart of the cosmopolitan imagination in so far that this is a way of viewing the world in terms of its immanent possibilities for self-transformation and which can be realized only by taking the cosmopolitan perspective of the Other as well as global principles of justice

There has been widespread recognition of the salience of cosmopolitanism for an understanding of the present time. While cosmopolitanism has become influential within normative political theory,[4] it has been taken up in a different guise in disciplines such as history, sociology, anthropology and cultural studies where the tendency has been towards a more situated or rooted understanding of cosmopolitanism as always contextualized. This has specific methodological implications for social and political analysis and points to the need for a new conceptual framework to understand the interconnectivity of the world and go beyond national frames of reference. It would not be inaccurate to speak of a cosmopolitan turn in social science. Recent contributions by sociologists and social theorists have attempted to open up new ways of understanding the social world and to explore the methodological implications of cosmopolitanism for social science.[5] Ulrich Beck, who has been at the forefront of sociological cosmopolitanism, has argued for a methodological cosmopolitanism to replace the methodological nationalism of much of social science. There has been widespread recognition of the diminishing significance of the nation-state and the related notion of 'society' as a territorially

---

[4] See for example Brock and Brighouse (2005) and Tan (2004).
[5] See for example the special issue of the *British Journal of Sociology* 57 (1), 2006 on cosmopolitan sociology, edited by U. Beck and N. Szaider and the special issue of the *European Journal of Social Theory* 10 (1) 2007 on cosmopolitanism. See also the special issue of *Theory, Culture and Society* 19 (1–2) 2002; Holton 2009; Kendall *et al.* 2009.

bounded reality (Touraine 1998; Urry 2000).[6] Within mainstream political science Pippa Norris (1997) has argued for the importance of cosmopolitanism. But there is little of a substantive nature on the relation between normative accounts and methodological considerations for empirical social science. Recent publications have stressed the relevance of cosmopolitanism to non-Western societies (see Hawley (2008), Fojas (2005), Kwok-bun (2005) and Pollock (2006). However this is largely an undeveloped field but undoubtedly one where the future of cosmopolitan analysis lies.

The main approaches to cosmopolitanism can be summed up as follows. First, there is cosmopolitanism as a political philosophy that is concerned with normative principles relating to world citizenship and global governance. In such accounts, as most prominently in the work of Held and Archibugi, cosmopolitanism is seen as a new kind of political framework based on global conceptions of rights and justice and in which democracy can be established on a new basis beyond the nation-state (Archibugi 2003, 2008). This can be termed global cosmopolitanism. Second, there is cosmopolitanism in the sense of liberal multiculturalism where the emphasis is on plurality and the embracing of difference in the creation of a post-national political community (Calhoun 2003a; Stevenson 2002). In such approaches, which include Habermas's discourse theory and which may be termed post-national cosmopolitanism, the focus is less on global governance than on nationally specific forms of political community. Third, there is cosmopolitanism as transnational movements, such as diasporas and hybridity (Clifford 1992; Hannerz 1996; Nederveen Pieterse 2004, 2006). Culturally oriented approaches in anthropology, cultural studies and sociology are increasingly stressing the cosmopolitan nature of transnational processes and global culture, such as new modes of cultural consumption and lifestyles, identities and communication. In such approaches, which can be termed transnational cosmopolitanism, there is a strong emphasis on hybridity and the mixed nature of cultural phenomena, as well as a concern with aesthetic cosmopolitanism (Szersznski and Urry 2002). Finally, a fourth development has become apparent in a view of cosmopolitanism as a methodological approach

---

[6] See the special issue of the *European Journal of Social Theory* 10 (2) 2007 'Does the Prospect of a General Sociological Theory Still Mean Anything (in Times of Globalization)?'.

for social science responding to the challenge of globalization. As is best illustrated in the work of Ulrich Beck, it is possible to speak today of a cosmopolitan condition as the reality of contemporary society and which necessitates a new methodological approach. In this case, cosmopolitanism is not confined to identifiably transnational processes as such, but pervades the very nature of social relations and institutions more generally. In the work of William Connolly it extends into the domain of affect theory (Connolly 2002).

These approaches are varied, but it can be noted that underlying all is a view of cosmopolitanism as a new orientation in the world today and which has important implications for both normative theory and empirical analysis. Cosmopolitanism as a theoretical approach suggests a critical attitude as opposed to an exclusively interpretative or descriptive approach to the social world. In this sense it retains the normative stance of traditional notions of cosmopolitanism while offering a critical evaluation of current developments. The appeal of cosmopolitanism is partly due to the legacy of postmodernism in so far as this has opened up new ways of thinking about culture and politics. Although postmodernism has faded in its appeal as a foundation for social science, its impact has been considerable in the attention it has given to the mixed and overlapping nature of culture and the relativization of universal standpoints. This confluence of postmodernism and cosmopolitanism is noticeable in much of the literature that concerns cultural issues as well as postcolonial questions. Indeed, it is in postcolonial theory that important insights have been made in disengaging cosmopolitanism from purely Western assumptions (Breckenridge *et al.* 2002). Another and related topic is aesthetic cosmopolitanism, especially in relation to the spaces of encounters and dialogue that are constituted in contemporary arts (Paperstergiadis 2006). However, it would be a mistake to see cosmopolitanism as a product of postmodernism. Its roots are much older and it should rather be situated in the context of modernity and the constitution of the subject around new modes of experience and interpretation. In addition, the relevance of cosmopolitanism for social science is due in no small part to theories of globalization that emphasize its non-economic dimensions. The growing interest in cultural and political expressions of globalization, as in the work of Robertson (1992), has invariably drawn attention to the interaction of the global with the local. One of the central claims of this book is that this dynamic opens up a range of considerations that bring globalization theory in the direction of a new conception of cosmopolitanism as a mode of world disclosure and as a way in which to theorize the transformation of subjectivity in terms of relations of self, Other and world.

The distinctive approach adopted in this book will be termed critical cosmopolitanism in order to emphasize its essentially critical and transformative nature.[7] Invoked in this conception of cosmopolitanism is a new definition of social reality as opposed to a set of cosmopolitan principles or a cosmopolitan agent or political project. Rather than seeing cosmopolitanism simply as an ideal, as is indicated by the title of this book, the cosmopolitan perspective requires a particular imagination – the cosmopolitan imagination. In this respect, the aim is to advance the sociological approach to cosmopolitanism in a way that draws on the insights of some of the main contributions to cosmopolitan theory. The specific challenge now is to link the political philosophy of cosmopolitanism with the sociologically oriented approaches and the contributions of global history. Although the concerns of the various approaches are clearly different, there are common themes and a rich body of literature that is rarely brought together. The basic view of cosmopolitanism taken in this book is that it is rooted in two contexts: a new definition of social reality of immanent possibilities and a conception of modernity that emphasizes its multiple and interactive nature.

The notion of social reality that is referred to here is an essentially relational one. The social refers less to a clear-cut definition of 'society' as national society or a territorially or culturally bounded entity, but a field of social relations in which conflicting orientations are played out. In addition to this emphasis on conflict, contingency is an important methodological dimension of the cosmopolitan imagination for the analysis of the social world. Social action occurs increasingly in situations of uncertainty and there the outcome of individual or collective decisions is often determined by global contexts. The relational conception of the social does not exhaust all senses of the real, for reality is also a form of human experience. As will be argued throughout this book, cosmopolitan orientations and attitudes give expression to specific forms of experience of the world which also entail the interpretation of the world. The cosmopolitan imagination is both an experience and an interpretation of the world (Wagner 2008).[8]

---

[7] The term has been used by others, for example Mignolo (2000). See also Rumford (2008).
[8] On experience and interpretation, see Wagner 2008.

Four dimensions of the social that are constitutive of the cosmopolitan imagination can be highlighted. First, a cosmopolitan view of the social stresses, cultural difference and pluralization. This concern with cultural pluralism and heterogeneity ties cosmopolitanism closely with radical or postmodern approaches in multiculturalism; it suggests a view of not just social groups, but of societies as mixed and overlapping as opposed to being homogeneous. The recognition of cultural difference as both a reality and a positive ideal for social policy is one of the principal features of the cosmopolitan imagination. Second, the cosmopolitan moment occurs in the context of global–local relations. As mentioned, cosmopolitanism is not reducible to globalization but refers to the interaction of global forces with local contexts. This interaction takes many forms, ranging from, for instance, creolization and diasporic cultures to global civil-society movements. Third, the negotiation of borders. Territorial space has been displaced by new kinds of space, of which transnational space is the most significant. In this reconfiguration of borders, local and global forces are played out and borders in part lose their significance and take forms in which no clear lines can be drawn between inside and outside, the internal and the external. A cosmopolitan perspective on the social world gives a central place to the resulting condition of ambivalence in which boundaries are being transcended and new ones established. Thinking beyond the established forms of borders is an essential dimension of the cosmopolitan imagination. Fourth, the reinvention of political community around global ethics, and what Bryan Turner (2006: 140), has referred to as a 'cosmopolitan epistemology of a shared reality'. Without a normative dimension, cosmopolitanism loses its significance as a concern with finding alternatives and with transcending the immediately given. The challenges raised by the previously mentioned dimensions of the social all raise normative questions relating to difference, globalization and borders. The social cannot be separated from cosmopolitan principles and the aspiration to establish a new kind of political community in which national interests have to be balanced with other kinds of interests. Foregrounded in this are notions of care, rights and hospitality.

The definition of the social that emerges from these considerations introduces both a critical and a sociological perspective into the cosmopolitan imagination. The important point to be stressed is that cosmopolitanism has a social dimension as opposed to either a political or cultural dimension conceived of in isolation from a concept of the social. A more complete account of this notion of critical cosmopolitanism requires a perspective that goes beyond the limits of the present to a historical contextualization. While globalization is generally associated with relatively recent developments, although by no means confined to current times, cosmopolitanism clearly has a much longer history. This will be discussed in detail in Chapter 1. The approach taken in this book is that the cosmopolitan imagination has been integral to the spirit of modernity and can be fully understood only by an analysis of the dynamics of modernity. The following four points sum up the main direction of the argument.

First, one of the key dynamics of modernity is the continuous transformation of present time by political designs for the future. The consciousness of modernity emerged with the experience of the unlimited possibilities of human freedom and the vision that human beings can create the world in a new image. Modernity signalled the break from the past and a great optimism about the future. The cosmopolitan vision of a new order was a central orientation within modernity and modernity itself was also greatly animated by cosmopolitan ideas of world openness and self-transformation. Second, modernity opened up the social and political world to new orders of interpretation in which the universe of meaning and interpretation was continuously expanded as a result of the encounter with new contexts. This has cosmopolitan implications for human experience in the constant self-problematization of what was previously taken for granted. This dimension of modernity had in addition a broadly critical thrust in the tendency towards self-confrontation in light of the encounter with the Other and with new modes of interpretation arising out of exchange, encounters and dialogue. Third, while modernity has often been associated with Western or European civilization, it should be seen as having a far wider civilizational relevance. Modernity can emerge in any civilization and while the Western tradition has indeed been important in shaping other experiences of modernity, this too has been a highly differentiated one. Rather than speak of modernity in the singular, it should be seen as having multiple forms. In this respect the civilizational dimension is particularly important, since the different forms modernity takes can be attributed more to civilizational differences than to, for instance, different national traditions. Fourth, the multiple nature of modernity is in itself an interesting instance of cosmopolitanism, but more significant for cosmopolitan analysis is the inter-civilizational dynamic by which civilizations interact and as they do so they undergo change. This perspective draws attention to the role of cultural encounters, exchange, dialogue and the overlapping nature of civilizations as multiple orders of interpretation.

The implications of this approach to cosmopolitan analysis are far-reaching and go beyond conventional assumptions about both cosmopolitanism and modernity as Western or as universal. Locating cosmopolitanism as an orientation within modernity avoids a narrow view of cosmopolitanism as a recent development and a product of global culture or Westernization. Cosmopolitanism can instead be seen as one of the key dynamics of modernity and a context in which societies deal with the normative challenges raised by difference, the reconfiguration of borders, and the many questions brought about by globalization. If modernity is conceived of in multiple and inter-civilizational terms, cosmopolitanism loses its connection with simple notions of universalism. This means that the only acceptable kind of cosmopolitanism today can be post-universal, that is a universalism that has been shaped by numerous particularism as opposed to an underlying set of values (see Connolly 2002; Julien 2008; Tong 2009). This does not mean an entirely relativistic postmodernism, but the recognition that universal claims or normative principles are always limited and often context bound and, as Connolly has argued, can extend into the domain of the neuropolitical. Concretely it means that cosmopolitan orientations simply take different forms and can be found in many different cultural contexts and historical periods.

One of the most important developments in recent times within social and political science is the recognition that the Western understanding of the world needs to be considerably revised. At least three reasons for this can be given. First, the enhanced speed of globalization in all its forms has led to a more connected world. Second, there has been increasing recognition of postcolonial critiques of Western political thought and from within mainstream Western social science recognition of alternative routes to modernity. Finally, major shifts in the international political order have led to a post-Western world in which new centres of political power have arisen. Europe has become more important as a global economic and political actor and, in Asia, China and India have emerged as major economic powers. This all points to what can be called a post-Western world, in the sense that the global world can no longer be considered primarily Western (Delanty 2003). The diversity of cultures, social movements and forms of political community do not correspond to a simple model of Westernization. For these reasons the notion of a post-Western world is relevant to the current situation in which contradictory global, regional and nationalist tendencies are in evidence.

Within Europe itself there has been considerable attention paid to the tremendous transformation of the nation-state as a result of Europeanization. However, there has been less attention paid to the implications of the emerging post-Western world for European self-understanding. In particular, current scholarship has not properly assessed the multiple ways in which political community is shaped by different cultural contexts and the implications of divergent routes to modernity for inter-cultural understanding and political coopera-tion. The collapse of communism has not only signified the integration of Europe largely on the terms of Western Europe, but it also signifi-cantly has shifted the core of the European integration project east-wards, thereby questioning a purely Western European definition of the project; it also draws attention to different civilizational back-grounds of Europe and thus 'multiple Europes', and challenging a Western European definition of the modern nation-state and its role in European integration. At the same time, Europe's global cen-trality appears to be on the decline now that Asia is increasingly gaining prominence as an economic as well as a cultural and political player (Delanty 2006). The question arises to what extent European modernity is still the dominant modernity, also now that the West is divided, and whether other modernities are gaining in importance (Therborn 2003).

What is needed is an understanding of how political community is being shaped today in light of new kinds of experience. The challenge is to avoid an over-emphasis both on Westernization and on global differentiation and also global polarization. On the one side, there is much evidence – within Europe as well as in the rest of the world – of societal differentiation and, with this, in many cases, challenges to Western cultural and political models; on the other hand, there is some-thing like a global normative political culture taking shape around issues relating to democracy, human rights and climate change, and which is in evidence in increased cosmopolitanism in terms of identities and other dimensions of political community. The upshot of this is that political community cannot be understood simply in terms of the importation of a single Western model or global uniformity and nor can it be understood in the terms of a retreat into particularistic nativism or anti-Westernism. It has been increasingly recognized that there has been a worldwide shift towards cosmopolitanism, a development that is evident in cultural orientations, cognitive shifts and in more overt political forms, as well as in transnational identifications. This shift, however, has taken place in a context of colliding global and nativisitic forces. While there has been increased attention given to the transformation of the nation-state within Europe, wider analysis has been limited. What is urgently needed is a greater understanding of cosmopolitan trends.

Three levels of analysis are required, of which the third is the most important. First, any analysis will have to take as its starting point the context of the local and in particular major national, regional and civilizational traditions. Second, the impact of the culture of the Other, ranging from the influence of other nations to global forces, must be brought to bear on the analysis of the Self. In addition to this interplay of the local and the global by which Self and Other interact, there is also the cosmopolitan dimension of ways of thinking, cognition and feeling that derive neither from the native culture nor from the culture of the Other, but from the interaction of both. This is often referred to as universal or world culture, by which is meant the development of an orientation to the world as opposed to either nativism or the adoption of the culture of the Other. This analysis insists on the distinction between the cosmopolitan and the global, since the former is constituted in shifts in self-understanding that arise when both Self and Other are transformed. This approach allows for a richer and more culturally robust understanding of the relation between, for instance, the political community of the nation-state and that associated with transnational civil society or global culture. The notion of a 'third culture' is relevant here (Restivo 1991). Cosmopolitanism is a third level of culture in which diverse social actors – communities, nations, civilizations – can engage with the world. Such a third culture should be understood as a means of interconnecting different positions into forms of world disclosure that transforms the culture of all parties. The 'fusion of horizons' that Gadamer (1975) believed to lie at the core of the hermeneutics of cultural understanding must be understood today as achieved through inter-cultural communication on a global scale.

It is arguably the case that in the present day cosmopolitanism has become one of the most important expressions of modernity and some of its most innovative expressions can be found in the non-Western world. While Europe – and in particular the Europeanization of the nation-state – has been a focus of much discussion around cosmopolitanism, an important but neglected area is Asian cosmopolitanism. Whether in Europe or in Asia, the notion of cosmopolitanism implied by the analysis developed in this book is post-Western. This is an important dimension of the general conception of cosmopolitanism being advocated. As a result of the worldwide impact of global forces and the growing importance of societies that have emerged from non-Western modernities, a genuinely global assessment of the current day needs to be less confident about the centrality of the West and the equation of globalization with Westernization. Europe, as will be argued in Chapter 9, is itself increasingly post-Western in that it can now be seen to be a product of diverse modernities and evolving a post-national identity. Europe today is no longer a Western enclave centred around the core founding states, but a larger and more diverse political community in which the Central and Eastern heritage has become more prominent. But it is in the wider world that the post-Western constellation is most visible and nowhere is this clearer than in Asia.

The direction of the analysis given here shifts the emphasis from substantive cultural or political entities, such as specific societies or social agents, towards processual dynamics such as forms of cultural interaction, developmental processes and modes of self-transformation. In methodological terms, the cosmopolitan approach advocated in this book stresses the interrelated nature of cultures. Rather than seeing cultures as different, the cosmopolitan perspective sees them as related. If anything captures the cosmopolitan perspective, it is the attempt to understand the processes by which societies undergo change in their moral and cultural capacities. The self-transformative moment is central to cosmopolitanism and distinguishes it from other processes, such as globalization or transnationalism which are concerned with the question of the transformation of the subject. Without a transformation in self-understanding it does not make much sense to speak of cosmopolitanism. Thus for this reason cosmopolitanism is not a simple matter of diversity or transnational movement. Cosmopolitanism concerns self-problematization and while diversity will, by the pluralizing nature of cosmopolitanism, be inevitable, the reflexive and critical self-understanding of cosmopolitanism cannot be neglected. Cosmopolitanism must be seen as one of the major expressions of the tendency in modernity towards self-problematization and reflexivity. The normative implications of global culture and transnationalism are best seen in terms of cosmopolitan shifts in self-understanding and the articulation of new cultural models that open up different conceptions of political community and social organization.

This, then, is the answer to the criticism that cosmopolitanism pertains only to elites. The methodological approach associated with critical cosmopolitanism has as its primary aim the relational field of social relations and cultural modes of interpretation through which societies undergo change. As will be argued in Chapter 2, this can be related to the micro dimension of social analysis, collective actors, or whole societies or models of modernity. Cosmopolitanism is thus best understood as a dynamic or orientation rather than a concrete identity or a specific culture and, as such, it can arise anywhere and at any time. It does not simply refer to cases or situations that are called cosmopolitan by those involved in them. The critical aspect of cosmopolitanism concerns rather the internal transformation of social and cultural phenomena through self-problematization, pluralization and developmental change arising out of competing cultural models in the context of a third culture. The cosmopolitan imagination entails a view of society as an ongoing process of self-constitution through the continuous opening up of new perspectives in light of the encounter with the Other. In the analysis to be developed in Chapters 2 and 7, this is discussed along the lines of the logic of translation, here understood as cultural translation. It is the nature of translation that the very terms of the translation are altered in the process of translation and something new is created. This is because every translation is at the same time an evaluation. Translation was once a means to communication and to render another culture intelligible, but with the advent of modernity translation became a cultural form in itself and can be understood as a paradigmatic third culture. With the principle that every culture can translate itself and others, came the possibility of incorporating the perspective of the Other into one's own culture.

A further rejoinder can also be made to the objection that cosmopolitanism is an elite movement or an abstract ideal that has no substance. As many contributions have argued, cosmopolitanism is rooted in real experiences, such as those of migrants and ethnic communities formed out of transnational migration or national upheaval (Sassen 2007). It is in these situations that the 'fusions of horizons' is negotiated as an interpretation of those experiences. Cosmopolitanism has a popular form and like nationalism can take 'banal' forms in everyday life. But the rooted nature of especially recent cosmopolitanism is much more than what is found in individual experiences; it has major societal expressions in, for instance, establishing an international normative order based on human rights and multicultural forms of political community in which cultural difference gains positive recognition. There are thus many ways it is possible to claim that cosmopolitanism is situated and therefore 'real'.

It follows from this perspective that cosmopolitanism must somehow invoke a sense of openness as opposed to a closed or particularistic view of the world. This orientation, which can be regarded as central to the cosmopolitan imagination, can be referred to as an orientation towards world openness or world disclosure. It is in the interplay of Self, Other and World that cosmopolitan processes come into play. The abstract category of the world provides a frame of reference for relations between Self and Other that gives to the cosmopolitan imagination its distinctive characteristic of transcending Self and Other and bringing into play the transformative and self-reflexive moment. The notion of the cosmopolitan imagination relies on a specific meaning of the idea of the imaginary or imagination. As used in this book, it is the sense intended by Cornelius Castoriadis's notion of the imaginary as the way in which societies symbolically constitute themselves. For Castoriadis (1987), all societies possess an imaginary dimension, since they must answer certain symbolic questions as to their basic identity, their goals and limits. Cosmopolitanism can certainly be seen as one such imaginary component of society and can be contrasted to, for instance, Benedict Anderson's (1983) somewhat affirmative conception of the imaginary as a national imaginary. Cosmopolitanism as a creative process can thus be seen as entailing the opening up of normative questions within the cultural imaginaries of societies. In this sense, cosmopolitanism refers to an orientation that resides less in a specific social condition than in an imagination that can take many different forms depending on historical context and social circumstances. Conceived of in terms of an imaginary, it is not then a matter of an ideal that transcends reality or a purely philosophical or utopian idea but an immanent orientation that takes shape in modes of self-understanding, experiences, feelings and collective identity narratives. The imaginary is both a medium of experience and an interpretation of that experience in a way that opens up new perspectives on the world.

Both the concept of modernity and that of the social that is proposed in this approach are non-reductive and multi-perspectival. Modernity has been characterized as a site of tensions and the social a field of symbolic conflicts.[9] The notion of cosmopolitanism that is being advanced under the general heading of critical cosmopolitanism takes on a similar characteristic. Cosmopolitanism makes sense only as a site of tensions in which different principles and orientations are played out. The most significant tension that constitutes the field of cosmopolitanism is the interaction of the global and the local. It is in this respect that cosmopolitanism represents a different reality from globalization in that it concerns rather the field of tensions when global forces interact with the local. This is not a simple condition of the latter merely reacting to the global as an external reality. The local and the global are intertwined in complex ways and in ways that have created new spaces in which a cosmopolitan reality has been constituted. Such spaces are not beyond or outside the national or local, which should not be seen as external and merely reactive to globalization.

Another instance of the cosmopolitan moment resides in the interaction of Self and Other. In this case, too, the cosmopolitan dimension occurs in the interactive moment when a transformation in self-understanding happens as a result of the interaction. In short, cosmopolitan space is the space of new dynamics, interactive moments, and conflicting principles and orientations. This approach, then, places cosmopolitanism as the heart of social transformations and a key dimension of social change today. While specifically relevant to the present day, cosmopolitanism is also highly relevant to historical and comparative analysis and in particular to global history.

The approach to cosmopolitan analysis developed in this book attempts to move beyond the current conceptions. The political philosophy of cosmopolitanism for the greater part operates on a normative level of analysis and has relatively little to contribute to empirical analysis or to social theory. Normative considerations relating to

---

[9] I refer here to Arnason (1991).

moral and political standpoints are important for a critically oriented social science, but they need to be embedded in a framework that is empirically meaningful. With the exception of studies on global politics, where the empirical and the normative have been more success-fully linked, the empirical analytical dimension has been weak. However, it would be a mistake for cosmopolitan theory to lose the link with the normative. The tendency in recent cosmopolitan theory in social science is to reduce cosmopolitanism to transnational space or cultural diversity. For many theorists looking beyond global politics, cosmopolitanism is chiefly characterized by hybridity and is a product of transnational movements. In such accounts the critical factor is opposition to nations and thus an opposition is set up between nation-hood and cosmopolitanism. The critical cosmopolitanism position developed in this book offers a different view. Transnational move-ments, cultural diversity and hybrid cultures do not in themselves con-stitute cosmopolitanism, although they are undoubtedly important preconditions for cosmopolitanism. More important is the critical moment in which changes in self-understanding occur as a result of global challenges. This angle to cosmopolitanism offers what can be regarded as essential, namely an evaluative standpoint. For instance, a cosmopolitanism perspective does not simply involve accepting the views of the Other but requires in some way a problematization of one's own assumptions as well as those of the Other. Without mutual criticism and self-problematization, cosmopolitanism loses its force and become reduced to the mere condition of diversity. As argued in this book, the cosmopolitan imagination points in the direction of a discur-sive approach to the encounter with the Other. As will be discussed in Chapter 10, this has important implications for notions of inter-cultural dialogue as well as for multiculturalism.

It can be finally remarked that while there is clearly an opposition between nationalism and cosmopolitanism, there is not a fundamental division in that cosmopolitanism does not signify the end of the nation. Cosmopolitanism certainly involves a post-national conception of poli-tical community and in methodological terms an alternative to metho-dological nationalism. However, it should be seen as an orientation within political community and in wider terms the social world and modernity rather than specifically as an alternative to nation-states and nationalism. There is no reason why national identities cannot embody cosmopolitan forms of identity or why nation-states cannot incorporate cosmopolitan principles. Indeed, there are many examples of the mutual implication of national and cosmopolitan projects, identities and forms of political community to reject a purely dichotomous view. The national has never been entirely national, but has always been embroiled with immanent cosmopolitan orientations.

1 | The rise and decline of classical cosmopolitanism

Introduction

Cosmopolitanism is today one of the most important ways of making sense of the contemporary world and, as will be argued in this chapter, it has been an influential movement within modernity. However it is in fact a product of antiquity and can be said to be one of the oldest intellectual movements that have shaped the way we think about the world. In this chapter I want to outline and discuss the history of the cosmopolitan idea in order to provide a background for contemporary cosmopolitanism. I am making a distinction between classical and contemporary cosmopolitanism roughly in line with the re-emergence of a new kind of cosmopolitanism in the present day along with a notion of globality. The older cosmopolitanism, which I am calling classical cosmopolitanism, has been generally associated with a concern with universalism and can be contrasted to the post-universalism of contemporary forms of cosmopolitanism. Moreover, unlike cosmopolitanism today, classical cosmopolitanism from antiquity to the Enlightenment has had a more pronounced Western orientation, though as I shall argue it cannot be entirely dismissed as Eurocentric and it is possible to find non-European expressions of cosmopolitanism throughout history.[1]

My aim in this chapter is to make two arguments, which in a sense are arguments about the double face of classical cosmopolitanism. The first is to show that while classical cosmopolitanism has indeed been a significant feature of the European cultural and political heritage, it is in fact less Eurocentric than is often assumed. To pursue this I shall endeavour to argue that the cosmopolitan imagination in Europe has had a hermeneutical and a self-critical dimension which can be related to an inter-cultural understanding of the world. The argument developed in

---

[1] There is clearly a difficulty with this in that the term cosmopolitanism is used to make sense of phenomena that are not self-consciously cosmopolitan.

this chapter goes beyond the limits of a European cosmopolitanism to point to the existence of alternative cosmopolitan orientations in non-Western civilizations.

The second aim of the chapter is to show that in addition to the hermeneutical conception of cosmopolitanism as entailing cultural dialogue between civilizations, classical cosmopolitanism was also closely related with one of the main political philosophies of Europe, namely republicanism. Sometimes in tension with republicanism, cosmopolitanism was often inseparable from it. This connection between republicanism and cosmopolitanism corresponds to the distinction between a closed vision of the human polity and an open one. It was a distinction that reflected the ambivalence of the European political heritage towards an inclusive and exclusive view of political community. Despite the often compelling force of the cosmopolitan imagination, it was the inclusive and closed vision that gained ascendancy in modern Europe. In this chapter this story is one of the rise and the decline of cosmopolitanism, which became overshadowed by nationalism. In telling the story of the decline of classical cosmopolitanism in this way, the aim is not to suggest that nationalism and cosmopolitanism are contrary forces, for they were often intertwined. The thesis is that cosmopolitanism represents the immanent possibilities within modernity and which has often been contained within nationalism as an unrealized potential.

The theme of the ambivalence of cosmopolitanism developed in this chapter will be central to later chapters when it will be argued that cosmopolitan moral and political orientations are expressed in many different forms, including national culture and global culture. The particular and the universal are not entirely different perspectives but are bound up with each other. Indeed, I shall argue that cosmopolitanism captures precisely this ambivalence. Although the story of the rise of cosmopolitanism has often been told with an emphasis on its Greek origins and its revival with Kant's Enlightenment project, all too neglected in this narrative is the inter-civilizational dimension including non-Western expressions of cosmopolitanism. This is the ambivalence of a universalism and a particularism that lies at the heart of the cosmopolitan imagination. However, the purpose of this chapter is to provide a critical reading of the history of classical European cosmopolitanism in order to have a basis for looking at contemporary theories of cosmopolitanism as well as new and alternative expressions.

The origins of cosmopolitanism

The origins of cosmopolitanism lie in the ancient civilizations and can be directly related to the emergence of civilizations based on universalistic principles. Greek, Chinese, Hindu and later Islamic and Christian civilizations gave rise to ways of thinking that promoted an inclusive vision of human community. The diversity of peoples and the pursuit of a civilizational unity was the central animus that inspired cosmopolitan thought in several civilizations. Ancient Greek thought gave rise to what Baldry (1965) referred to as an attitude of mind centred on the unity of humanity. The Chinese notion of '*Tian Zia*' – meaning literally 'all under heaven' – implied a notion of world society and can be seen as an early form of cosmopolitanism. Mo Tzu (480–390 BC) promoted a cosmopolitan or universal love, an outwardly oriented disposition of mind which is devoted to achieving the benefit of others.[2] His notion of 'love is defined in terms comparable Kant's principle of treating all men as ends in themselves' (Dallmayr 1996; Schwartz 1985: 146–7). Menicus, the Ancient Chinese philosopher, advocated a notion of global peace based on Confucian principles of harmony. The Confucian notion of harmony, which he espoused, has been much misunderstood in its association with sameness, but is highly pertinent to current debates on unity and diversity since it is based on the positive recognition of difference.

The word cosmopolitan is itself of course Greek, *kosmopolites*, meaning citizen of the world, and is generally first attributable to Diogenes the Cynic (*c*.412–323) who said 'I am a citizen of the world', a statement that was to reverberate throughout the history of cosmopolitanism. This declaration of cosmopolitanism was both an act of individual freedom and also a recognition of the external category of the world. It was this latter aspect of the repudiation of local forms of belonging that has been a source of inspiration for all subsequent forms of cosmopolitanism. This gave to cosmopolitanism a concern with forms of belonging that go beyond the community into which one is born to a concern with the wider world of a global humanity. However, for Diogenes cosmopolitanism was a moral sensibility and an individual act of liberation by which he rejected his immediate community in Sinope. His love of the world must be seen in the context of his denouncement of

[2] I am grateful to Baogang He for some of these points.

the local order to the polis. The Cynic belief in cosmopolitanism was in fact a limited individualistic pursuit of an ascetic ideal that had no real substance beyond the rejection of that which is conventional. Despite the limited nature of the Cynics's notion of cosmopolitanism, it had one important legacy: it gave to the cosmopolitan imagination a critical sensibility. Cosmopolitanism can be a way of relativizing one's own culture and identity, even if an alternative is not articulated. Yet, the Cynics did change irreversibly the view that the polis was the exclusive measure of political community. It is important to consider that the Cynics were challenging the relatively closed world of the classical Greek polis where the highest ideal was civic devotion to the political community. This was a republican order that had no place for cosmopolitan values since the republic was an internally ordered community that distinguished sharply between citizens and non-citizens. It was this distinction between an inside and an outside that cosmopolitanism challenged.

A century later the Stoics gave to cosmopolitanism its enduring political orientation. The Stoics developed cosmopolitanism as a consequence of their moral philosophy, which was an attempt to create a morality based on virtue. For the Stoics a distinction had to be made between what people can do and what is beyond their control. They held that internal virtue should prevail over external circumstances and that virtue could be related to a law of nature. In line with this concern to establish an affirmative morality based on rationality, they emphasized the need to create a new political community based on cosmopolitan principles. The Stoics believed that human beings are naturally social and have the potential to be members of a shared cosmopolitan community (Sellars 2006: 133). The new polis was the cosmos, a political community of a more universalistic nature than the traditional closed polis. They stood not for the rejection of the polis, as was the case with the Cynics, but demanded its reinvention based on new values of civic engagement. A further and important dimension of Stoicism was the recognition of the role of human emotions in the shaping of morality and enlargening its scope. As argued by Martha Nussbaum (2001), this is directly related to the cosmopolitan tradition that they inaugurated in that love of humanity is not something that can be explained by reason alone. For the Stoics divinity is present in every person and it is this that gives to humanity the unity than can be the basis of a cosmopolitan ethic. Berges has pointed out that notwithstanding this deistic argument, Stoic cosmopolitanism was based on a strong view of human sociability and the view that sociability can be fulfilled only in a community that encompasses the whole of human society (Berges 2005: 11).

With the Stoics, the republicanism of the classical polis is opened up to new interpretations as opposed to being rejected in the name of individual freedom. Zeno of Citium (333–264 BC) advocated an ideal cosmopolitan city based on wider membership and claimed that civic obligation derives from deep subjective feelings of belonging. The Greek Stoics are also a good illustration of the connection between republicanism and cosmopolitanism, since Zeno's cosmopolitanism was essentially one that sought to reorient the closed world of the republican polis rather than reject it altogether. From its inception cosmopolitanism is an orientation that challenges a narrow and exclusivist patriotism, but it is also opposed to the view that Toulmin attributes to it, namely the idea that political community must reflect a disembodied globalism, such as a predetermined universal 'natural order' that can only be discovered and determined by science (Toulmin 1992). For this reason, then, from the beginning cosmopolitanism asserts the entanglement of the local in the global without prioritizing one over the other. This reading of ancient cosmopolitanism suggests a view of cosmopolitanism as a dimension that mediates between the national or local and the global; it is not one, but a reflexive relation between both. The cosmopolitan is not someone whose roots are once and for all settled. Cosmopolitanism entails the positive recognition of difference and signals a conception of belonging as open. As a critical sensibility, then, it is opposed to closure and particularism.

The historical context is important. Stoicism arose at a time when the Greek polis of the classical age was in decline and when the Hellenistic Empire of Alexander the Great was spreading Greek culture eastwards into Persia and as far as India. This was a time when Greek culture and language became universalized with the recognition of a wider political community beyond Greece. In short, it became increasingly difficult to think of political community exclusively in the closed terms of the republican polis. It would be misleading to say that cosmopolitanism was a direct product of the Hellenistic Era of Alexander the Great (356–323 BC), since the cosmopolitan movement was already in evidence before the conquests, but without this wider context it is difficult to make sense of the opening up of the Greek mind to the wider category of the world. In this respect it marks a departure from the political horizons of Plato. While Greek cosmopolitanism was influenced by the earlier critical philosophy of Plato, the world of Plato was a different one. Plato's republic was not a universal cosmopolitan order but a vision of how the classical polis should be governed. The Cynics's concern with self-scrutiny and self-problematization can be related to the cosmopolitan spirit to relativize one's own culture in light of the encounter with others. However, it was the Hellenistic era, which can be regarded as an early form of globalization, that greatly promoted cosmopolitanism as a political and moral philosophy leading it to be easily taken up by Roman and later Christian thinkers. The Hellenistic Empire, after the conquests of Egypt, Asia Minor, Persia and parts of India, connected a huge territory across Europe, Africa and Asia in which numerous cities and political entities were interlinked in a vast trading and cultural world based on the Greek language. It is impossible to call this inter-civilizational constellation Western and it was only loosely Greek, which was a lingua franca. Hellenism was a transnational cultural world as opposed to being an ethnically based culture. The multiethnicity and transcultural nature of the Hellenistic Empire offered a context for cosmopolitan thought to emerge. The earlier distinction between barbarians and Greeks becomes less sharp, not least due to the extension of the Greek world into non-Greek cultures. Indeed, it could be argued that the loosening of the distinction of the barbarian and the Greek marks the birth of cosmopolitanism.

With the Stoics the idea of political community is enlarged to take account of a new age of empire in which the traditional idea of a republican self-governing political community as based on a city is re-imagined as a larger entity. In this re-shifting of the horizons of the city the republican ethos acquires a new meaning with the need to include within it a wider community.[3] Greek classical Stoicism did not develop cosmopolitanism beyond a general recognition for a world-state or wider political community. However it is thought that it had some influence in social reforms, such as those in Sparta where the distinction between citizens and non-citizens was eased. Roman Stoicism, in inheriting Greek thought, articulated a much stronger notion of a cosmopolis as a mode of belonging based on law. Greek Stoicism became influential in Rome from the early republic and Stoic tutors were employed by several emperors. In the writings of Seneca and above all of Cicero, who are the main

---

[3] See Heather (1996: Chapter 1).

philosophical representatives of Roman Stoicism, political community now becomes the community of the Roman Republic with its members being citizens. The Graeco-Roman civilization that emerged out of the fusion of Greek and Latin culture was greatly influenced by Stocism and the cosmopolitan ideal. This was expressed in the notion of the *oikoumene*, meaning 'the whole world' or 'the inhabited world' and designated a vision of human community beyond the immediate context (Romm 1992). Inglis and Robertson (2005) argue that an ecumenical sensibility arose in the Hellenistic period after the death of Alexander the Great and was expressed in new conceptions of universal history based on a view of the 'world as one place'. As a result of the Roman conquest of the Hellenistic world Greek intellectuals began to see themselves as part of an interlinked world. This consciousness of the wholeness of the world was projected back onto a view of history and the necessity to find ways of narrating the whole world rather than just parts. The most famous of these cosmopolitan accounts of history was the *Histories* of Polybius in the second century BCE where a conception of Roman power is told that emphasizes the centrality of global interrelations of peoples, places, actions and events (Inglis and Robertson 2005).

With the expansion of the Roman Republic into an empire the notion of cosmopolitanism emerged in a new key since the Roman world now incorporated the Hellenic. By equating the city with a world republic, cosmopolitanism became an alternative political identity to the narrow and nationalistic republican vision of Rome and its myth of exclusivity. The Roman Empire was based on a principle of universal rule that had no territorial limits. As a geopolitical configuration as opposed to a linguistic world, the empire was defined not by territory but by the limits of its political system and a vast social, cultural and economic world. Though its imperial centre was of course Rome, this was a decidedly non-Western empire, including a vast territory that was more Mediterranean than European. It would be wrong to conclude that cosmopolitanism was simply a philosophy of empire. Despite its association with the Hellenistic and Roman Empires, cosmopolitan political thought was less concerned with nationalistic justification than with articulating a new vision of the human city. In both periods it is interesting to note how the narrow world of the republican city is challenged by the broader vision of a world community that comes with the expansion of imperial rule. As the cosmos and polis merged, so too did the Roman *orbis* and *urbs*.

As a geopolitical entity, the Roman Empire was a civilizational constellation embodying a vast array of cultures. It shifted the eastwardly Hellenic civilization westwards. The Roman Empire was above all a Mediterranean civilization. Its diversity reflected the multiethnic world of the Mediterranean as well as the wider European continent including much of Germany and England. Although we often see Europe divided between an East and a West, this distinction made no sense in Roman times when a conception of Europe did not exist. Although we often see it as the birth of Europe, it was Asian, African and European. It was culturally cosmopolitan in the sense of being very mixed. The pre-Christian Roman religion adopted many pagan traditions from all over the Mediterranean world with which it came into contact in its continuous expansion. The Roman Empire, while expanding in many directions from Rome after the Punic Wars and the conquest of the Hellenic territories, was in its time a world empire. In his studies of the Mediterranean, Fernand Braudel portrayed the interaction of a plurality of civilizations within the unity of the Mediterranean: Christian, Jewish, Islamic and Orthodox civilizations interacted and the cross-fertilization of their cultures produced the world of the Mediterranean, which he associates with the multiethnic Roman Empire. Braudel never developed his concept of civilization, which remained a vague, suggestive notion entailing both unity and pluralism within it and at the same time included an inter-civilizational dynamic that was creative and transformative (Braudel 1972/3). Cultural trade, diasporas, translations, cultural diffusions and cross-fertilizations produced the world of the Mediterranean and its civilizations.

An important part of the Roman contribution to European civilization has been commented on by Rémi Brague, namely a specific relationship to culture as the transmission of what is received (Brague 2002). Roman civilization was based on a culture that was based on the reworking of those cultures it came into contact with, in particular Greek, Hebraic, Near Eastern and African. These cosmopolitan currents were of course often checked by the republican tendencies of the metropolitan centre. This dynamic tension at the heart of the Roman Empire gave to Europe one of its creative impulses, namely the constant reworking of all cultures, including the heritage of the past. The implication of this is that the European heritage is not primarily based on an essential culture or a European people but on a medium of cultural translation. Brague stresses Europe's logic of distanciation from its own

origins, leading to a culture that can only see itself through the eyes of
the Other. So what distinguishes Europe is its mode of relating to itself,
which is one of distance. Brague argues that because Europe borrowed
everything from sources outside itself – which he associated with the
Roman heritage – it is forever unable to see the present in terms of a
narrative that can claim an origin of its own. European culture thus is a
culture of, what he calls, 'secondarity'.

The Latin language, in replacing Greek, was the practical basis of
cosmopolitanism in the lands of the Roman Empire. But this was only
one variety of cosmopolitanism. Sanskrit, for instance, can be seen as an
Asian cosmopolitan equivalent of Latin. Sheldon Pollock refers to a new
age of vernacular cosmopolitanism following the classical cosmopolitanism of antiquity and is present in Southern Asia and in Western
Europe. If cosmopolitanism is seen as a literary communication that
travels without obstruction from any boundaries and thinks of itself as
unbounded, then the world of writers and readers that both Latin and
Sanskrit produced can be termed cosmopolitan. These languages were
written to be readable across space and time (Pollock 2002: 22–3). The
literary and cultural diffusion of this vernacular cosmopolitanism is
remarkably similar in extending the space of cultural communication
beyond elites. The vernacularization of universal languages and literary
practices enable us to see how people were cosmopolitan without having to actually profess to be. This is a cosmopolitanism of action as
opposed to an idea. Moreover, as Pollock argues, it was a cosmopolitanism that was not the product of a conquest state and church, but the
result of a more diffuse cultural world of adventurers, writers, traders
and readers. Nor was there the same degree of legal standardization
that was a feature of the Roman cosmopolis. The Sanskrit cosmopolis
can be seen as a way in which the cultural horizon of those who came
into its orbit was widened and gave expression to a vision of human
community that was not bounded by space. In the Sanskrit imagination
the world was wider than the world that fell under imperial conquest.
This contrast with the Sanskrit cosmopolitanism and the Western,
Graeco-Roman one draws attention to a dimension of cosmopolitanism
that has been largely eclipsed by the equation of cosmopolitanism with
its Western classical lineage. Again, to follow Pollock, there are two
cosmopolitanisms, not a European universalism and a narrow Asian
particularism (Pollock 2002: 29). We can add to Pollock's notion of
a Sanskrit cosmopolis, a Chinese one and an Arabic one. Thus the

emergence of Mandarin Chinese as the official language of the Chinese Empire made possible a medium of communication based on a common script but one that was neither alphabetically nor phonetically uniform. In this way a common medium of communication was possible.

A fuller account of the implications of vernacularization for cosmopolitanism will require a consideration of alternative models of modernity. This will be examined in Chapter 7. The important point for the present discussion on the rise of classical cosmopolitanism is that it underwent internal transformation due to the vernacularization of a universal language. This illustrates two points. One is that a universalistic culture such as that of Latin was only one universalism, and can be contrasted with other universalistic languages, such as Sanskrit, Arabic and Chinese. As world religions, Hinduism, Islam, Buddhism and Confucianism established the basic preconditions for Asian cultures to create dynamic and hybrid societies in which cosmopolitanism could take root. In addition, all of these universalistic cultures were themselves internally transformed by the logic of vernacularization to produce particular cultures. The civilizations that formed around these vernacular cultures thus contained both universal and particular elements. Chinese civilization, for instance, was formed out of the continuous absorption and transformation of Indian Buddhism which developed in a different direction following its encounter with Confucianism.

Classical cosmopolitanism is best seen in terms of its civilizational origins in the great civilizations of the 'Axial Age'. According to S. N. Eisenstadt, the major civilizations of the world have been products of the 'Axial Age' civilizations (Eisenstadt 1986). These civilizations emerged in the second half of the last millennium BCE in ancient Greece, Israel, India, China and Iran where far-reaching breakthroughs occurred and which led to lasting revolutions in the relation of culture and power. The Axial Age saw the birth of the world religions which provided enduring reference points for intellectual elites to articulate different visions of the world based on universalistic principles. It is possible to see in each of these world religions the basic orientations towards cosmopolitanism. Although not a theory of cosmopolitanism as such, Eisenstadt's thesis has a clear relation to the cosmopolitan perspective in that it suggests a view of all civilizations having a common concern and in having this orientation all civilizations can be seen in terms of a radical field of interpretations. The Axial Age civilizations gave rise to the belief in the possibility of bridging the gap between the transcendental and the mundane orders; they were based on the belief in the capacity of human agency to realize in the mundane orders some of the transcendental and utopian visions.

In the case of Christianity the relation between the cosmopolitan imagination and the new universalism is most evident since there was a direct influence of Stoicism on the early church. This was represented in St Paul's vision of a universal church. The Pauline philosophy was particularly relevant to the cosmopolitan imagination in that, to follow Alain Badiou's interpretation, Paul proposed a new universalistic truth that transcended the distinction between Greeks and Jews (Badiou 2003). Paul, a Greek-speaking Jew who was a Roman citizen of what is present-day southern Turkey, sought to overcome such differences. Differences that appear to be significant, such as the difference between Greeks and Jews, become less important in light of a new conception of truth. Christianity was based on a universalistic principle of belief in personal salvation. The tension within Graeco-Roman political thought between the polis and the cosmos was reflected in the Christian idea of two kingdoms, an idea which was exemplified in Augustine's 'City of God'. But where the Stoics sought a reconciliation of the human order of the city and with the wider order of the cosmos, Christian thought separated these domains and ultimately subordinated the human city to the heavenly city. The city of God can be seen in terms of the cosmopolitan principle of a transcendence of the local and particular in the name of a higher and more inclusive human community. However Christian doctrine conceived itself from the beginning as the source of all authority and moved in the direction of a church rather than a community. Christianity in time repudiated its classical roots in the Graeco-Roman civilizations, proclaiming itself as the new and the modern against the paganism of antiquity. There were certainly limits to Christian cosmopolitanism and eventually the church had moved away from any direct association with cosmopolitan thought.

Since the eleventh century any chance of Christianity developing along cosmopolitan lines was halted with the final split that came with the Orthodox Greek tradition, and a later Russian offshoot, representing a different version of Christianity. Since 1054 there was no pan-European religion, but three major ones which were frequently locked in combat: Catholicism, Orthodoxy and Lutherism. For several centuries in Northern and Southern Europe and in Russia these religions provided a framework of stability, while for others, unresolved religious conflicts had the consequence that modernity developed in an uneven manner. In short, Christianity had become divisive and any unity it offered was not strong enough to be identifiable with cosmopolitan principles. Christian cosmopolitanism ultimately eradicated the distinction between Self and Other as one of mutual recognition based on the pursuit of justice, positing instead a higher principle of unity. Cosmopolitanism entails the transcendence of the particular in order that the particular can be universalized, but the City of God ultimately stood for the transcendence of the Human City and neutralized the tension between the particular and the universal. An exception to the trend might be the example of Dante, who argued for the Christian unity of Europe under a world or universal monarchy. However even this was essentially a vision of a renewed Holy Roman Empire and had only limited cosmopolitan significance.

The birth of modern cosmopolitanism

Classical cosmopolitanism is primarily a development of the modern age, at least in its most well-known formulation. The previous discussion has drawn attention to its origins in the ancient or axial civilizations of the great world religions. This context should be seen as one of civilizational preconditions rather than in any sense a fully developed cosmopolitan condition. The ancient expressions of cosmopolitanism were relatively marginal and not connected with mainstream trends. Ancient cosmopolitanism, as in the Stoic tradition, tended to be part of a broader philosophy and this too was the case with its Christian revival. It was with modernity that cosmopolitanism took on a distinctive political and cultural identity and became more integral to the overall movement of modernity. The development of a cosmopolitan imagination was greatly influenced both by modern secularism and by new ways of thinking about otherness, developments that were centrally connected with geographical discoveries as well as scientific advancement. From the Renaissance to the Enlightenment the spirit of cosmopolitanism spread throughout Europe. This was a period in which nationalism, while on the rise, was not yet the dominant force that it was to become, and for many cosmopolitanism and nationalism were not opposed. However, the primary inspiration for cosmopolitanism was not the critique of nationalism but the critique of the present, and the present, in the eyes of the cosmopolitans, was one of absolutism and dogmatism. In so far as it cultivated an attitude of world openness, a transcendental sensibility around the centrality of the human person and rights, the Enlightenment can be considered to be cosmopolitanism even when the term was not explicitly used.

The following are three main manifestations of the modern phase of classical cosmopolitanism. First, there is the tradition of Renaissance humanism and Enlightenment civic republicanism from Erasmus to Kant where the emphasis was on the political and moral unity of humankind by a world-state or international order of cosmopolitan law. Second, there was the individualistic and culturally oriented cosmopolitanism of the Enlightenment and Romantic movement based on science, literature and travel and where it represented a broadening of the mind. Third, from the Renaissance to the Enlightenment there was a different and more hermeneutical kind of cosmopolitanism present in cultural encounters between East and West and which can be found in those attempts of Enlightenment thinkers in Europe to understand better the culture and thought of Asia.

The cosmopolitanism of antiquity was revived along with much of classical literature and thought by the Renaissance. The humanists, such as Erasmus, revived cosmopolitanism in their belief in the unity of human nature and the possibility of new kinds of political life based on what people share by virtue of their common human nature. The notion of the unity of human nature tended towards a cosmopolitan ethic not merely in putting unity over human diversity, but as a consequence of a new emphasis on the secular political community. The vision of a harmonious human nature determined by natural law was particularly important in shaping new ideas about the nature of political authority and social relations. The rise of cosmopolitanism since the Renaissance can be related to the secularization of politics and the notion of a republican self-governing political community, which gave rise to the idea of a republican international order. Cosmopolitanism can be associated with the various strands of republican and natural law political thinking, including Erasmus, Rousseau, Grotius, Pufendorf and, most importantly, Kant.

The idea of a world-state can of course be related to the early empires of Europe, from the Roman Empire to its various successors from Charlemagne to the Germanic Holy Roman Empire. The fourteenth-century notion of a universal monarchy was one of the many political visions of a legal framework to include all of Europe. The cosmopolitan ideal however should be more properly related to later developments that emerged along with republican and federalist thinking, since many of these visions of political community in the Middle Ages were animated by concerns that are only loosely related to cosmopolitanism. The idea of a world state can be attributed to Johannes Althusius in the early seventeenth century when federalist ideas first emerged as alternatives to warring states. Many of these early cosmopolitan proposals were in the form of peace plans, a famous example being Abbé Charles de Saint-Pierre's 'Project for Making Peace Perpetual in Europe' in 1713. In the course of the eighteenth century several Enlightenment thinkers, including Montesquieu, advocated federal and confederal political ideas. In 1752 David Hume's 'Idea of a Perfect Commonwealth' was a plea for a new kind of a political framework that was neither a nation-state nor an empire. These ideas were taken up by the American federalists, Madison and Hamilton with a theory of federal government. The eighteenth-century notion of a commonwealth of nations had a strong cosmopolitan dimension to it, though the cosmopolitan idea was not always invoked. Unlike earlier it was not based on notions of Christian unity but on the need to give unity, in most cases, to Europe. It was inevitable that many such political designs were constrained by the inter-state system established with the Peace of Westphalia in 1648. Notions of world government or federal unity for the greater part remained on the level of ideas which had a later resonance in proposals for European unity. One of the more consequential developments however was the rise of international law theory, as in the writings of Grotius and Pufendorf. Generally advocated from within the philosophy of natural law and social contract theory, these ideas were important in giving political and legal substance to cosmopolitanism. These early modern conceptions of an international order were ambivalent. On the one side, there was a clear move towards a cosmopolitan view of politics and, on the other, this was often limited to the negative task of eliminating war and establishing a lasting social contract between states.

The ambivalence of eighteenth-century cosmopolitanism as somewhere between a new universalism and international law was encapsulated in the political thought of Immanuel Kant, who is without doubt the main figure in classical cosmopolitanism and a pivotal reference point for contemporary cosmopolitanism. In his major works on cosmopolitanism – 'Idea for a Universal History with a Cosmopolitan Purpose' in 1784 and 'Perpetual Peace' in 1795 – he put forward a theory of cosmopolitanism that was based on a philosophy of history and a moral theory that finally broke the last link with the early modern tradition of natural law. Kant argued that history – by which he meant European history – was leading to the creation of a republican order of free states united in a common republican world order. For Kant, drawing on a long tradition going back to Aristotle, humanity is united by an essential moral nature and purpose. In his theory of history he claimed providence would ultimately guarantee that the moral nature of human beings would guide them to establishing, first, republican governments and, second, on that basis a wider republican world order. In Kant republicanism and cosmopolitanism are complementary political philosophies.

Kant's political theory was republican in its emphasis on the moral autonomy of the political community to be free from coercion and to determine the legal structure of society. In this respect Kant's thought was republican rather than liberal since the purpose of political rule was not merely the removal of coercion for individuals to pursue their individual interests; rather for Kant politics has itself a moral purpose of a more positive nature in establishing the rights of a sovereign people. Although Kant did not develop this into a theory of democracy, he was primarily concerned with establishing a new notion of national sovereignty that would be a basis for a cosmopolitan order of states. It would be wrong to claim that Kant's political theory was at odds with classical liberalism, for he too was concerned with establishing the conditions of liberty. For Kant individuals are not just free beings but are also rational in that they are in principle capable of acting on the basis of moral principles. It is in this respect that he stands within the republican tradition of political thought. The distinction between Kant and liberalism is undoubtedly a thin one since the main lines of division within German political thought are between Kant's attempt to ground politics in a universal morality based on reason – a heritage revived by Habermas – and the rejection of universal morality by Nietzsche, Heidegger and Schmitt. Kant's conception of republicanism was based on three principles: a principle of freedom for all members of society, the centrality of a common legislation and a principle of legal equality. Like much of classical liberalism, Kant was opposed to democracy which he believed was despotic since he viewed it as based on an undifferentiated notion of popular rule and thus in opposition to the separation of powers by which the legislator, the executive and the judiciary are formally separated. However, Kant defended a notion of representative rule, but confined it to the legislator. Despotism prevails, Kant argued, 'if the laws are made and arbitrarily executed by one and the same power' (1991: 101). Government, the business of the executive, had a purely instrumental purpose in carrying out the will of the legislator.

Kant was clearly a moral universalist, but the universalism that his political philosophy espoused was cosmopolitan in being based on a notion of rights that extend beyond the national community. Kant's republican position is in fact decidedly cosmopolitan and it was his concern with cosmopolitan issues that shaped his political thought in a direction that was in marked contrast his rival, Hobbes (Williams 2003). This is possibly because he was greatly influenced by Greek and Roman Stoicism (Nussbaum 1997). In 'Idea for a Universal History with a Cosmopolitan Purpose' he put forward a theory of world government that reflected the Enlightenment self-confidence in the capacity of human beings to reshape the world in the spirit of rationality. It was a forward-looking vision that still owed much to the optimism of the French Revolution, which gave a new relevance to republicanism. Until now the cosmopolitan imagination was largely speculative and individualistic, but with the French Revolution it appeared the *ancien régime* of autocratic monarchies might be swept away and new political institutions designed along the principles of republicanism and cosmopolitanism.

In 'Perpetual Peace' Kant revised his arguments with a certain pessimism that 'the positive idea of a world republic cannot be created' (Kant 1991: 105). His position was influenced by the *realpolitik* of the day that saw peace established between Prussia and France. In place of this world republic is instead the possibility of cosmopolitan law, on the one side, and on the other an incremental movement towards a cosmopolitan order. However, he did not think it was realistically possible for a world state to emerge, in the sense of a world republican government. It would appear that his mature position was that states should ideally become republican, which he believed to be a real possibility. Republican states are less likely to go to war with each other than non-republican states. However the best chance for the future is for these republican states to ground themselves in a cosmopolitan legal order. In this argument for a developed conception of international law based on a theory of morality, Kant provided an important foundation for legal and political cosmopolitanism. He saw as the main objective of a cosmopolitan legal framework the need to constrain the actions of states in a binding international framework in which war would be eliminated. He held that a contractual system such as the Westphalian system was not enough to deal with the state of nature that existed within the inter-state system. In this respect cosmopolitan theory goes significantly beyond contractual theories in that it demands a moral foundation beyond purely strategic interests. The legal framework that Kant argued for fell short of the idea of a universal republican order in accepting the autonomy of states, but went far beyond contractual declarations of peace in advocating an external legal order to which states will submit themselves.

It would be wrong to see Kant's proposal only as one that argued for international law. The major innovation that Kant introduced was in distinguishing between international and cosmopolitan law. The former is essentially a law that pertains to states while the latter concerns a conception of international law that rests ultimately not on the rights of states but on the rights of individuals. Cosmopolitan law entails recognition of the right of hospitality: 'hospitality means the right of a stranger not to be treated with hostility when he arrives on someone else's territory' (Kant 1991: 105). The right to hospitality in Kant is a right that can be asserted against the state and the state is obliged to recognize and protect individuals on the basis of their rights. This was a radical idea, especially in its application to the international order. The core tenet of modern cosmopolitanism was established with the famous claim:

The peoples of the earth have thus entered into a universal community, and it has developed to the point where a violation of rights in one part is felt everywhere. The idea of a cosmopolitan right is therefore not fantastic and overstrained; it is a necessary complement to the unwritten code of political and international right, transforming it into a universal right of humanity. (Kant 1991: 107–8)

There was much that was unclear in Kant's proposals, in particular it was unclear how this international cosmopolitan legal would emerge. Kant ultimately relied on a vague notion of providence, with the hint that the force of moral reason would finally prevail. Several passages in 'Perpetual Peace' suggest that he saw history leading towards a situation in which people become progressively more and more interconnected and, as a result, a cosmopolitan right to hospitality becomes a necessity.

It may too be that he thought pragmatically that republicanism was conducive to cosmopolitanism. He certainly held that a cosmopolitan legal order could be a basis for a federation of states, though not a world state. Such a federation is more like, as Habermas (1997: 181) argues, a 'negative substitute' for a world republican state than an end itself. In fact for Kant the only end is the end of individual moral autonomy. Kant's cosmopolitanism ultimately rested in a belief that cosmopolitanism would be gradually extended from nations to the wider international order rather than being a framework that can be established in an act of foundation. In this respect he has been proven correct in that the cosmopolitan principles operative in the world today have been shaped by global public opinion and civil-society movements rather than being direct outcomes of national sovereignty. In his other writings Kant certainly drew attention to the role of public reason and debate which he saw as the hallmark of the Enlightenment. In other words, the establishment of cosmopolitanism in the world can only come about through critical publics. As Habermas has argued: 'In contemporary terms, Kant's "negative substitute" works precisely because pluralistic publics may promote peace by reshaping political institutions in accordance with cosmopolitan right. In some instances, they may even create and then continually reshape new, international institutions based on the principle of interlinked public spheres in world citizens exercise their sovereignty' (1997: 181). The true significance of Kant's advocation of cosmopolitanism may thus reside in the notion of a broadening of the sphere of public reason into a cosmopolitan public sphere. Kant's belief in a common human understanding and a universal moral capacity implies a cosmopolitan public sphere in which public reason is exercised.

The centrality of Kant to cosmopolitan thought largely resides in the foundations he established for the legal and political dimensions of cosmopolitanism which, as argued here, were closely related to his republican approach. The Enlightenment context of his work and the theme of the public sphere draws attention to another strand of eighteenth-century cosmopolitanism which also had a lasting impact on the cosmopolitan imagination. The Enlightenment era was the era of a culturally oriented cosmopolitanism around science, literature and travel. Kant's vision of a cosmopolitan republic and other conceptions of international law were all part of a cultural turn towards a broadening of vision beyond the narrow world of *ancien régime* loyalties which still dominated the Westphalian inter-state system established in 1648. The great diversity of movements that constitute the Enlightenment era were cosmopolitan in spirit. The Enlightenment intellectuals declared their allegiance to humanity as opposed to a specific country. Voltaire's proclamation that he was 'a citizen of the world' encapsulated this spirit. The notion of a 'citizen of the world' was a term used by many of the eighteenth-century philosophers, such as David Hume. Many of course were themselves more European than national by nature, a famous example being Leibniz, who was highly versatile linguistically and culturally and also believed in the necessity for a political unity of humankind. The eighteenth-century Enlightenment intellectuals appealed to the unity of humankind but, with some exceptions such as Kant and Leibniz, they did not see that necessitating anything like political action. It was a state of mind, largely symbolic but one that was a product of the philosophical concern with universalism that was a feature of the age. Despite the superficiality of much of Enlightenment cosmopolitanism, which of course was the cosmopolitanism of a tiny elite, it established an important reference point and mediation of older cosmopolitan ideas with modernity. The tension within modernity between particularism and universalism owes much to the rise of modern forms of cosmopolitanism.

Romanticism cultivated a moral cosmopolitanism that was not explicitly political and was also not part of a philosophical system, but simply postulated a common humanity. In particular the pursuit of personal and political freedom by the revolutionary romantics, such as Byron, constitutes a cosmopolitanism in so far it was not constrained by any borders and was European as opposed to national in orientation. This, too, can be said about the less revolutionary idea of a World Literature, which has been associated with Goethe, who declared the end of national literature in favour of a new age of World Literature. Revolutionary romanticism was cosmopolitanism in a more far-reaching sense than many other movements of the age in that it was formed out of a creative self-transcendence and, in the case of Byronic romanticism, formed through wandering and isolation. The rejection of the social in the name of a hyper-individualism was different from the universalistic orientation of the mainstream Enlightenment, and in part a reaction to it, but nonetheless it was an important aspect of the cosmopolitanism of the era.

It is easy to dismiss these proclamations as constituting a meaningless rootlessness that was the luxury of elites and irrelevant to, if not contemptuous of, the masses who lived uncosmopolitan lives. This was Rousseau's objection to at least a certain kind of cosmopolitanism when he stated, in the Geneva version of *The Social Contract*, that the cosmopolitans 'boast of loving everyone so that they might have the right to love no one' (Rousseau 1997: 158). This was a view famously reflected in Fougeret de Montbron's essay *Le Cosmopolite* in 1753 when he declared that all countries were the same to him and that consequently he had no commitment to any. Much of this cosmopolitan in fact had a critical function in expressing an attitude of hostility against the narrowness of *ancien régime* patriotism. This may explain why in 1762 the *dictionnaire de l'Académie française* defined the cosmopolitan as 'someone who adopts no country and is not a good citizen' (cited in Rosenfeld 2002: 25). Montesquieu admired England and a century later de Tocqueville admired America because they found their own society inadequate. The capacity to view one's own society from the perspective of another is a central characteristic of the cosmopolitan imagination and marks it off from a national perspective. But it does not reduce the cosmopolitan position to the rejection of the national or local context. Kant's own advocation of cosmopolitanism had little to do with rootlessness. Unlike Leibniz, Kant was famously local in never having travelled outside Königsberg. The beginning of international travel in the eighteenth century, both within Europe and beyond, was an important influence in shaping the cosmopolitan imagination. In terms of the distinction between the Cynic and the Stoic cosmopolitan tradition, it can also be noted that it was the latter and more politically relevant conception that lay behind some of the more important cosmopolitan developments of the Enlightenment.

The culture of the Enlightenment may have been an elite culture at least in its most well-known forms, but this would be to ignore the diffusion of ideas in the wider society. The social reality of Enlightenment cosmopolitanism went beyond the idiosyncratic personalities in that the culture of the new cosmopolitanism was based on learned societies, academies, journals and the wider intellectual and aesthetic public sphere (see Jacobs 2006). Moreover, the Enlightenment movement was not confined to the elites. While its most famous figures were elites and many were members of the aristocratic order, there was a popular Enlightenment within the burgeoning public sphere that arose along with a reading public. There was a relatively large polemical literature by unknown and mostly anonymous authors proclaiming in pamphlets cosmopolitan virtues and peace plans for Europe (Rosenfeld 2002). Cosmopolitanism was a clear strand in national self-awareness in the eighteenth-century historical narratives (O'Brien 1997). In a study of the twenty-year period from 1780–1800 Kleingeld (1999) has documented six varieties of cosmopolitanism in German thought. The Enlightenment was built on the idea of a Republic of Letters and common to its various streams was the belief that knowledge and above all science can offer a common basis for humanity to build a positive future. Two centuries later we have good reason to be sceptical about the unifying nature of knowledge and universalistic ideas, but in its time it was an important step in the direction of a more cosmopolitan world and a departure from the older unifying ideas of Christianity. The cosmopolitanism of the Enlightenment goes beyond the stances of its philosophers to constitute a shared public culture. The intercommunication between the Enlightenment intellectuals, according to Schlereth (1977: 5–9) in his study of the cosmopolitanism of the eighteenth century, made possible a shared culture, which was also a transatlantic one. This shared public culture was initially one confined to the Republic of Letters, with much of it based on the *philosophes*'s common classical education, but gradually extended to include much of the wider society and, as it did so, the use of classical sources faded.

The political and cultural values of the Enlightenment brought cosmopolitanism in the direction of a universalism that has been much criticized today. In its dominant forms it was without doubt highly Eurocentric, reflecting a Western perspective on the world and viewing the non-European world through the lens of Europe. This received view of the Enlightenment, which has been much influenced by the work of Edward Said, is in need of some qualification (Said 1978). This brings us to the third dimension of modern cosmopolitanism, namely inter-civilizational dialogue. Both the Renaissance and the Enlightenment were greatly shaped by the encounter with the non-European world. The discoveries and explorations of the age opened the European mind to alternative worlds, which included Utopias. The beginnings of global travel and travel writing in the eighteenth century contributed to the cosmopolitanism of the Enlightenment and its concern with knowledge, including knowledge of other cultures. One aspect of this, and which has not been given sufficient attention, is the dialogic relation between East and West that was established in the Enlightenment period. This was important not just with respect to an understanding of the

Enlightenment, but is important with regard to the shaping of the cosmopolitan imagination more generally since one dimension of cosmopolitanism that has come into focus today – namely inter-civilization dialogue – was established in the Enlightenment period. Although the terms of that dialogue may be different from those of the present day, it is possible to detect the beginning of a cosmopolitanism that goes beyond the limits of an internal European–American 'Republic of Letters'.

Many of the major philosophers of the eighteenth and early nineteenth centuries were greatly interested and inspired by Asian cultures.[4] It is possible to see in this a cosmopolitanism that derived from the concern with universal humanity and the desire to extend the horizons of the European world in much the same way that the Stoics earlier aimed to extend the horizon of the Greek polis to the world opened up by the conquests of Alexander the Great. The Enlightenment's encounter with Asia was varied, as with other aspects of Enlightenment thought, but cannot all be dismissed as a fascination with the pursuit of the exotic. One of the most famous examples was Montesquieu's *Persian Letters*, published in 1721, where we are offered from the sceptical perspective of two Persian travellers a critical look at French court society. This tradition of satire was reflected in other works, such as Oliver Goldsmith's *The Citizen of the World* in 1762 which appeared to be praising ancient Chinese civilization as a way of criticizing European Christian civilization. The use of China for the purpose of critique and anti-clericalism was particularly characteristic of French Enlightenment intellectuals, such as Pierre Bayle and Voltaire, for whom China represented an atheistic civilization that did not need religion. The appeal to China in eighteenth-century Enlightenment thought displayed a cosmopolitan concern that went beyond a purely critical function. As Clarke (1997: 49) points out in his invaluable study of what he calls 'the oriental Enlightenment', the *philosophes* were attracted to what they saw as the benevolent and more harmonious 'despotism' in China where learning appeared to be an important part of government. Indeed, the key to good government was held to be merit through learning rather than hereditary right. It was in this vein that the physiocrat François Quesnay's *Le despotisme de la Chine* was written in 1767. Malebranche promoted the study of Chinese philosophy for its own sake as did Leibniz in what is possibly

---

[4] See Clarke (1997), Halbfass (1988) and Lach (1970, 1977).

the most significant work on the age on the overall unity of European and Chinese philosophy, *Discourse on the Natural Philosophy of China*. In this work he sought to explore common links between the basic concepts of Chinese thought and European thought, claiming an overall unity of purpose. The Enlightenment's embracing of China declined from the end of the eighteenth century, when tensions between China and the West came more acute. It was gradually realized that, after all, Chinese civilization was not based on freedom. Rousseau, with his republican philosophy of freedom, was a critic of China. From about this time onwards India dominated the later Enlightenment, especially for German philosophers.

Sanskrit texts made their appearance in Europe from the late eighteenth century. According to Schwab (1984) this can be compared to the impact of Greek texts on the European renaissance. With the translation of the Upanishads, Europeans gained a new understanding of Indian thought that was far-reaching and greatly influenced philosophers such as Schopenhauer who, like Leibniz earlier, drew parallels between Asian and European philosophy. This was all in the name of the overall unity of humankind, a notion that was reflected in the discovery of a linguistic unity of the Indo and European languages. Political concerns were relatively unimportant in the encounter with India, which appeared to open up a spiritual and more cultural kind of cosmopolitanism. Johann Gottfried Herder played a role in the European encounter with India and influenced the idealist movement's sympathetic view of Hindu philosophy. Often dismissed as the founder of cultural nationalism, Herder's interest in culture had a cosmopolitan dimension to it that has rarely been appreciated. While he was responsible for the historicist conception of the uniqueness of national cultures this was a view that had little to do with modern ethnic nationalism. Like most Enlightenment intellectuals of the age, Herder believed that all cultures were based on an underlying universal order of values. For Herder this universalism resides less in a higher order, such as science, but has crystallized in national cultures in different historical ages. He believed that Hindu thought was not fundamentally different from European thought. For instance, he was attracted by the Indian concept of world-soul which influenced the German Romantics in their notion of the transcendent wholeness of the natural world (Clarke 1997: 62). The notion of monistic wholeness in Hindu thought had a direct relation with the German Idealist movement from Fichte and Schelling to Hegel.

Of the Idealists it was Schelling who was the most interested in India, but it was Friedrich Schlegel who made the most systematic attempt to place India as the source and origin of European culture. For Schlegel in his *Essay on the Language and Wisdom of the Indians* in 1808 India was superior to modern Europe. Hegel, too, though less embracing of the East than Schlegel, included Indian thought in his account of the world-spirit. Although his philosophy of history gave Europe a more superior position in the development of thought, his concern with the East revealed a serious attempt to understand another civilization in order to learn from it and to gain self-knowledge. The critical function of India and the East more generally was inseparable from the Enlightenment's critique of Europe and in this respect it was a reflection of the cosmopolitan concern with the embracing of otherness. A limitation certainly was that this was ultimately a concern that was more bound up with European self-understanding than with Asia. Despite this limitation and the at times superficial engagement, much of the Enlightenment encounter with Asia cannot be understood in the terms of Said's orientalist critique as a strategy of power. This was an age that preceded European imperialism and in the case of the German philosophers in particular there is much to suggest that the encounter reflected the cosmopolitan spirit of understanding another culture in order to gain self-knowledge.

The decline of classical cosmopolitanism

The cosmopolitanism of the Enlightenment was closely connected with the republicanism of the age. The decline of the cosmopolitan idea in the nineteenth century can in part be explained by the transformation of republicanism into varieties of nationalism. Modern and ancient forms of cosmopolitanism shared a common concern with freedom. As a philosophy of freedom it had tremendous appeal for Enlightenment intellectuals and nationalist leaders alike. Both nationalism and cosmopolitanism were inspired by the idea of freedom, be it the freedom of movement or the right of the nation to be free of tyranny. The emergence of the modern notion of the self-legislating subject, which lies at the heart of modern philosophical thought, gave to both nationalism and cosmopolitanism the basic animus of freedom as a political and personal goal and ideal to be pursued. Cosmopolitanism found a certain home in both republicanism and liberal nationalism, though a point was eventually reached when that relation became strained.

Like cosmopolitanism, republicanism is an older movement than nationalism and with ancient origins, but differs from cosmopolitanism in its conception of peoplehood in terms of a territorial community of self-legislating subjects. Although having numerous forms, republicanism, in particular in the American tradition, tended towards particularism in its view of the political community as a community of fate. But much of that tradition – including the Jeffersonian tradition – was open to the cosmopolitan orientation to the world and to the principle of human freedom. The most famous example of cosmopolitanism and republicanism co-existing was the French Revolution. The principles of 1789 were held to be universal and applicable to all nations fighting injustice and tyranny. In this sense, the spread of the French Revolution and the ideas it gave rise to across Europe in the first half of the nineteenth century reflected the force of the cosmopolitan idea of a human republic based on freedom. Tom Paine wrote: 'The true idea of a great nation is that which extends and promotes the principles of universal society; whose mind arises above the atmosphere of local thought, and considers mankind of whatever nation or profession they may be as the work of the Creator' (cited in Schlereth 1977: 106). *La Patria* signified a belief in equality, justice, tolerance and freedom for the Enlightenment. Thomas Schlereth, in his study of Enlightenment cosmopolitan thought, refers to this kind of cosmopolitanism as humanitarian nationalism and a contrast to an unchecked nationalism (Schlereth 1977: 109). But of course it is evident that this mixture of republicanism and cosmopolitanism can equally be seen in terms of nationalism, since it was the nationalism of the French republic that promoted this kind of cosmopolitanism. In time, with the transition from a revolutionary notion of the French nation to the nascent centralized republican state, the subordination of cosmopolitanism to nationalism is precisely what happened and cosmopolitanism became linked with the French aspiration to be a world power.

If republican cosmopolitanism was a national project and one closely associated with the new patriotism of the French state, the other face of cosmopolitanism reflected minority nationalism. Liberal nationalism was the dominant nationalist movement of the early nineteenth century and was shaped by the Enlightenment's belief in freedom as a general aspiration for all peoples. It can be contrasted to the nationalism of the established nation-state. Liberal nationalism emerged in the 1820s – along with the Greek national cause – and, although like all nationalist movements of the age it was elitist in leadership, it embodied a populism that was to prove enduring. The cosmopolitan dimension of this nationalism consists of a view that had gained widespread support in the nineteenth century that nations of a certain size had a right to become independent. The famous examples of such nationalist causes are Belgian, Bulgarian, Greek, Irish, Italian and Polish nationalist movements, which had gained the support of many liberals, most notably from the 1870s the Liberal Party in Britain under the leadership of William Gladstone. Liberal nationalism within a broad cosmopolitanism found a major expression in Giuseppe Mazzine's Young Europe League, founded in Berne in 1834, an organization that promoted the idea of self-determination as the principle by which the political map of Europe should be drawn. The movement, which was republican in spirit, led to several other such leagues, such as Young Italy, Young Ireland and Young Poland, which all pursued the goal of national liberation. For this movement there was no contradiction between a European cosmopolitanism and the creation of sovereign nations. Kok-Chor Tan (2004) has argued that there is not a contradiction between the principle of self-determination that is the basis of liberal nationalism and cosmopolitan political aspirations. Indeed, nationalism itself is a demonstration of the cosmopolitan principle that people can imagine a political community beyond the context of their immediate world. Moreover, cosmopolitanism requires an acknowledgement of national forms of belonging.

Despite their common association with republicanism and the ideas of the Enlightenment, nationalism and cosmopolitanism were eventually to part company. What ultimately divided them was the transformation of nationalism into a territorial ideology to which became associated an exclusivist notion of peoplehood that was at odds with the cosmopolitan ideal. On the one side, nationalism promoted a territorial basis of belonging and, on the other, cosmopolitanism proclaimed freedom to consist in non-territorial forms of belonging and the idea that individuals can transcend and move beyond and between national territories. But the entwinement of nationalism and cosmopolitanism did not completely unravel and both remained embroiled in each other even as nationalism gained ascendancy. So, for example, many nationalist movements sought to incorporate minorities into the national community.

The ambivalence of nationalism is clearly evident in the complicated relationship between citizenship and nationalism (Habermas 1992).

Cosmopolitanism, along with republicanism, shares a basic belief in citizenship as a rights-based status acquired through birth. This, as we have seen, was part of the modern concept of the person as a bearer of rights as opposed to a subject. The birth of the modern notion of citizenship marked the decline of the idea of society based on a natural order in which some are signalled out by rank or class for social privilege. It was only with the transformation of the idea of the nation into an exclusivist nationalism that the idea of citizenship became interchangeable with a particularistic nationality and lost its cosmopolitan dimension. The modern notion of the nation must be distinguished from later state- and territorial-based forms of nationalism as well as from exclusivist ethnic notions of the nation. The idea of the nation was universalist in its advocating of a notion of political community that sought to bring diverse people together into a national community. Inclusive forms of nationalism were compatible with cosmopolitanism in so far that they were not particularistic. This notion of the nation was particularly pronounced in the eighteenth-century German idea of the nation, as expressed, for instance, in the writings of Herder, Hegel and Fichte. Fichte's 'Address to the German Nation' in 1808 is one such example of a universalistic notion of the nation in a country and age that had not yet witnessed the rise of the modern nation-state.

The idea of cosmopolitanism received its first major negative connotation in the works of Marx and Engel. One of the most famous passages in *The Communist Manifesto* in 1848 declared: 'The bourgeoisie has through its exploitation of the world market given a cosmopolitan character to production and consumption in every country' (Marx and Engels 1967: 7). The association of cosmopolitanism with the global reach of capitalism gave to it a new meaning that is both cultural and economic. Marx and Engels did not claim that the bourgeois class was cosmopolitan; rather it is the market and commodities that are cosmopolitan. The notion of cosmopolitanism used here is clearly more akin to more recent theories of globalization. It is also a striking contrast to another argument in *The Communist Manifesto* concerning the universalism of the proletariat:

The working men have no country. We cannot take from them what they have not got. Since the proletariat must first of all acquire political supremacy, must rise to be the leading class of the nation, must constitute itself *the* nation, though not in the bourgeois sense of the word. (Marx and Engels 1967: 29)

So against the cosmopolitanism of the market is the new universalism of the communist revolution, which is also a reassertion of the universalism of the nation. With this claim, the older Enlightenment idea of cosmopolitanism of Kant is buried.

Few works capture the decline of the cosmopolitan idea better than Frederich Meinecke's work, *Cosmopolitanism and the National State*, originally published in German in 1907. Meinecke (1970) was struck by the gradual demise of the cosmopolitanism of the nineteenth century and the concomitant rise of nationalism and the national state. For Meinecke, a German liberal nationalist, this was a positive development and reflected a broadly liberal view of nationalism as the inheritor of the cosmopolitan project. It was his conviction that 'the true, the best German national feeling also includes the cosmopolitan idea of a humanity beyond nationality and that it is unGerman to be merely German' (Meinecke 1970: 21). This view had a genuine basis in German thought. Kant had stated of the Germans that they 'have no national pride, and are too cosmopolitan to be deeply attached to their homeland' (Kant 1974: 180). Meinecke, who introduced the distinction between the 'cultural nation' and the 'political nation', argued the German Enlightenment notion of the cultural nation had been cosmopolitan, but in resting on an intellectual universalism it was too weak to be politically effective since it lacked a clear focus on the state. The political nation needed more lofty ideals, he argued.

Clearly this was a position that had not been shaped by the two world wars that were to follow and it is not impossible to imagine that Meinecke and other German liberal patriots of the age, such as Max Weber, who held similar uncritical views, might have been less enthusiastic about the rise of the national state had they been writing at a later period. But until 1914 it was possible for German liberals to be hopeful about the promise of the nation-state and to find a way of accommodating German particularity within a universal concept of European culture (Harrington 2004). This was, after all, a country that had only recently been unified and a country where the intellectuals and professional elites were highly cosmopolitan, having, as Greenfeld (1992) remarks, only lately discovered nationalism. However, it was obvious to everyone that cosmopolitanism alone was not going to solve the problems of the age. The demise of cosmopolitanism in Germany was symptomatic of its European fate. Everywhere a xenophobic fear of diversity gained ground and with this too came a crisis of the international normative order. The League of Nations, created after the First World War in 1919 in an attempt to revive the older cosmopolitan ideal, became helpless in the face of the new nationalism.

For much of the early twentieth century the notion of cosmopolitanism was associated with the outsider and indicated a fundamentally pejorative condition of deracination. The cosmopolitan was epitomized by the Jew and came to signify the outsider within. This anti-Semitic use of the term cosmopolitan still informs popular French uses of the term in the present day. The xenophobic and racist climate that developed in Europe from the First World War onwards represented not merely a turning away from the cosmopolitanism of the nineteenth century, in Meinecke's terms, but the reversal of it. Gone was the idea of the national community as the embodiment of cosmopolitan ideas; instead was a view of the cosmopolitan as an Other to be excluded from the national community. With this too came a shift in many countries from an inclusive citizenship based on birth to an exclusive one based on ethnicity. This led to the demise of cosmopolitan republicanism and the rise of a patriotic state-based republicanism which sought to eradicate cosmopolitanism.

Towards the end of the nineteenth century, population increase as a result of urbanization and industrialization led to greater and more mixed cities. In an age of empire-building the increasing mix and flow of peoples led to a shift in the meaning of cosmopolitanism in the direction of a fear of otherness. Nationalism lost its liberal underpinnings and with scientific racism on the rise, fear and notions of otherness combined to forge xenophobia. The cosmopolitan became a label attached to the socially uprooted and with the decadence of the cosmopolitan city to which the national state had an ambivalent relation. As pointed out by Eleanor Kofman, migrants, outcasts and refugees were the new cosmopolitans and were defined as such not as individuals but by their association with the city (Kofman 2005). Indeed, the great cosmopolitan cities were often colonial trading outposts – Shanghai, Tangiers – where peripheral peoples settled. The resulting multiple identifications that such metropoles tended to nurture did not fit in easily with the national project towards uniformity and single identities. This is equally true of the Soviet Union where the term cosmopolitanism was equated with the critical intellectual and with a more general association with Western bourgeois decadence.

The cosmopolitan city is a product of forces that the national state does not control and which it is unable to homogenize. Intellectuals, artists, political refugees and déclassé individuals of various kinds that the late nineteenth century produced represented a cosmopolitanism that was perceived to be a threat, since these groups were separated from the elites, but not directly under political or class power in the way the working class were. Cosmopolitanism thus signifies rootlessness with which goes, allegedly, a lack of loyalty to the nation. It is in the figure of the Jew that this suspicion of cosmopolitanism is most evident, since with the Jew rootlessness is combined with otherness. The Jew was the cosmopolitan who as outsider embodied a particular vision of modernity as a relation of Self and alternity (see Cheyette and Marcus 1998). Vienna was the melting pot of cosmopolitanism and nationalism in the *fin-de-siécle* period. According to Ernst Gellner:

The influx of nationalies into the expanding imperial capital meant that by the end of the nineteenth century almost everyone went over to a Völkisch-national position. The only liberals, or with Jewish links, i.e. the cosmopolitans. They could choose, in their public persona, to be proud of their universalistic liberalism and spurn the ethnic totem poles as shameful. (Gellner 1998: 138)

Here again we have an example of cosmopolitanism as part of the dark imaginary of nationalism and without which it would not have been able to define itself. It will of course be noted that many of these cosmopolitan cities – Paris, Berlin, Vienna – were national capitals and were, especially in Central Europe, multiethnic. The national project, on the one hand, sought to domesticate this cosmopolitanism by giving it a universalistic form and, on the other hand, it sought to suppress cosmopolitanism. The condition of cosmopolitanism was nationalism. As with national capitals, universalistic projects such as world exhibitions and monumental architecture were intended to make the nation part of a universalistic Western civilization. In this centralizing mission cosmopolitanism was absorbed into the universalism of the nation-state, but without its critical, self-transformative and ambivalent relation to fixed reference points. Despite this, the figure of otherness and rootlessness could not easily be domesticated. In terms of a wider conception of modernity, it could be suggested that nationalism and cosmopolitanism reflected different aspects of modernity: the homogenizing project of the modern national state and the pluralization of modern culture and social relations. Ernst Gellner described this in graphic terms as a struggle between an atavistic and closed nationalism and a liberal cosmopolitan nationalism open to the world. Many primordialist nationalist movements, he argued, defended their völkisch cause against 'bloodless' and 'rooted cosmopolitanism' (Gellner 1998). It is evident, then, that by the twentieth century cosmopolitanism has given way to nationalism. The polyethnicity, which William McNeil (1986) believed was a feature of history prior to the arrival of the modern nation-state, disappeared and was replaced by a national citizenry.

What of the fate of internationalism, the cosmopolitanism of the inter-state system? To the extent to which the Kantian notion of a cosmopolitan order of republican states survived the first half of the twentieth century, it was as an international order based on sovereign states. From the League of Nations to the United Nations and the 1948 Declaration of Human Rights, an international normative order had been set up. However this was an order based on sovereign nation-states. This, too, was the case with the international socialist movement, which since the collapse of the Third International, developed on national lines and eventually became absorbed into national political parties or trade unions. There were some exceptions, notably the International Brigade during the Spanish Civil War and, possibly, the case of the resistance movement to German occupation during the Second World War.

The inter-civilization cosmopolitanism of the Enlightenment was briefly revived by what can be called 'cultural internationalism' (Iriye 1997) in the period prior and subsequent to the First World War. Cultural internationalism was a challenge to the rising tide of nationalism and militarism of the age. Iriye argues this survived until the 1930s and was evidenced in the cultural concerns of the League of Nations, which fostered cosmopolitan exchanges between Europeans and Chinese, and was also reflected in the cultural pursuits of Comintern, which set up a journal called *World Culture*. 'In part this reflected the awareness that intra-Western internationalism was not enough; that just as the League of Nations included non-Western members, postwar cosmopolitanism must become truly global' (Iriye 1997: 61).

The Universal Races Congress in London in 1911 is another such example. Robert Holton has argued that this was an important expression of cosmopolitanism (Holton 2002). This has also been noted by Gilroy, who has argued that the significance of the Congress lay in its concern with the cultural interaction of peoples as opposed to an over-integrated conception of culture (Gilroy 1993: 2). Other examples of cosmopolitan encounters include the first pan-African Congress in London in 1900. The sociologist Tönnies, who presented a paper at the Universal Races Congress, claimed the event was in the tradition of the older liberal cosmopolitanism of nineteenth century (Holton 2002: 161). This kind of internationalism can be seen as a product of an emerging global consciousness from the end of the nineteenth century and which was reflected in world-time as in the Greenwich Meridian, the refounding of the Olympic Games and the foundation of the Nobel Prizes. The opening of the Suez Canal in 1869 signalled what was often called a 'world unicity'.[5] In China, until the Cultural Revolution, unlike in Russia, cosmopolitanism and communism reinforced each other. According Levenson, cosmopolitanism emerged as an anti-traditionalist and modernist critique of Confucianism with the May Fourth movement in the twentieth century and was taken up by the Communist Party as part of its anti-imperialist mission (Levenson 1971).

Conclusion

The fate of the cosmopolitan idea cannot be easily summed up. As outlined above there has clearly been a movement away from cosmopolitanism from the end of the nineteenth century. The appeal to cosmopolitanism in the Enlightenment was on the whole prior to the emergence of modern nationalism, which when it finally triumphed absorbed much of the cosmopolitan spirit. However, as argued in this chapter, nationalism was itself influenced by cosmopolitanism and that there is not a fundamental tension between cosmopolitanism and nationalism. In any case cosmopolitanism tended to be overshadowed by another 'universalism', namely the idea of civilization, which reflected the anti-cosmopolitan appeal to the superiority of Western civilization. Notwithstanding the apparent decline in the cosmopolitan ideal, which was clearly marginalized as a result of the two world wars of the twentieth century, I have argued for a perspective on the European political and cultural heritage that sees cosmopolitanism as intertwined with republicanism in that both universalistic and particularistic visions of political community have together shaped the way we think about the world. On the whole, cosmopolitanism has reflected

[5] I am indebted to David Inglis for these examples.

the universalistic impulse while republicanism has stood for a particular understanding of political community. In this sense cosmopolitanism represents an immanent transcendence of the possibilities within modernity for the fusion of horizons. The next chapter will explore the revival of cosmopolitan thought in the second half of the twentieth century. Here it will be shown that the immanent possibilities of modern society for cosmopolitan transcendence have taken on a greater force.

2 | Contemporary cosmopolitanism and social theory

The idea of cosmopolitanism is most recognizable as a term of political governance and with a history that extends to the Enlightenment and to classical antiquity. Although the origins of cosmopolitanism lie in an essentially moral view of the individual as having allegiances to the wider world, it was to acquire a political significance once it was linked to peoplehood. As argued in Chapter 1, the main tradition in modern cosmopolitan thought, which derives from Immanuel Kant, sought to extend republican political philosophy into a wider and essentially legal framework beyond the relatively limited modern republic. With this came the vision of a world political community extending beyond the community into which one is born or lives. Cosmopolitanism thus became linked with the universalism of modern Western thought and with political designs based on recognition of the rights of the individual as opposed to the state. Yet, from the end of the nineteenth century to the middle of the twentieth century the national imagination for the greater part prevailed over the cosmopolitan imagination. After the Second World War cosmopolitanism gained a new significance. The foundation of the United Nations and the affirmation of international law as in the UN Declaration of Human Rights and in the new legal category of crimes against humanity were among the events that gave cosmopolitanism a significance and reality that it previously lacked. As a result of the tremendous transformation of the world in the post-1989 period, there has been renewed interest in cosmopolitanism.

Until recently cosmopolitanism has been predominantly viewed as a political philosophy. The dominance of political philosophy has tended to overshadow the contribution of social theory and social science. The fact that social theory, and more specifically sociology, has been relatively absent from cosmopolitan theory is not entirely surprising. The separation of the social from the political in the modern imagination had the implication that cosmopolitanism was equated with the political in opposition to the social. Cosmopolitanism thus reflected the revolt of the individual against the social world, for to be a 'citizen of the world' was to reject the immediately given and closed world of particularistic attachments. Not surprisingly it became associated with the revolt of the elites against the low culture of the masses. Sociological theory, which arose in the age of the nascent nation-state and industrial society, tended towards a view of the social as bounded and moreover was sceptical of notions of freedom that were associated with cosmopolitanism. The social world as territorially given, closed and bounded by the nation-state and the class structure of the industrial societies did not sit comfortably with the openness of the cosmopolitan idea, with its universalistic orientation. Moreover, since Auguste Comte, sociology as a positive science was opposed to the cultural and political claims of the Enlightenment intellectuals who were associated with a mode of critique not grounded in positively given facts. Whether Kantian political cosmopolitanism or the cultural cosmopolitanism of the intellectuals and elites, cosmopolitanism was thus marginalized by twentieth-century preoccupations.

Viewed from a different perspective – a broader vision of social theory as a critical reflection on modernity – the decline of the cosmopolitan imagination associated with the Enlightenment and the rise of the nation-state could be seen as the beginning of a different kind of cosmopolitanism, one less premised on the assumptions of a world republic or on elites and also one less Eurocentric. In contrast to the dominant Enlightenment notion of cosmopolitanism as a transnational republican order, current developments in social theory suggest a post-universalistic cosmopolitanism that takes as its point of departure different kinds of modernity and processes of societal transformation that do not presuppose the separation of the social from the political or postulate a single world culture. Current debates in political theory draw attention to the revival of the Kantian ideal, which it is argued is relevant in the present context of globalization, the alleged crisis of the nation-state and the need for global civil society (Bohman and Lutz-Bachmann 1997). I do not wish to argue against such normative positions, but to highlight a different and more sociological approach to cosmopolitanism which is relevant to a critical social theory of late modernity. Viewed in such terms, the emphasis shifts to the very conceptualization of the social world as an open horizon in which new cultural models take shape. In this approach, which I term critical cosmopolitanism, the cosmopolitan imagination occurs when and wherever new relations between Self, Other and World develop in moments of openness. It is an approach that shifts the emphasis to internal developmental processes within the social world rather than seeing globalization as the primary mechanism and is also not reducible to the fact of pluralism. This emphasis on the internal transformation of the social world highlights the relevance of cosmopolitanism as a form of immanent transcendence as opposed to an externally induced transcendence.

The point of departure for this kind of critical cosmopolitan social theory is the recognition that the very notion of cosmopolitanism compels the recognition of multiple kinds of cosmopolitanism, including earlier kinds of cosmopolitanism, and which cannot be explained in terms of a single, Western notion of modernity or in terms of globalization. Cosmopolitanism refers to the multiplicity of ways in which the social world is constructed through the articulation of a third culture.[6] Rather than see cosmopolitanism as a particular or singular condition that either exists or does not, a state or goal to be realized, it should instead be seen as an ethical and political medium of societal transformation that is based on the principle of world openness, which is associated with the notion of global publics. Today global publics are playing a critical role in such processes of transformation. In equating world openness rather than universalism as such with cosmopolitanism, the basis for a more hermeneutic and critical cosmopolitan sociology will hopefully be established. In sum, then, the argument of this chapter is that a sociologically driven critical cosmopolitanism concerns the analysis of cultural modes of mediation by which the social world is shaped and where the emphasis is on moments of world openness created out of the encounter of the local with the global. Viewed in these terms, cosmopolitanism is a form of world disclosure that arises out of the immanent possibilities of the social world for transformation.

The chapter proceeds as follows. The first section locates the notion of critical cosmopolitanism within the cosmopolitan tradition through a critical reading of the different approaches, which are summed up under the headings of moral cosmopolitanism, political cosmopolitanism and cultural cosmopolitanism. The second section outlines an alternative theoretical conception of critical cosmopolitanism with a focus on how it opens up a different vision of modernity. The third section elaborates

---

[6] The notion of third culture derives from Restivo (1991).

on some of the methodological assumptions of a critical cosmopolitan analysis. The overall aim of the chapter is to develop a conception of the complexities of cosmopolitanism as an emergent social phenomenon that has major implications for a critical social theory of modernity and sociological inquiry.

Types of cosmopolitanism

Cosmopolitanism has a long tradition and takes many forms. It is possible to discern within contemporary cosmopolitanism three broad strands, which can be divided for the purpose of illustration into strong and weak forms. These are moral cosmopolitanism, political cosmopolitanism and cultural cosmopolitanism.

The dominant conception of cosmopolitanism can be termed moral cosmopolitanism due to the strong emphasis in it on the universalism of the cosmopolitan ethic. In the most well-known version of this, which goes back to antiquity, the basis of cosmopolitanism is the individual whose loyalty is to the universal human community. This has generally been identified with the universal human community, with the Cynics and later the Stoics. While having resonances in later Western thought, this kind of cosmopolitanism has been revived in recent times. A much discussed essay by Marta Nussbaum can be seen as a contemporary example of cosmopolitanism as a moral universalism (Nussbaum 1996). In her account, the Stoic conception of the citizen of the world does not require surrendering local identifications, which can be a source of great richness in life. She argues the Stoics suggest that 'we think of ourselves not as devoid of local affiliations, but as surrounded by a series of concentric circles'. From an inner circle centred on the self to outer ones based on the family, local groups, nation, the circle expands to include humanity as a whole. Citing the Stoic philosopher Hierocles, she states 'our task as citizens of the world will be "to draw the circles somehow toward the centre"' (Nussbaum 1996: 9). Thus, in this conception of cosmopolitanism there is nothing contradictory about local and personal identifications, on the one hand, and the cosmopolitan emphasis on humanity as a whole. Education has a fundamental role to play in cultivating cosmopolitan values. Nussbaum gives four arguments for making cosmopolitan education the focus of education as opposed to national citizenship. First, through cosmopolitan education we learn more about ourselves. Second, we live in a connected world requiring greater international cooperation. Third, we need to recognize that we hold moral obligations to the rest of the world. These obligations are often implicit in our values. Four, moral obligations do not stop at national borders. Nussbaum's essay is a plea for the recognition of a moral universalism that is implicit but often not acknowledged in much of human conduct. Education has a special role to play in developing it into a more self-consciousness awareness of obligations towards humanity. What is implied in this is a critical role for education in opening up new perspectives and ways of thinking about the world. Nussbaum's essay, while being a signal work in shaping the new cosmopolitanism, was limited by being confined to a purely moral orientation that neglected the political dimension as well as cultural variants of cosmopolitanism; it was a cosmopolitanism based on a common loyalty to humanity.

Habermas's communication theory, too, can be seen as an example of an approach that is strongly informed by a moral universalistic kind of cosmopolitanism (Habermas 1996, 1998). This is a universalism that consists only of communicative competences and the related capacity for deliberative reasoning. Rather than a universalism of common values, Habermas defends a moral universalism that is primarily based on the capacity for dialogue and properly understood as a post-universal conception of rationality. For Habermas, this is a capacity that is separate from cultural traditions and particular cultural contexts. The essential contribution to cosmopolitan theory made by Habermas is a notion of dialogic reason whereby different positions are problematized and scrutinized. Through dialogue and debate all cultural assumptions must be critically examined. While consensus may be possible, the communicative process makes possible a situation in which both sides can subject each other to critical judgement. From such encounters, changes in self-understanding can result, leading to new ethical and political orientations leading in turn to changes in subject formation. Habermas's work has only been loosely related to cosmopolitanism and what has generally been emphasized is his later political philosophy of European post-nationalism. His discourse theory has generally not been discussed with respect to cultural questions such as those pertaining to inter-cultural communication.

A weaker conception of cosmopolitanism can be found in liberal communitarian approaches to multiculturalism, as in the idea of universal recognition of the moral integrity of all people. Moral cosmopolitanism suffers from a major drawback in so far as it lacks a nuanced sociological dimension and assumes a too-strong universalistic sense of universal humanity. It has been criticized for failing to see cosmopolitanism as 'rooted' and not necessarily universalistic. Cultural cosmopolitanism, to be discussed below, offers a less dualistic view of the relation between the particular and the universal, while political cosmopolitanism suggests an alternative to the individualism that underlies moral conceptions of cosmopolitanism. As Ferrara argues, cosmopolitanism is first of all a normative concept (Ferrara 2007).

The revival of cosmopolitanism in recent times is largely due to the rise of an explicitly political conception of cosmopolitanism relating to citizenship and democracy. Strong and weak versions can be found. Strong conceptions of cosmopolitanism can be found in notions of world polity as advocated by John Meyer or notions of cosmopolitan democracy as put forward by David Held and others (Held 1995; Meyer *et al.* 1997). The Kantian notion of a cosmopolitan world order of republic states can today be regarded as less an ideal than a compelling normative dimension of what Archibugi terms a global commonwealth (Archibugi 1995, 2008). Such approaches generally take globalization as the basis for a new conception of a transnational democracy beyond the nation-state. These are strong positions in that they see cosmopolitanism as manifest in a fundamentally new political context brought about by globalization. There is also a firm commitment to universalism in these approaches, which on the whole are normative in their approach and do not engage with actually existing political systems.

A less strong, but nonetheless very important, expression of cosmopolitanism can be found in the argument made by Karl Jaspers in *The Question Concerning German Guilt* in 1945. Jaspers (2001) was struck by the new category of 'crimes against humanity' as invoked in the Nuremberg Trials and argued that it was the realization of Kant's notion of a cosmopolitan order. The significance of the legal category 'crimes against humanity' was significant in many respects for cosmopolitan thought. In line with Kant's argument, it was more extensive than international law in appealing to a normative principle beyond statehood and national legal system (see Fine 2000, 2007). International law was primarily a law between states and did not recognize crimes committed in the name of states. Crimes against humanity overrode national conceptions of legality in removing immunity for those acting under orders or in the name of a national objective. In introducing into international law a category of criminal guilt and individual responsibility, crimes against humanity marked an innovative step in the direction of a cosmopolitan legal order. Of course, in the specific context of the Nuremberg Trials there were limitations. Jaspers was aware that only the crimes against humanity committed by the vanquished Germans were being judged and that the tribunal was not an international court, but one of the victors and thus was not strictly speaking cosmopolitan since only one side was being judged. Despite these and other limitations, Jaspers believed that a significant step had been taken in the direction of a cosmopolitan legal order. In this respect he has been proved correct in that subsequent developments have given a firmer foundation for crimes against humanity.

Weaker conceptions of political cosmopolitanism can also be found in theories of citizenship. Here the universalistic assumptions of cosmopolitan democracy are more nuanced. Where for T. H. Marshall full citizenship had been achieved with the rise of social rights associated with the welfare state, theorists of citizenship today have identified a wide range of new challenges to citizenship (see Turner 1993). Marshall's trajectory of civic to political to social rights must now be completed by cultural rights, a sphere of rights that incorporates the cosmopolitan dimension. Cultural rights concern at least three areas. In place of the individual as the bearer of rights, the emphasis shifts to rights largely for minorities, but also lifestyle rights including consumer rights, cultural rights and rights relating to new technologies and environmental concerns (Chaney 2002; Delanty 2000; Stevenson 2000, 2002).

It is in reconciling the universalistic rights of the individual with the need to protect minorities that the cosmopolitan moment is most evident. In this context cosmopolitan citizenship is understood in terms of a cultural shift in collective identities to include the recognition of others. Cosmopolitan citizenship is marked by a decreased importance of territory – as measured by the place of one's birth – in the definition of citizenship rights as well as a lesser salience on an underlying collective identity, in other words a political community does not have to rest on an underlying cultural community. Cultural rights are thus possible in the space that has been created by multiple and overlapping identities. As Seyla Benhabib has argued: 'Cosmopolitanism, the concern for the world as if it were one's *polis*, is furthered by such multiple, overlapping allegiances which are sustained across communities of language, ethnicity, religion, and nationality' (Benhabib 2004: 174–5).[7] In her Tanner lectures she put forward a nuanced theory of cosmopolitanism as consisting of mediations as opposed to reduction or totalization (Benhabib 2008: 19–20). Her thesis is that cosmopolitanism, as reflected in rights, is not reducible to rights as such but is more a way of framing issues. Cosmopolitanism takes the form of 'democratic iterations' which have a mediating role between cosmopolitan norms, on the one side, and, on the other, democratic movements and public opinion. It is an unavoidable feature of cosmopolitanism understood in this way that it leads to more, not less, contestation since meaning is constantly transformed and with it self-definitions are also transformed. That the normative level of rights, which have been disaggregated from nationality, is appropriated in political struggle by people who use such universalistic language to achieve their objectives is an instance of cosmopolitanism as a form of immanent transcendence.

The contemporary relevance of cosmopolitanism has arisen as a result of cultural pluralization arising from migration, ethnic multiculturalism, cultural diversity of all kinds and the growing demands for the recognition of different life choices (see Cheah and Robbins 1998). Iahwa Ong draws attention to the creation of a 'flexible citizenship' arising out of transnational migrations in the Pacific-Asian world where practices of multi-location of refugees and business migrants and their families have redefined the meaning of citizenship (Ong 1999; see also Kwok-bun 2005). In addition, but of more relevance to Europe, there is considerable evidence to suggest that national rights and international human rights are becoming increasingly blurred (see Eder and Giesen 2001; Soysal 1994). It is now more difficult for states to equate nationality and citizenship since many rights can be claimed on the basis of human rights. In short, membership rights are not exclusively defined in terms of a community of descent or of birth but of residence. These examples illustrate the rise of a cosmopolitan concept of citizenship, which varies from being a modification of the traditional understanding of citizenship in liberal political theory to an emphasis on global citizenship and post-national kinds of membership (Smith 2007).

---

[7] See also Benhabib (2008).

There can be little doubt that cosmopolitanism has been greatly enhanced as a sociologically pertinent topic due to the tremendous transformation in rights that has occurred in recent times. However, while the domain of rights is one of the main sites of cosmopolitanism it is not the only one. From the perspective of the cosmopolitan social theory one dimension of cosmopolitanism that is striking and not adequately recognized is the construction of political community around competing visions of the social world: political community is increasingly being defined in and through global communication with the result that the 'we' is counter-posed not only by reference to a 'they' but by the abstract category of the world. This is a point that has a more general application to the constitution of society and will be returned to later in this chapter. It will suffice to mention in the present context that a sociological perspective on cosmopolitan peoplehood suggests not merely an allegiance to the world community as opposed to national community, as Nussbaum (1996) argues, or the establishment of cultural rights, but a reframing of identities, loyalties and self-understandings in ways that have no clear direction. This suggests an understanding of cosmopolitanism as a form of world disclosure. Thus for Appiah, in his defence of 'rooted cosmopolitanism', cosmopolitans are people who construct their lives from whatever cultural resources they find themselves attached to. Appiah thus cites a comment made by Gertrude Stein in 1936 that 'America is my country and Paris is my hometown' (Appiah 1998: 91; see also 2004, 2006). The cosmopolitanism he espouses is one that celebrates cultural variety within states as well as across them. Rejecting the global humanist strand of Enlightenment cosmopolitanism, Appiah defends the liberal pluralist heritage as one that asserts the freedom to create oneself. Although this is a position that is largely a modification of liberal cosmopolitanism, there is the interesting suggestion of culture as an ongoing process of construction as opposed to being embodied in a particular way of life. This perspective reinforces the notion of cosmopolitanism as a mode of cultural framing which is not reducible to rights or particular identities, but concerns cultural models by which the social world is constituted. In sum, the significance of cosmopolitanism goes beyond post-national membership, but this is inadequately brought out in the existing approaches concerned with the political dimensions of cosmopolitanism.

The third strand in cosmopolitan theory can be termed cultural cosmopolitanism to distinguish it from the previous models. Hannerz's essay 'Cosmopolitans and Locals in World Culture' was a seminal work in shaping a view of cosmopolitanism as, what he called, 'a mode of managing meaning'. A genuine cosmopolitanism, he argued, 'is first of all an orientation, a willingness to engage with the Other. It entails intellectual and aesthetic openness towards divergent cultural experiences, a search for contrasts rather than uniformity' (Hannerz 1996, originally 1990: 103). In a similar vein, James Clifford (1992) has argued that the distinction between non-cosmopolitan locals and a cosmopolitan travelling culture can no longer be upheld. In place of this us/they polarity should be an emphasis on what he calls 'discrepant cosmopolitanism'. A major reorientation of cosmopolitan theory was initiated by the volume *Cosmopolitics: Thinking, Feeling Beyond the Nation*, which Pheng Cheah and Bruce Robbins edited in 1998. The inspiration for most of the contributions was the cosmopolitan turn within postcolonial theory, such as Homi Bhabha's (1990, 1994) 'vernacular cosmopolitanism' and James Clifford's 'discrepant cosmopolitanism'. These approaches are characterized by a pronounced anti-nationalism in favour of radical cosmopolitanism whose reference points are hybrid cultures. But in others this is marked by an easing of the dichotomy of nationalism versus cosmopolitanism and the universalism of the older nationalism. As Cheah (1998: 3) stated in the Introduction, 'We should not and perhaps cannot accept the old cosmopolitan ideal of transcending the distinction between strangers and friends'. In place of the classical unitary cosmopolitanism, is a concern with the multiple forms of cosmopolitanism. This includes a concern with cosmopolitanism as multiple attachments and attachment at a distance. These contributions mark a move away from Nussbaum's moral universalism. In his contribution to the volume, Richard Rorty put forward an argument for a contingent scale of loyalties: 'what makes you loyal to a smaller group may give you reason to cooperate in constructing a larger group, a group to which you may in time become equally loyal, or perhaps more loyal' (1998: 54). In his assessment of the present situation of postcolonial cosmopolitanism, Cheah suggests that the emphasis on hybridity has certain limits. On the one side, the new hybrid cosmopolitanism overplays culture to the detriment of its material basis and, on the other hand, it does not appreciate that much of it is carried by nationalism in a new guise: 'the forms of transnational activity we are witnessing today are not new cosmopolitanisms but are instead aporetic cases of nationalism as given culture in a cosmopolitan force field' (Cheah 1998: 292). Cheah's later work has given a much stronger emphasis on the need to locate cosmopolitanism within popular nationalism, especially if cosmopolitanism is to be able to seriously address emancipatory politics in the South (Cheah 2006). The neglect of this dimension results in an elitist, northern world perspective on cosmopolitanism. This leads him to a more critical attitude to 'discrepant cosmopolitanism' and the view that cosmopolitanism can transcend nationalism, since this neglects the fact that the nation-state is a necessary condition for progressive global local networks in the South where economic poverty is the main cause of oppression (Cheah 2006: 104–5).

To go beyond the limits of purely cultural analysis to an analysis of societal processes and orientations is clearly important. The first explicitly sociological discussion of cosmopolitanism is without doubt Émile Durkheim who was concerned with global issues to an extent that has often not been appreciated (Inglis and Robertson 2008). While this was an undeveloped part of this work, it nonetheless was a significant dimension. Durkheim believed that there was a possibility that at some point in the future humanity might be organized as a single society and that the organic solidarity that was characteristic of modernity could develop not just within national societies but also between societies, making possible a world patriotism. In *The Elementary Forms of Religious Life*, published in 1912, as Inglis and Robertson (2008: 19) point out, he drew conclusions about the emerging world culture of his time:

There is no people, no state, that is not involved with another society that is more or less unlimited and includes all peoples ... There is no national life that is not dominated by an inherently international collective life. As we go forward in history, these international groupings take on greater importance and scope. (Durkheim 2001: 322)[8]

Despite these interesting remarks, cosmopolitanism remained undeveloped in Durkheim's work. In contrast, Robert Merton's 'Patterns of Influence: Local and Cosmopolitan Influentials', originally published in 1948/9, was a more methodologically oriented application of cosmopolitanism (Merton 1968). Merton's analysis of different types of 'influential' persons, locals and cosmopolitans, was based upon interviews

[8] Quoted in Inglis and Robertson (2008: 19) who have developed a detailed reading of the cosmopolitan concerns of Durkheim's sociology.

with 86 persons in a small town, 'Rovere', on the east coast of the
United States. The distinction rested on their orientation to Rovere:
'the localite largely confines his interests to the community. Rovere is
essentially his world. Devoting little thought or energy to the Great
Society, he is preoccupied with local problems, to the virtual exclusion
of the national and international scene. He is, strictly speaking, parochial'. The cosmopolitan, in contrast, while being concerned with the
local community is 'also oriented significantly to the world outside
Rovere, and regards himself as an integral part of that world. He resides
in Rovere but lives in the Great Society. If the local type is parochial, the
cosmopolitan is ecumenical' (Merton 1968: 393). Merton's study offers
an interesting and methodologically sophisticated approach to the analysis of cosmopolitanism as a social orientation among individuals.
It also marked a departure from normative conceptions of cosmopolitanism. However Merton's concerns were restricted to an empirical
investigation into social types and his account of the cosmopolitan
personality was limited in many respects. Indeed, the Great Society to
which the cosmopolitan turned was the national society rather than the
wider world.

Since Merton several social theorists have attempted to reconceptua-
lize the idea of society in a cosmopolitan direction, although this is not
always explicitly stated. These developments concern major changes
in the cultural fabric of society leading to the erosion of the very notion
of a bounded conception of the social (see Gane 2004). The key to all of
this is the notion of societal pluralization. Examples of a more sociologically inclined cultural cosmopolitanism are to be found in theories
of mobilities and forms of consumption, hybridities, networks and even
modernity itself. Central to all these accounts is the positive value of
diversity, which is often equated with the modern cosmopolitan city (see
Sennett 1977). As argued by Calhoun, cosmopolitanism is not only an
elite phenomenon, but is fully compatible with a commitment to roots,
solidarity and belonging (Calhoun 2003a, 2003b). A critic of elite
cosmopolitanism, Calhoun asserts that no one lives outside particularistic solidarities (see also Lu 2000). Consumption-oriented approaches
have demonstrated the complex nature of cosmopolitan orientations
(Thompson and Tambyah 1999). As noted in Chapter 1, Pollock
(2002) has associated cosmopolitanism with non-Western cultures.
Werbner (1999) draws attention to working-class migrants who exhibit
cosmopolitan orientations that are different from and challenge the

cosmopolitanism of the global elite (see also Nava 2002, 2007). In a more recent publication Werbner (2008) has demonstrated the centrality of a new cosmopolitanism to anthropology: the new cosmopolitanism is rooted and situated and is not premised on the assumptions of a Western model of the world.[9] In a similar view, Lamont and Aksartova (2002) write about 'ordinary cosmopolitanisms' in working-class people of different ethnicities.

Manuel Castells's notion of networks as open and flexible structures suggests a basis for a cosmopolitan sociology (Castells 1996). For Castells, society exists today in the form of networks rather than territorial spaces. What is significant about the network are the modes of connectivity by which different things are related. Networks are open structures connected by nodes rather than hierarchical structures. Under the conditions of globalization the network is organized through informational flows. This notion of cosmopolitanism offers a new view of society, but is not without problems and can be criticized on three grounds. First, Castells tends to see networks as horizontal and tendentially open democratic systems, whereas it is easy to show that in fact networked systems are differentially organized systems of power and have their own hierarchies. Second, there is no basis for distinguishing between globalization and cosmopolitanism: the global context is the primary reality and everything else is a reaction to it. This neglects cosmopolitan resistances to globalization. Third, his notion of a network is largely a technocratic one determined by informational technologies and does not give any room to communicative spaces and global publics. The implication of this is that only societies that are integrated into the global informational economy can be cosmopolitan. This approach excludes earlier and alternative kinds of cosmopolitanism and fails to appreciate the significance of global publics in the constitution of the social.

According to Urry (2000, 2002), who aligns his position more explicitly with cosmopolitanism, the key feature of the current situation is the fact of mobility. For Urry, mobility is an ontological condition and is expressed in processes as different as global complexity and reflexive modernity: people, commodities, cultures, technologies are all mobile and their reality is one of mobility. Mobilities are not just

---

[9] For a debate on the significance of cosmopolitanism to contemporary anthropology, see Rapport and Stade (2007).

flows but networked relations and are globally organized in new kinds of spaces and temporal processes. In his theory, which is a development of Castells's and influenced by Bruno Latour, the idea of society is redundant and with it all of classical sociology because it suggests an entity that is bounded, territorial and constituted by the state. Global processes have undermined the nation-state creating an entirely new context for social relations, which instead of being relations between people are relations between mobile and immobile elements. This thesis lends itself to a cosmopolitan perspective since it sees the social world in terms of open as opposed to closed processes. The difficulty with this argument is twofold. On the one side, the argument that society has become redundant makes unwarranted assumptions about the concept of society in classical sociology as entirely defined by the categories of the nation-state and thus neglects earlier and more cosmopolitan notions of society which cannot be reduced to territorially bounded ideas. On the other side, it exaggerates the novelty of current mobilities. Aside from neglecting earlier mobilities, such as Marx's definition of capital, the main drawback with this approach is that too much explanatory power is given to global mobilities and hyper-chaotic phenomena. For instance, it is by no means evident that nation-states outside the relatively small part of the world within the European Union are losing power. If anything they are gaining power, as the examples of the United States and China suggest. Moreover, if the concept of society is jettisoned it will have to be replaced by something similar. From the perspective of a cosmopolitan social theory, global mobilities are of central importance, but the fact of mobility is not the key feature of the cosmopolitan movement. Indeed, many kinds of mobilities are not cosmopolitan in the sense used here. They may be open structures, as Urry argues, but the openness that he associated with cosmopolitanism is in fact global fluidity, or 'cosmopolitan global fluids' (Urry 2002: 133). The problem here, again, is the reduction of cosmopolitanism to globalization. In opposition to this emphasis on mobility as the chief characteristic of cosmopolitanism, the argument in this chapter is that cosmopolitanism cannot be entirely separated from the normative vision of an alternative society and that this imaginary is also present as a cultural model within the cultural traditions of societies as a form of immanent transcendence. Identities and modes of cultural belonging, while being influenced by global mobilities, are not reducible to mobility.

The aspect of globalization that is more pertinent is the abstract presence of the global public within the social world.

The turn to networks and mobilities from action thus does not solve the problem of comprehending the social world in terms of cosmopolitan challenges. An alternative to these approaches is the notion of hybridity. From the vantage point of Actor Network Theory (ANT), Bruno Latour advances a different notion of networks conceived of in terms of the idea of a hybrid (Latour 1993, 2005). He argues the social as society explains nothing; it is, he says, like the notion of ether in late nineteenth-century physics, namely a necessary illusion we have lived to learn with. In his view, the central issue is associations, that is the social concerns relations between things and what social actors do, rather than something that lies behind them and constituting, as in Durkheim and Bourdieu, a reality or objectivity of its own. This idea, which extends the notion of the network, suggests a cosmopolitan sociology in that the object of study is the relation between things. This relational dimension is very important in sociology, since the object of study is very often the relation between things, as in, for example, Marx's famous definition of capital. For cosmopolitanism, the significance resides in the notion of hybridity. While Latour's writings have mostly concerned hybrids of nature and society, the notion of hybridity has had a wider resonance in cultural approaches to globalization. Jan Nederveen Pieterse (2004) has written extensively on globalization as creating hybrid cultures arising out of transnational movements of people and cultures. Globalization involves grey zones, for example, creolization, which exist alongside other processes produced by globalization and entail not just networks and contacts, but also conflict. It is this dimension of conflict and resistance that is often neglected in the approaches inspired by Castells's work on the network society.

While avoiding many of the difficulties of global networks, the notion of hybridity does not fully account for cosmopolitanism. First, like Urry's mobilities, if everything is a hybrid then the concept loses any explanatory usefulness. Most societies and cultural entities have arisen out of a process of syncreticism whereby different elements are combined to produce something new. Second, there is a sense in which it could be argued most aspects of contemporary societies entail some degree of mixing as a result of the cross-fertilization of cultures. In this respect the connection with cosmopolitanism is evident but only to a limited degree. Cosmopolitanism is more than the simple fact of cross-fertilization since many hybrid phenomena – for example national socialism – are not in any coherent sense of the term cosmopolitan. It is easy to refer to many examples of multicultural communities, which may be called hybrid, but are not cosmopolitan in their denial of universal norms. In short, hybridity is a major aspect of cosmopolitanism but it is not itself the defining feature. Without some notion of an alternative society, cosmopolitanism has a limited normative application (see Fine 2003). One major dimension to cosmopolitanism, then, is that it opens up normative questions. Now, while this normativity has been more central to political cosmopolitan approaches discussed above, what is lost in ANT conceptions of cosmopolitanism as hybridity is precisely this normative orientation. Nature, for example, has been one of the key reference points in reshaping politics along cosmopolitan lines as is evidenced by the cosmopolitan politics of the environmental movement. For the same reason, the notion of the network as a new societal reality is also limited as a model for cosmopolitanism.

From a wider historical sociology cosmopolitan possibilities are increasingly being noted in modernity itself in terms of the interaction of different modernities. Several theorists have developed a notion of multiple modernity and have related this to a culturally nuanced notion of cosmopolitanism. The work of S. N. Eisenstadt (2003) and Johann Arnason (2003) have been at the fore of such developments which have led to an entirely new approach to modernity based on multiplicity and which is highly relevant for cosmopolitan social theory. This perspective will be returned to in Chapter 7 for a more detailed discussion, but for present purposes it can be remarked that this notion of multiple modernities challenges the classical theories of modernization and signals a particular view of the contemporary world in terms of a multiplicity of cultural and political projects based on civilizational transformation.[10] The cosmopolitan thrust of the argument is that civilizations are internally plural based on frameworks of interpretation, which can be appropriated in different ways by many social actors within and beyond the contours of a given civilization.

The idea of modernity as plural was already introduced by postmodernism, which by general agreement has not displaced modernity but opens the concept up to different readings. As Zygmunt Bauman (2000)

---

[10] For a detailed analysis, see Arnason (2003), Arjomand and Tiryakian (2004) and Ben-Rafael and Sternberg (2005).

has argued, the current form of modernity is not postmodernity, but what he calls 'liquid modernity', which is characterized by social forms based on transience, uncertainty, anxieties and insecurity and resulting in new freedoms that come at the price of individual responsibility and without the traditional support of social institutions. Although Bauman does not link this condition to cosmopolitanism, such a connection can be established with respect to social relations based on contingency. From a wider historical sociology of modernity cosmopolitan possibilities are more evident in a conception of modernity that stresses the interaction of different modernities. The notion of multiple modernity can be seen as a basis for a cosmopolitan conception of modernity as an interconnecting third culture (see Chapter 7).

It will suffice to remark in conclusion that theories of multiple modernity have led to a new conception of cosmopolitanism that gives particular emphasis to post-universalism. A post-universal cosmopolitanism is critical and dialogic, seeing as the goal is alternative readings of history and the recognition of plurality rather than the creation of a universal order, such as a cosmopolis. This is a view that enables us to see how people were cosmopolitan in the past and how different cosmopolitanisms existed before and despite Westernization. It may be termed 'cultural cosmopolitanism', that is a plurality of cosmopolitan projects by which the global and the local are combined in diverse ways. In this sense cosmopolitanism would be mostly exemplified in diasporas and in transnational modes of belonging. Such expressions of cosmopolitanism can be related to what is often called cultural globalization, that is expressions of globality that are evident in resistances to the culture of the metropolitan centres and manifest in creative appropriations and new cultural imaginaries which, unlike earlier cosmopolitan projects, are more present in popular culture than in high culture.

However, critical cosmopolitanism is not merely about plurality. Although this is one key aspect of cosmopolitanism, it is not the main or only aspect: cosmopolitanism is not a generalized version of multiculturalism where plurality is simply the goal. A post-universalistic conception of cosmopolitanism should rather be seen in terms of moral and political shifts in self-understanding that occur as a result of the impact of global tensions. Of particular importance in this respect is the tension between the global and the local, on the one side, and on the other the universal and the particular. It is possible to see these tensions as constituting the basic animus of cosmopolitanism. So against notions of

globalization and universality, on the one side, and plurality and particularism on the other, the cultural dimension of cosmopolitanism consists more in the creation and articulation of communicative models
of world openness in which societies undergo transformation in their
self-understanding as a result of coming into contact with each other.
The inevitable diversity that comes from the pluralization of cultural
traditions should not detract from processes of communicative transformation that arise as a result of responses to the presence of global publics.
Cosmopolitan culture is one of self-problematization and while diversity
will, by the pluralizing nature of cosmopolitanism, be inevitable, the
reflexive and critical self-understanding of cosmopolitanism cannot be
neglected. Cosmopolitanism must be seen as one of the major expressions
of the tendency in modernity towards self-problematization and subject
formation.

Defining cosmopolitanism: the global public and world openness

Underlying many cultural conceptions of cosmopolitanism discussed
in the foregoing analysis is a failure to distinguish globalization from
cosmopolitanism. Yet there is clearly a connection, but the distinction
needs to be clarified. The trend towards cultural cosmopolitanism
offers some of the most promising developments and avoids the characteristic bias towards universalism typical of the other approaches
discussed above. Cosmopolitanism concerns a dynamic relation
between the local and the global. This is suggested by the term itself:
the interaction of the universal order of the cosmos and the human
order of the polis. Cosmopolitanism thus concerns the multiple ways
the local and the national is redefined as a result of interaction with
the global. The resulting situation will vary depending on the precise
nature of the interaction. Hybridization, creolization and indigenization may be the result of interactions in which the local appropriates
the global or, in the case of global diasporas, where the local is
transformed into a new cosmopolitan global flow. Where, as in the
example of the global diaspora, the outcome of local global relations is
a phenomenon that is neither local nor global. These examples, which
could be seen in terms of instances of localization, have been much
discussed under the general terms of cultural globalization (Appadurai
1996; Hannerz 1996; Nederveen Pieterse 2004; Tomlinson 1999).

In contrast, examples such as McDonaldization and other instances of McSociety illustrate the predominance of the global over the local. The extent to which any global process can entirely impose itself on the local is, of course, disputed (see Beck *et al.* 2000).

The previous points are a reminder of the essentially contingent, multi-levelled and indeterminate nature of globalization, which is an unavoidable context for almost every aspect of the social world as structured and framed by global processes. The global is not outside the social world but is inside it in numerous ways. The aspect of this, decisive for cosmopolitanism, that needs to be emphasized is the notion of the global public. By this is not meant a specific public, but the global context in which communication is filtered as a reality creating process. The global public is the ever-present sphere of discourse that contextualizes political communication and public discourse today. It has been long recognized that social reality entails processes of social construction entailing knowledge and socio-cognitive structures, but what is only becoming clearer in recent times is that this now occurs in the context of risk, uncertainty and contestation – in other words contingency. The role of the public in this is of course also well documented, as is evidenced by the significance which is now attached to the public sphere, which must be conceived as having a cosmopolitan and hermeneutic dimension (Eder 2005; Kögler 2005; Strydom 2002). While debates continue on the question of the global public sphere as a transnational space, what is more important is the emergence of a global public, which is less a spatially defined entity than a manifestation of discourse as a third culture. The discursive construction of the social world takes places within the wider context of global communication in which the global public plays a key role. The global public has a major resonance in all of communication in the sense that it structures and contextualizes much of public discourse and has what Strydom (1999b, 2002, 2006) calls a cognitive function in shaping discourse.

It is no longer possible to see national societies or any particular social form in terms of autonomous actors isolated from the global context. The global public is inside as well as outside national publics and is the central dynamic in cosmopolitanism, conceived of as an opening up of discursive spaces and which has a critical function in shaping the social world. This is one reason why, as remarked earlier, it is so difficult to define peoplehood or political community more generally today. Dynamics and boundaries of inclusion and exclusion are constantly changing, making society a category that can be analysed only as a process. This idea of the social as a process is reflected in Luhmann's concept of society as existing only as 'world society' (Luhmann 1990). But this world society exists only as a concretely existing society in so far as it is a plural condition dispersed in numerous discourses. Moreover, and a point of considerable significance is that the Self, or the 'We', is not merely defined by reference to an 'Other', a 'They' that is external to the Self – whether in adversarial terms or in more exclusives modes – but is defined by the abstract category of the world as a form of third culture. The constitution of the social world in and through globally filtered processes of communication cannot be seen in the simple terms of Self and Other, terms which are often attractive illusions for many social scientists and social commentators. A cosmopolitan-oriented social theory should rather have as its goal the identification of the broader context of the constitution of the social world in which Self and Other are articulated in self-problematizing ways within discursive processes. It is thus possible to speak of world openness in cosmopolitan terms in situations where the global public impinges upon political communication and other kinds of public discourse creating as a result new visions of social order. To speak of cosmopolitanism as real is thus to refer to these situations of immanent transcendence, and which we may term the cosmopolitan imagination, where the constitution of the social world is articulated through cultural models in which codifications of both Self and Other undergo transformation.

To an extent, this cosmopolitan dynamic is something that goes on even in relatively closed societies, including earlier societies. However it is only with the enhanced momentum of globalization and more extensive modes of communication that it takes on a specifically cos-mopolitan significance. Under the conditions of advanced globalization the radical impetus within modernity has a more general sphere of application. This has nothing to do with the alleged crisis of the nation-state or with the transformation of sovereignty. The notion of cosmo-politanism put forward here is distinct from traditional notions of Kantian cosmopolitanism. Rather than seeing the cosmopolitan imagi-nation in an international order, it is, as Beck and Sznaider (2006) argue, more reflexive and internalized. The notion of an 'internalized cosmopolitanism' that they suggest is therefore a contrast to notions of the 'world system', 'world society' or 'world polity', as proposed variously by Immanuel Wallerstein, Niklas Luhmann and John Meyer.

For Wallerstein the 'world system' is essentially the world economy and emerged out of the rise of the West: it is based on the dominance of a single centre over the periphery. Cosmopolitanism in contrast concerns less the homogenizing capitalist world economy than different combinations of periphery and centre. Luhmann's 'world society' and Meyer's approach regard the global level as the primary reality which simply impacts upon the local. The notion of critical cosmopolitanism put forward in this book stresses the mutual implication of centre and periphery and local and global levels as a transformative process of immanent transcendence. In sum, what is missing in these accounts is the cosmopolitan moment conceived of as a creative combination of different forces – centre and periphery, the local and global. While the central dynamic of cosmopolitanism comes from modernity, it is enhanced but not created by globalization. The notion of critical cosmopolitanism sees the category of the world in terms of openness rather than in terms of a universal system and as such it is more a matter of world disclosure. It is this world disclosing orientation that defines the cosmopolitan imagination. The emphasis on openness has also been stated by Hannerz (1990: 239) for whom cosmopolitanism is 'an intellectual and aesthetic stance of openness towards divergent cultural experiences'. The approach adopted in this book places a stronger emphasis on the socio-cognitive process by which new forms of social reality are constructed through an immanent transformation in communicative capacities and in subject formation.

Modernity takes different societal and civilizational forms but fundamental to it is the movement towards self-transformation, the belief that human agency can radically transform the present in the image of an imagined future. It is this impetus that constitutes the cosmopolitanism of modernity since through it different modernities interact. It lies in the basic self-understanding of modernity that there are no secure foundations for identity, meaning and memory. The term cosmopolitanism signals a condition of self-confrontation, incompleteness; modernity concerns the loss of certainty and the realization that certainty can never be established for once and for all. Globalization – as a process that intensifies connections, enhances possibilities for cultural translations and deepens the consciousness of globality – is the principal motor of modernity. Modernity is not a global condition as such, but a transformative condition and one which can be called cosmopolitan due to its plural nature and interactive logics. Cosmopolitanism is the key expression of the tendency within modernity to self-problematization and self-transcendence. On the basis of these remarks it can be established that cosmopolitanism has become one of the major expressions of modernity today due to the extent and speed of globalization. It follows, then, that the solutions to the problems of globalization do not come from globalization itself but from the immanent cosmopolitan possibilities within modernity itself.

No society can resist this and hope to survive. As Habermas has argued: 'A dogmatically protected culture will not be able to reproduce itself, particularly in a social environment rich with alternatives' (Habermas 2005: 23). The inescapability of cosmopolitanism can be partly explained by the very fact of globalization, which in penetrating to all parts of the world and into most spheres of activity in markets, in media, in education, has created a situation in which societies have become increasingly more and more embroiled in each other and in global processes. This has led some theorists to speak of global modernity (Dirlik 2003; Therborn 2003). However, this external or environmental situation is only one aspect of the cosmopolitan challenge to societies. The other is the internal, developmental transformation of cultural models arising as a result of learning processes associated with modernity. Societies as well as social groups contain within their consciousness and cognitive structures ways of responding to the challenges modernity presents. Whether it is due to societal complexity or the demands of living in multiethnic societies and competing conceptions of the common good, it is possible, following Habermas, to speak of a limited universality of problem-solving methods based on reasoned deliberation and recognition of the integrity of the individual (Habermas 1994, 2005). This is not a transcultural rationality, but rather a competence that is present in all of cultures to varying degrees and it therefore follows that such a universalism will take culturally specific forms. Without giving a detailed consideration of the problem of reconciling universalistic norms and particular cultural values, it will have to suffice for present purposes to state that there is considerable empirical evidence that bears out philosophical arguments concerning the reconciliation of universal claims and the limits of the particular context (Cowan *et al.* 2001). As Seyla Benhabib (2002: 25–6) has argued, 'cultures themselves, as well as societies, are not holistic but polyvocal, multilayered, decentred, and fractured systems of action and signification'. To put this in yet stronger cosmopolitan terms the point is that the diversity of cultures should be seen in terms of cultures being related rather than different. To think in such terms requires an epistemic shift in the direction of what Beck and Sznaider call 'methodological cosmopolitanism', as against assumptions of ontological difference that pervades much of academic and political thinking. Cosmopolitan sociology needs to move beyond a view of the social world as empirically given to one that captures emergent cultural forms and the vision of an alternative society. As a methodologically grounded approach, critical cosmopolitan sociology has a very specific task: to discern or make sense of social transformation by identifying new or emergent social realities. Therefore the cosmopolitan imagination is not identifiable with the mere condition of plurality or the attachments of the individual; it is rather more concerned with openness and societal transformative. Although particularly characteristic of recent social theory and relevant to trends within late modernity, it is a logic integral to modernity and, as Bryan Turner has argued, was a major concern of classical sociology, which cannot be reduced to methodological nationalism (Turner 2006). As pointed out earlier, cosmopolitanism was a theme in the work of Durkheim and can be found also in the writings of other classical sociologists, such as G. H. Mead. In *Mind, Self and Society*, Mead considered the 'question whether we belong to a larger community' and asked the question: 'Can we carry on a conversation in international terms?' He recognized in this classic work in symbolic interactionism wider societal processes of a global nature that require a cosmopolitan response, or in his terms 'international mindedness' (Mead 1934: 270–1). For Mead this was something rooted in the very categories of human experience.

The cosmopolitan imagination entails a view of society as an ongoing process of self-constitution. Alain Touraine has proposed the important notion of 'self-production of the society' in which struggles to define cultural models, or communicative frameworks of societal interpretation, constitute the fabric of the social. It is the nature of such struggles that they are incomplete and what is called 'society' is nothing more than the existence of such struggles. According to this definition of the constitution of the social: 'Society is not merely a system of norms or a system of domination: it is a system of social relations, of debates and conflicts, of political initiatives and claims, of ideologies and alienation' (Touraine 1977: 30). Despite his tendency to reduce the social to a dominant social movement and a notion of historicity that lacks a connection with modernity as a developmental process, his conception of the social in terms of subject formation and as an open and indeterminate field offers an important foundation for cosmopolitan social theory (see Delanty 1999). The key point in this is that he shifts the emphasis to cultural models, which are wider than group rights and collective identities, and contain what is a key aspect of cosmopolitanism, namely the transformative vision of an alternative society that is tied to subject formation.

The conception of cosmopolitanism put forward in this book is one that does not deny the relevance of nationhood. This is simply because most expressions of nationhood today entail cosmopolitan principles and orientations. Many popular nationalist movements in the South have emerged as a reaction against globalization. In seeking to reclaim the state from global capitalism, they often draw on cosmopolitan current (Yegenoglu 2005). Eckersley (2007) and Nash (2003) draw attention to 'popular cosmopolitan' movements which often are embroiled in national feelings rather than being in opposition to it. Westwood and Phizacklea (2000: 8) point out that 'nation-states in Latin America have been produced as much from diversity as the power of the homogenising national narrative'.

Cosmopolitan nationalism is also reflected in postcolonial conceptions of the nation, for instance as put forward by Homi Bhabha. According to Bhabha (1990), nations are not unified or homogenous but contain within their imaginaries alterity. The nation is formed in a narrative of transgression and negotiation with otherness and is, as a result, a hybrid entity. By means of the concept narration, Bhabha aims to capture the negotiation of identity in a continuous movement. Nations are built upon narratives which are incomplete and perspectival; they are stories that people tell about their collective existence and in them the past is constantly redefined. This is more true today than ever when marginal groups are coming to play a greater role in defining national identity: women, migrants, indigenous peoples etc. are less outside the nation than within it. Related to this is a shift in the narrative construction of the nation from the centre to the peripheries and a male worldview to a female one. The result of this shift to margins is more and more different kinds narratives of nationhood. As a hybrid and multivocal category the nation is thus already cosmopolitan. In a similar vein feminist scholars have argued that something like a feminization of the nation is occurring as a result of recodifications of the nation by migrant women, leading to a move beyond earlier male constructions of women as the docile voice of the nation (Anthias and Yuval-Davis 1989; Yuval-Davis 1997).

The dimensions and dynamics of cosmopolitanism

The definition of cosmopolitanism proposed in this chapter has related it to the tendency within modernity towards self-problematization and on the basis of this it has been further linked to processes of globalization, which have led to a global public that is present in all of communication and public discourse now central to the constitution of the social world. The upshot of this is that the relations of Self and Other that pervade the social world are constituted within the broader context of the world as represented by the global public. This thesis goes beyond the postmodernist arguments concerning alterity and the otherness of the self since it is concerned with the ways in which social reality is constructed through a third culture. Cosmopolitanism does not arise merely in situations of cultural diversity or taking the perspective of the Other. It is not an identity as such that can be contrasted with national identity or other kinds of identity, except in a restricted sense of the term. In this sense cosmopolitan sociology is not an alterative to all previous kinds of social theory.[11] Critical cosmopolitanism does not take an extreme position in dismissing all that is not cosmopolitanism since cosmopolitanism is a process that comes into play when third cultural orientations are in evidence. Moreover, as used here, cosmopolitanism does not simply refer to cases or situations that are called by those involved in them cosmopolitan, although this dimension of cosmopolitan self-description is by no means irrelevant; the critical aspect of cosmopolitanism concerns the internal transformation of social and cultural phenomena through self-problematization, self-transcendence and pluralization. It is in the interplay of Self, Other and World that cosmopolitan processes come into play. Without a learning process, that is an internal cognitive transformation, it makes little sense in calling something cosmopolitan. As used here, the term refers to an immanent developmental change in the social world arising out of competing cultural models and modes of cognition. This suggests a

---

[11] For a critique of methodological cosmopolitanism as advocated by Beck, see Chernilo (2006a, 2006b).

processual conception of the social as an emergent reality formed out of re-interpretations of experience.

It is useful to distinguish three main dimensions of cosmopolitanism: the historical level of modernity, the macro or societal level of the interaction of societies or societal systems, and the micro level of identities, movements and communities within the social world. With regard to modernity, cosmopolitanism arises when different modernities interact and undergo transformation, producing a new field of tensions within the project of modernity. The central animus within modernity as discussed earlier – the self-transformative drive to re-make the world in the image of the self in the absence of absolute certainty – provides the basic direction for cosmopolitanism. European cultural and political modernity was formed out of the interactions and mutual interpenetration of different models of modernity, in particular the French and German, but also the British and later American modernity. It may be suggested that in the present time European modernity is undergoing a further cosmopolitan transformation arising from the encounter with the non-European world, as a result of migration, multiculturalism and globalization. There is another dimension to this, which cannot be explored here, which is that the formative influences on European modernity were Asian and that the rise of European modernity was dependent on these earlier forms of cosmopolitanism.

The cosmopolitan perspective with regard to modernity is the context in which to view the macro and the micro dimensions of cosmopolitanism. In macro terms, it is possible to speak of cosmopolitanism as an outcome when two or more societies interact and undergo change of a developmental nature in their model of modernity as a result. While modernity itself can be seen in terms of cosmopolitanism, one of the major expressions of that dimension of cosmopolitanism is in the actual interrelations of societies. In this respect, Europeanization can be cited as one of the most relevant examples of cosmopolitanism. Europeanization entails horizontal links existing between European societies, vertical links between European societies and the EU, and transversal links between European societies and the global, as well as between the EU and the global (see Chapter 8). The resulting cosmopolitanism is more than the co-existence of difference. Rather than simply co-existence of the various levels as the outcome, what in fact is occurring is the co-evolution of the societal levels and which might be reflected in a transformation in self-understanding. From a macro-societal perspective what is also significant are changing core–periphery relations, with the core having to redefine itself from the perspective of the periphery. This point has a more general application to cosmopolitanism as a condition that concerns the formation of an emergent reality. As stated earlier, cosmopolitanism, viewed from a critical perspective, is a condition of immanent transcendence through world openness and self-transformation.

The micro dimension of cosmopolitanism concerns individual agency and social identities, that is aspects of cosmopolitanism reflected in internal societal change understood in terms of subject formation. This is the dimension of cosmopolitanism that is most commonly commented on, but the examples that are generally given tend to focus on transnational or post-national phenomena. The analysis in this chapter is that this dimension must not only be looked at in the wider context of the macro and historical framework of modernity, but it must also be seen as more than a simple empirical condition, as in the frequently given example of a shift from national community to transnational community or the replacement of national identities with cosmopolitan ones. The micro dimension of cosmopolitanism is exemplified in changes within, for example, national identities rather than in the emergence of new identities. So cosmopolitanism is not to be equated with trans-nationalization, as is the tendency in political cosmopolitanism as discussed above. The relativizing of cultural values in contemporary society and the experience of contingency has led to a greater self-scrutiny within national identity: there are few national identities that do not contain self-problematizing forms of self-understanding. Rather than find cosmopolitanism embodied in a supra-national identity, it makes more sense to see it expressed in more reflexive kinds of self-understanding. Taking the example of Europeanization, a cosmopolitan European identity can be seen less as a new supra-identity rather than a growing reflexivity within existing identities, including personal, national and supra-national identities, as well as in other kinds of identities (see Chapter 8). In addition to the transformation in identity, there is also the transformation in communication and in cultural models.

Considerable emphasis should be placed on the interactive dimension, which can be seen as a precondition and amplifier of cosmopolitanism, without being equated with cosmopolitanism as such. It is out of the interaction of communities, societies, individuals from different cultures, that the cosmopolitan imagination is generated. As Tarrow has commented, 'it is through people's relations to significant others that cosmopolitan attitudes are shaped. What is new in our era is the increased number of people and groups whose relations place them beyond their local and national settings without detaching them from locality' (Tarrow 2005: 41). The cosmopolitan imagination is consti- tuted not in the fact of such forms of interaction, but in the awareness of them. In this sense it is possible to see cosmopolitanism as a form of reflexivity in which global issues enter into the self-consciousness of people and movements.

The indicators of cosmopolitanism go beyond shifts in identity to wider discursive and cultural transformation. In methodological terms, cosmopolitan indicators are necessarily ones concerning socio-cultural mediation. If the cosmopolitan moment arises in the construction and emergence of new identities or forms of self-understanding, cultural frames and cultural models, then mediation is the key to it. This emphasis on mediation between, for example, competing conceptions of the social world accords with the cosmopolitan idea in all its forms: the desire to go beyond ethnocentricity and particularity. In this sense then critical cosmopolitanism is an open process by which the social world is made intelligible; it should be seen as the expression of new ideas, the opening of spaces of discourse, identifying possibilities for translation and the construction of the social world. Following Bryan Turner's analysis, it can be related to such virtues as irony (emotional distance from one's own history and culture), reflexivity (the recogni- tion that all perspectives are culturally conditioned and contingent), scepticism towards the grand narratives of modern ideologies, care for other cultures and an acceptance of cultural hybridization, an ecume- nical commitment to dialogue with other cultures, especially religious ones, and nomadism, as a condition of never being fully at home in cultural categories or geopolitical boundaries (Turner 2001; Turner and Rojek 2001: 225). This is also reiterated in the arguments of other social theorists, such as Calhoun (2003b), Gilroy (2004) and Kurasawa (2004) that cosmopolitanism does not entail the negation of solidarities, as liberal cosmopolitan theorists, such as Nussbaum (1996) argue, but is more situated and, as Appiah (2004) argues, it is also 'rooted'.

This notion of cosmopolitanism goes beyond conventional associa- tions of cosmopolitanism with world polity or with global flows. I am stressing the socially situated nature of cosmopolitan processes while recognizing that these processes are world-constituting or constructivist ones. Such processes take the form of translations between things that are different (see Chapter 7). The space of cosmopolitanism is the space of such translations. It is the nature of such translations that the very terms of the translation are altered in the process of translation and something new is created but which also contains the elements of what has gone before it. Without this dimension of self-transcendence, cosmopolitanism is a meaningless term. Conceived of in such terms, cosmopolitanism entails the opening up of normative questions within the cultural imaginaries of societies. The research object for critical cosmopolitan sociology concerns precisely this space, the discursive space of translations, dialogue and exchange. But more attention needs to be given to the empirical manifestations of cosmopolitanism and to methodological considerations.

Ulrich Beck (2000, 2002, 2006) has been at the forefront in advocating a 'methodological cosmopolitanism' as an alternative to 'methodological nationalism', which has allegedly prevailed until now.[12] The basis of his case for a new methodological cosmopolitanism is the simple recognition that social reality has become cosmopolitan. Beck refers to the following transformations in the nature of social reality that point to the necessity for a cosmopolitan perspective in theory and in methodology. The awareness of the interconnected nature of the world as one consisting of risks and crises challenges the perspective of the nation-state. What is internal and external cannot be easily separated, but nor is it possible to live in a world without borders with the result that new borders are constantly being drawn. In addition, there is the principle of the recognition of difference and that of empathy leading to the interchangeability of situations. In addition, there is the mélange principle of the mixing of local, national, ethnic and religious cultures. Beck interprets these developments not in terms of a conventional model of globalization, in the sense of top-down economic-led processes, but as what he terms 'cosmopolitanization'. This is a multidimensional process and includes new institutional forms, such as the International Court of Justice and the United Nations. This is not simply globalization, he argues, but a product of the intensification of social relations all over the world as opposed to being globally

[12] This is a disputed point. See Chernilo (2006a, 2006b, 2007).

induced. Cosmopolitanization is a globalization 'from within'; it emerges from the internal transformation of societies.

This leads to a second concept: 'cosmopolitan realism'. Cosmopolitanization is real and not merely a state of mind. Its reality consists of the fact that people are living in an interconnected world and experience it as such. Beck thus rejects the view that cosmopolitanism is a choice or is voluntary, and possibly associated with a mobile global elite. It is, on the contrary, part of the social reality of contemporary societies. This can be viewed as a 'banal cosmopolitanism' in that it has become part of everyday life even if it is not conscious: 'Cosmopolitanism in this sense means latent cosmopolitanism, unconscious cosmopolitanism, passive cosmopolitanism which shapes reality as side effects of global trade or global threats such as climate change, terrorism or financial crises. My life, my body, my "individual existence" become part of another world, of foreign cultures, religions, histories and global interdependencies, without my realizing or expressingly wishing it' (Beck 2006: 19). Where Kant's cosmopolitanism was about imposing order on an unordered world, Beck sees the new cosmopolitanization of society as less ordered and chaotic. This does not mean nation-states cease to exist, for clearly they do and much of the cosmopolitanization of reality occurs within a world of nation-states, but they are in the process of becoming what he calls 'zombie categories', redundant concepts inherited from the past that are still in currency because there is nothing to replace them.

Beck further distinguishes between cosmopolitanization and a cosmopolitan outlook or perspective. The latter is the basis of cosmopolitan institutions and arises as a result of the increasing impact of the 'world risk society' in everyday life and in politics. Global risks sharpen ethical and political consciousness promoting a cosmopolitan outlook on the world. This kind of cosmopolitanism is not a matter of mere love of humanity but arises in a climate of heightened global threats and risks forcing new definitions of reality and new ways of looking at the global problems and it consists, too, of the capacity to see the local and the national as interconnected with the global: 'The cosmopolitan outlook calls into question one of the most powerful convictions concerning society and politics, which finds expression in the claim that "modern society" and "modern politics" can only be organized in the form of national states' (Beck 2006: 24). Cosmopolitanization also entails anti-cosmopolitanism in that it provokes resistance. On the basis of a critique of the fallacies of methodological nationalism and the existence of a cosmopolitan realism, Beck makes a strong case for 'methodological nationalism'. This rests on a distinction between normative or philosophical cosmopolitanism – roughly identical with classical cosmopolitanism and much of contemporary cosmopolitan political philosophy – and empirical-analytical cosmopolitanism. The latter is a social-scientific attempt to examine processes of cosmopolitanization in so far as they are really existing. This distinction is one between the cosmopolitan 'condition' and the cosmopolitan 'moment', with the former referring to the standpoint of philosophical cosmopolitanism and the latter its empirical manifestation in social reality. Beck's characterization of how methodological cosmopolitanism results in a major transformation of the research agenda of social science varies and is often unclear in terms of its novelty, but the main aspects are: risk-cosmopolitanism, with global public opinion as a side effect, the emergence of 'post-international' politics in which states are not the only actors, the increase in global inequality and its fragmentation into national inequalities which tend to disguise their global nature, and the banal cosmopolitanism of everyday life. Beck and Sznaider (2006: 17–18) develop this with the argument that social science can conceptualize and thematize the relational patterns of global, national, transnational and local links.

Beck's methodological cosmopolitanism is the most extensive application of cosmopolitanism to the social sciences. He avoids the excessive normativity that is a feature of much of the literature on cosmopolitanism, for, as he puts it, cosmopolitanism cannot ultimately be separated from what it is. It is in this sense that his concept of cosmopolitanism is highly relevant to the concern with immanent transcendence that is a feature of the critical theory tradition. Moreover he avoids setting up a dualism of nationalism versus cosmopolitanism in that he sees cosmopolitanization as occurring within nation-states and not as an exclusively universalistic condition: 'Cosmopolitan realism does not negate nationalism but presupposes it and transforms it into a cosmopolitan nationalism. Without the stabilizing factors that nationalism provides in dealing with difference, cosmopolitanism is in danger of losing itself in a philosophical never-never land' (Beck 2006: 49). Cosmopolitanism, he asserts, entails the recognition of difference, both internally and externally. In this sense, then, it involves both relativism and universalism. Beck's methodological approach is not without some problems. The main criticism that can be made is his tendency to conflate cosmopolitanism with transnationalization. The notion of cosmopolitanization, itself somewhat contrived, has an unclear relation to the concepts of transnationalism and globalization. Clearly Beck wants to examine the empirical manifestations of cosmopolitanism and thus requires a social scientific as opposed to a purely normative idea. But in rejecting normative cosmopolitanism, his notion of cosmopolitanization ends up very much like transnationalism or globalization in the sense of 'glocalization'. It is clearly evident from the extensive literature that globalization can be understood in terms of the interaction of local, national and global forces.

A related difficulty is that Beck's notion of cosmopolitanization tends to be over-generalized to include potentially everything and as result it is difficult to determine what is and what is not cosmopolitan. While he recognizes that cosmopolitanization can lead to anti-cosmopolitan movements, on the whole the direction of his argument is to see globalization – global risks etc. – impacting on national societies bringing about their cosmopolitanization in 'banal' ways and arising out of this is a growing consciousness which he calls the cosmopolitan outlook. What is needed is a more differentiated, and possibly a more limited application, of the term cosmopolitanism in order to avoid the conflation of cosmopolitanism and transnationalism (see Roudemetof 2005). However, the main advance Beck makes is to place the emphasis on the empirical forms of cosmopolitanism. Despite the tendency to over-generalize and to reduce cosmopolitanism to transnationalism, the value of a methodological cosmopolitan approach consists in advancing an empirical-analytical category that includes within it a focus on ethical and political orientations of a cosmopolitan nature. This combination of the empirical and the normative is one of the chief advantages of the concept of cosmopolitanism over the competing notions of globalization and transnationalism. It is also to the credit of his approach that he develops a notion of cosmopolitanism as a social process as opposed to being a specific condition or voluntary choice. This is what the somewhat awkward expression cosmopolitanization is intended to convey. It captures the sense by which cosmopolitanism can be an unintentional outcome of societal processes and is thus not reducible to identifiable individuals or beliefs or identities (Beck and Sznaider 2006: 7).

What is required is a sharper concept of cosmopolitanism as an empirical process. Beck's analysis does not go far enough when it comes to measuring or assessing the extent to which something is cosmopolitan and it is not sufficiently clear where the distinction between the normative/prescriptive and the empirical/descriptive levels of analysis lies. Part of the difficulty resides in the comprehensive notion of methodological cosmopolitanism, which in becoming a new methodological approach that replaces everything that has gone before is insufficiently clear when it comes to specific social and political examples. Methodological cosmopolitanism needs to be more methodological than in Beck's analysis where the indicators of cosmopolitanism are not sufficiently distinct from their preconditions and from what he calls a cosmopolitan outlook. The result is that cosmopolitanization leads to cosmopolitanism. An alternative approach would distinguish between the preconditions of cosmopolitanism and social indicators of cosmopolitanism. Transnationalization can be a significant precondition of cosmopolitanism, without being necessarily a cause, since cosmopolitanism can exist without transnationalism. In order to measure empirically cosmopolitanism in any of its forms – societal, individual etc. – indicators need to be established. It is here that the normative dimensions of cosmopolitanism are particularly important. It must be possible to demonstrate the extent to which given situations are manifestations of cosmopolitanism as opposed to postulating, on the one side, processes of 'cosmopolitanization' and, on the other, a resulting 'cosmopolitan outlook'. What needs to be explained and measured is precisely the latter and its relation to 'cosmopolitanization'.

In so far as cosmopolitanism, as opposed to its preconditions, concerns shifts in self-understanding and self-problematization in light of the encounter with the Other, what needs to be demonstrated is how in specific situations such forms of self-transformation occur and how these develop to become macro societal trends. As Skribis and Woodward (2008: 734) argue: 'In order to see cosmopolitanism as a useful analytical tool we suggest that it needs to be seen as a set of practices and dispositions, grounded in social structures, and observable in commonplace folk settings and practices.' In a further publication, Woodward *et al.* (2008: 211) develop a research approach that focuses on dispositions, which they argue is 'consistent with the idea that cosmopolitanism involves particular competencies, modes of managing meanings, and various forms of mobility'.

Similarly Lamont and Aksartova (2002) see cosmopolitanism as expressed in particular cultural repertoires that are drawn on by individuals in everyday situations. In this way cosmopolitanism is neither reducible to societal preconditions, such as transnational movements, nor to a global political community. The transnationalization of the life-world and increased mobility may lead to greater cosmopolitanism but whether or not this occurs is precisely what needs to be demonstrated. Mau *et al.* (2008) distinguish between transnationalization and cosmopolitanism by attempting to show that people with cross-border experiences and transnational social relations are more likely to adopt cosmopolitan attitudes with respect to foreigners and to issues of global governance. In their analysis cosmopolitanism refers to an empirically measurable attitudinal stance as opposed to specific kinds of actions and experiences for which they reserve the term transnationalization. In this way, they analytically separate the two and related concepts in a way that allows the former to be clearly identified. This approach has the advantage that it captures the normative dimension that is lost in Beck's notion of empirical cosmopolitanization, for in Beck's approach the normative is confined to the level of outcomes as in the notion of a cosmopolitan outlook. In the terms of Beck's approach, it is the cosmopolitan outlook that is subject to empirical investigation rather than cosmopolitanization, which should be seen as a precondition. Following Held (2002), Mau *et al.* (2008) distinguish three interconnected dimensions of cosmopolitanism as a measurable attitude: the recognition of the increasing interconnectedness of political communities, the development of an understanding of overlapping fortunes that require collective solutions at local, national and global levels, and the celebration of difference, diversity and hybridity and a related capacity to reason from the point of view of others and mediate traditions (Mau *et al.* 2008: 5). In a similar way, Roudemetof (2005) argues for an operationalization of the notion of cosmopolitanism in terms of a continuum of degrees of attachment to cultures, locales and regions. He distinguishes sharply between transnationalism and cosmopolitanism while seeing both in terms of different layers or as a continuum. He makes a convincing argument for a graduated approach that allows the researcher to see how some transnationals are predisposed towards localism while others are inclined towards cosmopolitanism: 'the specification of a continuum that consists of different degrees of attachment allows the researcher to view cosmopolitanism and local predispositions as relationships of degree, and not as absolutes' (Roudemetof 2005: 123). The overlapping nature of identities and loyalties is being increasingly recognized as a feature of cosmopolitanism, which is not a zero-sum game of local or global positions (see Phillips 2002). Indeed it is the capacity to imagine multiple forms of identification that marks the cosmopolitan moment (Woodward *et al.* 2008).

Globalization or transnationalism has greatly transformed people's lives whether they are aware of it or not, but it is not this that is cosmopolitanism as such. Roudemetof stresses the element of attachment or belonging as a criterion or indicator of cosmopolitanism (see also Roudemetof and Haller 2007). Faced with the reality of transnational experiences and global forces, people opt for different kinds of attachment, with some opting for greater degrees of identification with locales, nations and global community. Norris (2000), in a study on cosmopolitan orientations, found that the most important indicators of cosmopolitanism are those associated with generational change and with education. Those born after 1945 are more likely to display cosmopolitan attitudes than those born earlier. Norris defined cosmopolitanism in terms of cosmopolitans who in turn are defined by identifying more broadly with their continent or with the world, and who have a greater faith in the institutions of world governance. She found that the most salient indicator of an emerging cosmopolitan orientation comes from generational change.

Such approaches have provided much needed empirical applications of cosmopolitanism without necessarily proclaiming a new methodological cosmopolitanism. However, they are limited by being confined to the analysis of the attitudes of individuals, who are located somewhere on a continuum of locals and cosmopolitans. The focus is ultimately on individuals who either are cosmopolitans or are not, or who adopt a combination of cosmopolitan and non-cosmopolitan attitudes. This limitation is indeed useful for the purpose of operationalizing abstract and fuzzy concepts such as cosmopolitanism, but it captures only one dimension of cosmopolitanism as a specific moral and political orientation expressed in the attitudes of individuals. An alternative proposal for the analysis of cosmopolitan trends can be outlined as follows. In order to discover how cosmopolitan trends are in evidence a number of indicators need to be established that capture some of the main dimensions of cosmopolitanism, which go beyond the level of observable identities and attitudes to include macro societal trends and collective identities. These can be grouped into the following four categories or dimensions:

1. The increased degree to which people identify with, and express solidarity towards, people beyond the local and national to the wider world, collective identity narratives.
2. Changes in rights as a result of demands for the recognition of others; the impact of cosmopolitan values of care and hospitality on national politics.
3. The impact of global events on national politics; the expansion of global civil society movements; movements towards global co-operation.
4. Discursive shifts in the public sphere; emerging master narratives in which new ways of framing issues can be found; increased inter-cultural communication and transnational debates.

Much of the above-mentioned empirical studies remain confined to the first category, and generally to the individual identifications. While Beck has made a major and significant effort to address some of the other categories, as argued, his conflation of transnationalism with cosmopolitanization is unhelpful and the relation between the latter and the cosmopolitan outlook is unclear. However, with some adjustments the approach outlined here is not incompatible with Beck's intentions; indeed it advances his implicit acknowledgement of cosmopolitanism as a form of immanent transformation or transcendence. The fourfold categorization captures some of the major expressions of cosmopolitanism, from the level of collective identities to the levels of rights, movements and discourses in the public sphere.

It is possible to go one step further and specify four dynamics that have to be present, to varying degrees, in any specific dimension to demonstrate the extent of a cosmopolitan orientation. These relate to the very core of the cosmopolitan imagination and can be seen as capacities for immanent transcendence:

1. The capacity for the relativization of one's own culture or identity. In the encounter with the Other the self or native culture undergoes a process of learning or self-discovery. In this case, cosmopolitanism is to be understood according to the hermeneutic principle of under-standing the Other, as in Gadamer's theory of the fusion of horizons.
2. The capacity for the positive recognition of the Other. This goes beyond the use of the Other in self-transformation to an accommodation of the Other. It is possible to situate this capacity in many forms of multiculturalism and forms of alterity based on hospitality.

In this case, cosmopolitanism can be related to the theory of recognition, as in Charles Taylor's liberal communitarianism or Axel Honneth's notion of a moral struggle for recognition.

3. The capacity for a mutual evaluation of cultures or identities. In this case there is the possibility of inter-cultural dialogue extending beyond learning from the Other to a transformation of cultures and standpoints. This can be understood in terms of a notion of critical dialogue or deliberation and can be related to Habermas's theory of discourse.

4. The capacity to create a shared normative culture. This emerges out of the critical dialogue of standpoints and consists of a transcendence of difference and diversity towards a shared or common culture. It can be understood as a more developed third culture in which a translation of perspectives occurs.

These dynamics can be present to varying degrees in any dimension of cosmopolitanism and represent the depth of its normativity. For instance, the second form will entail supporting policies that are not necessarily in one's immediate interest, whereas the first dimension is compatible with a soft cosmopolitanism such as consumption. In the third case there is a move from alterity to plurality. In the fourth it is possible to speak of a third culture as a reality creating process. It is possible to see these dynamics as putting into play capacities that become progressively stronger as we move from the first to the fourth. Such capacities can be observed in terms of individuals, collective actors, societies or other large-scale social units. The advantage that this approach offers is that it allows for the critical evaluation of cosmopolitan orientations, dispositions and currents in society. As such it goes beyond descriptive analysis and attitudinal approaches in, first, bringing other dimensions to bear; second, in specifying different capacities which function as dynamics that intensify the cosmopolitan experience and imagination; and third in providing a way in which immanent transcendence can be conceptualized as an expansion in the communicative competence of society leading to societal transformation and subject formation.

Conclusion

Cosmopolitanism does not refer simply to a global space or to post-national phenomena that have come into existence today as a result of globalization. The argument advanced in this chapter is that it resides in social mechanisms and dynamics that can exist in any society at any time in history where world openness has a resonance. It is both an ethical and political orientation in the world and at the same time it is an analysis and interpretation of the world. Clearly cosmopolitanism has become relevant today, due not least to the impact of globalization. Cosmopolitanism concerns processes of self-transformation in which new cultural forms take shape and where new spaces of discourse open up, leading to a transformation in the social world. The cosmopolitan imagination from the perspective of a critical social theory of modernity tries to capture the transformative moment, interactive relations between societies and modernities, the developmental and dialogic. In this sense it goes beyond the internal history of cosmopolitan political thought, which was largely the focus of Chapter 1, to address the immanent potential within social reality for self-transcendence.

For these reasons, methodologically speaking, a critical cosmopolitan sociology proceeds on the assumption that culture contains immanent capacities for learning and that societies have developmental possibilities. The chapter has highlighted world disclosure as one of the central mechanisms of cosmopolitan transformation and which occurs on macro-societal and on micro dimensions as well as being played on in the continued transformation of modernities. Critical cosmopolitan social theory is a means of making sense of social transformation and therefore entails an unavoidable degree of moral and political evaluation. To this extent, cosmopolitanism is a connecting strand between sociology and political discourse in society and in political theory. It has a critical role to play in opening up discursive spaces of world openness and thus in resisting both globalization, understood as an external force, and nationalism.

3 | Global ethics, solidarity and the problem of violence

In this chapter I argue that one major dimension of cosmopolitanism is a concern with global ethics. Global ethics has a critical and dialogic character rather than being primarily grounded in 'thin' universalistic principles that transcend specific contexts. For this reason the question of global ethics is particularly interesting for critical social theory, which has been traditionally concerned with the critique of the present from the perspective of a critical-normative idea of the just society. As argued in the previous chapter, cosmopolitanism emerges out of shifts in the moral and political self-understanding of society and as such is a form of immanent transcendence whereby societies undergo change as a result of internal transformation as they respond to external and especially global challenges. It contains a strong ethical character and one that has a global frame of reference. Global ethics is above all an expression of cosmopolitan political community and can be seen as a multi-layered form of socio-cultural transformation. In the terms of the analysis in the preceding chapter, global ethics concerns the capacity to create a shared normative culture. It is not merely a product of a belief in global humanity and thus 'thin' (Dobson 2006). Societies can learn through ethics in the sense of shifts in their moral consciousness as a result of confronting common problems: collective learning takes the form of cognitive shifts which are primarily worked out in the communicative processes of the public sphere and shape collective identities. Global ethics is one such form of collective learning by which global issues enter into specific contexts. The outcome, I argue, is a 'thick' as opposed to a 'thin' cosmopolitan public sphere increasingly based on consciousness of the need for global ethics. Central to this are changes in the meaning of responsibility and solidarity for collective identities, especially in response to the experience of violence.

The first section discusses various conceptions of global ethics. I argue for a notion of global ethics that is centrally addressed to the problem of responsibility and solidarity as opposed to rights. The second part of the chapter then looks at the example of political violence and the argument is given that the nature of political violence today presents a cosmopolitan challenge suggesting the importance of a notion of global ethics as cosmopolitan solidarity. The centrality of violence in modern society has been much discussed in social and political theory. There has been surprisingly little attention given to violence in the now large literature on cosmopolitanism, which is often discussed as if the world were a peaceful one devoid of the turbulence of war. In this chapter I argue that violence, in particular new kinds of political violence, is a crucial context for the relevance of cosmopolitanism. The problem of violence highlights the need for a global ethics, not just in terms of rights such as human rights, but also in questions of responsibility and solidarity and in ways of both thinking and feeling. The third section develops this in terms of a cosmopolitan conception of the public sphere, which as argued in the previous chapter ties cosmopolitanism to a model of communication conceived of in terms of the cognitive notion of affect. Societies undergo transformation in their moral and political orientations through an expansion in their communicative and emotional structures, central to which is the cosmopolitan concern with the engagement with the perspective of the Other.

Debating global ethics

There is little consensus on how global ethics should be understood or of what its relevance consists. The emergence of global ethics is not simply an outcome of global civil society or of international law. It is rather a developmental process in which new ways of thinking, feeling, imagining and solidarity emerge and shape collective identities. The debate about global ethics is often confused as several problems – normative-philosophical, sociological, legal-political – are conflated. For instance, is the aim of a global ethics to find *within* the existing cultures of the world a common value system that can be called global and which might be the basis of a global ethics? Is the aim of a global ethics to impose a *Western* human rights regime on the rest of the world? Is the aim simply to create a normative framework to promote *diversity*, and thus consisting of a commitment to something like 'unity in diversity'? Or is the aim to create an entirely *new* 'one world' value system that people might choose if they were free to do so, as Peter Singer (2003) believes? There are complicated normative, cognitive and socio-cultural questions at stake here.

Communitarian political philosophy has been concerned to refute the very idea of a global ethics, including the Kantian idea of a cosmopolitan ethic based on reason. Michael Walzer argues that there are no global values upon which a global ethics can be based (Walzer 1983). Walzer distinguishes between 'thick' and 'thin' ethics, depending on how embedded they are in community. Thick ethics is firmly rooted in a living community and is therefore more real than thin ethics. He sees ethics as necessarily 'thick' and a global ethics cannot be 'thick' because it cannot be rooted in a cultural form of life. While he does not deny that people have moral views and feelings about people in other parts of the world, these sentiments do not amount to anything more than a 'thin' morality and certainly not to a global ethics. This is because for Walzer loyalties are prior to principles of justice. Justice is not primarily determined by a universal moral obligation.

A counter argument to this view can easily be made. First, Walzer reduces consciousness of global issues and concerns to trivial concerns. His assumption is that global issues are simply not important and that people primarily identify with local issues. This perspective totally neglects the tremendous impact of global issues and sets up a stark dichotomy between the local and global. He does not see that even a 'thin' morality can be sufficiently 'thick' to be significant. A second problem is that Walzer conflates culture with an underlying consensus. This view of culture as an ordered system of symbolic meaning has been heavily criticized. Culture is diverse, fragmented and based on contested values and fragile loyalties. This pluralization of culture has entered the sphere of democracy, presenting new challenges (see Gutmann 2003). Culture is no longer exclusively a basis for thick identities or a source of legitimation but is a site of dialogue. A more differentiated view of culture draws attention to its contested and layered nature. Such a view of culture would see global 'thin' ethics as being as 'thick' as allegedly national loyalties and constituted in cosmopolitan spaces and modes of identification that are multi-layered.

The communitarian position can be contrasted to liberal approaches where a stronger case for global ethics can be found. John Rawls has given an argument that offers a basis for global ethics (Rawls 1993, 1999). While Rawls's earlier work was based on a culturally neutral theory of political justice which presupposed the nation-state, he moved towards a greater recognition of the need for a conception of ethics that can address conflicts between different cultural worlds. This is especially evident in his last major work, *A Law of Peoples* (Rawls 1999) and an earlier essay in which he advocated the idea of an 'over-lapping consensus' and is relevant to the debate on global ethics (Rawls 1987). Rawls argues for a minimal universalistic ethics that is based on the recognition that despite the huge differences that divide them, people do share common ground. In this view, a global ethics might be constructed on the foundations of whatever common ground can be found between people who otherwise share very little. However, his mature political theory was limited by a notion of 'peoples' as distinct from each other and the cosmopolitan moment was at best a compromise between different conceptions of the common good.

While this argument is very useful in seeing how cultural conflict can be reduced with zero-sum conflict translated into negotiable conflict and commonalties gradually built upon, it mostly pertains to cases of cultural or moral conflicts over conceptions of the common good. It does not provide a basis for a global ethics in areas where there are no major conflicts, but where the challenge is to find common solutions to societal problems. Many of the challenges of a global ethics are not in fact impeded by the lack of common cultural values. Rawls's model, moreover, assumes that the common principles already exist in some form and only needs to be generalized. It is not a position that challenges existing ethical assumptions and, despite his accommodation of major conflicts over competing conceptions of the common good, does not seek fundamentally new or global perspectives. Although different in their approach to the idea of a global ethics, Rawls and Walzer are not so far apart. Neither position fully accepts a firm cultural foundation for global ethics. Rawls's deontological moral universalism did not give much room for global culture other than a recognition of the need for common ground. It is the nature of this common ground that it cannot be 'thick' in Walzer's sense. The result, then, is a self-limiting global ethics that would have to be too thin to be meaningful or relevant to the numerous developments that articulate in different ways global ethics. Such developments cannot be understood in terms of a notion of common ground, but are indicative of new cognitive models of the social world.

Anthropological arguments offer an interesting alternative to the liberal universalist position, but ultimately suffer from the same problems. Rather than look for universal moral values in global culture or in natural law or some kind of universal human traits, a recent tendency in political theory is to look for different cultural versions of universalistic values. These attempts aim to reconcile relativism and universalism. With regard to the debate about human rights, for instance, some critics argue that universal moral values exist in all human cultures and although the specific form these values take differs, they are nonetheless universalistic in spirit (Renteln 1990). Thus UNESCO and the UN-supported World Commission for Culture and Development argue that a global ethics has a foundation in the recurrent moral themes in all the major religions of the world. It has been noted by many scholars that the ontological and transcendental visions of the great religions of the world – Confucianism, Taoism, Hinduism, Buddhism, Zoroastrianism, Judaism, Islam and Christianity – all recognize in different ways the idea of human vulnerability, the fundamental equality of all human beings and the desire to alleviate suffering.

While these arguments tend to run into difficulty when they attempt to base a legal order (such as human rights) on traditional cultural values, such as those associated with religious cultures, a sound cultural basis has been established for values that are global. A particularly good example of such an approach is Sissela Bok's argument in her book *Common Values* (Bok 1995). She outlines three kinds of global values: those relating to duties of mutual support and loyalty, values relating to constraints on violence and dishonesty, and those relating to procedural justice. From this perspective we can begin to see how a global ethics might be conceived and which is not open to the charge of either minimalism or exaggerating cultural differences. The theologian, Hans Kung, in *Towards a Global Ethic* has also proposed a similar notion of a global ethics (Kung 1993). He outlines four shared principles essential to a global ethic: affirming respect for all life, economic justice and solidarity, tolerance and truthfulness, and equal rights and partnership between men and women. This is an interfaith and transcultural kind of a global ethics, which is oriented towards achieving global understanding.

The main drawback with the cultural values approaches is that such approaches tend to look for a global ethics on the level of cultural recognition, or inter-cultural understanding. The assumption appears to be that a global ethics already exists within the cultural traditions of different civilizations or ethnic groups and all that is required is the recognition of this. Hans Kung, for instance, argues that all the major religions have a global ethic because they believe in a God. It is difficult to see how a global ethics understood in such cultural terms might be related to the legal and political dimensions of globalization. At best such arguments establish, contra the 'clash of civilizations' thesis, that there is no civilizational obstacle against the possibility of global ethics. While these approaches also have the merit in demonstrating a wider conception of global ethics than in the narrow liberal model, they ignore the difficulty of cultural difference and naively suppose that one religious value system is translatable into another without self-problematization. For instance, it is unlikely an orthodox Jew or Christian fundamentalist will reach a fusion of horizon with a Buddhist or Muslim on the basis of common values alone since the basis of the values is their subjective cultural specificity and exclusivity. This can only be achieved through a critical engagement with cultural values.

Yet a degree of cultural contextualization is essential, but this does not have to be at the cost of a loss in universality. The cultural contextualization of human rights has been much discussed in recent times with respect to the debate about Asian values.[13] In this debate communitarian perspectives have introduced an important corrective of standard Western liberal democractic theory. It has been widely recognized that global ethics as reflected in the pursuit of human rights, freedom and democracy requires a mix of liberal individualism and communitarianism whether in Western or in non-Western societies. The cause of human rights is more likely to be advanced if human rights can be embedded in local cultures. A conclusion might be that while cultural traditions, such as the major world religions, provide resources for human rights, it is necessary to go beyond the particularity of cultural traditions to appreciate the ways in which discursive transformation occurs. Thus while human rights may be more advanced in Western societies, they are not generally seen as rooted in Christianity, which in itself has undergone internal transformation. This is similarly the case in non-Western societies where there is ongoing reinterpretation of cultural values in light of changing conceptions of rights around, for instance, feminism and minority rights as well as

---

[13]   See for example Bauer and Bell (1999), Bell (2000, 2007), Davis (1995), de Barry (1998), Kelly and Reid (1998) and Madsen (2002).

individual rights. As Charles Taylor argues, as obstacle to mutual understanding is the inability of many Westerners to see that their culture is one of many and that, contrary to what people think, 'world convergence will not come through a loss or denial of traditions all around, but rather by the creative reimmersions of different groups, each in their own spiritual heritage, traveling different routes to the same goal' (Taylor 1999: 142–3).

While much of the universal values and rights approach is concerned with the relativism-universalism problem, which it attempts to dilute, Hans Jonas in a classic work defended the possibility of a global ethics of collective responsibility (Jonas 1984). One of the first major works on a planetary ethics, Jonas was particularly responding to the rise of global threats to humankind, especially those emanating from modern technology. In his view, philosophical thinking on ethics, dominated by the Kantian tradition, has been too confined to a narrow notion of the subject of responsibility. He defended the case for a collective ethics and one that was global in terms of its responsibility, for only a global ethics could provide an adequate solution to the problems facing the world. While this was an important work in opening up ethics to new challenges, it remained trapped within a limited horizon, seeing the aim of global ethics solely in terms of human survival. Jonas assumed, too, that a global ethics might simply be based on a new version of the Kantian 'moral imperative'.

More recent theories of responsibility have shifted the debate on collective responsibility beyond Jonas's limited vision to a concern with risk and wider political and ethical concerns. Peter Singer is one such example of an approach that seeks to find a global ethics emanating from the moral and political necessity to find global solutions to global problems (Singer 2003). In his book, *One World: The Ethics of Globalization*, he argues a global ethics is a response to the need for global ethical solutions to global problems associated with climate change, the role of the World Trade Organization, human rights and humanitarianism, and foreign aid. His argument is that nation-centric solutions are no longer morally compelling and we need to adjust our ethics to the reality of the global world. But this requires the emergence of a global ethic of responsibility and Singer's argument remains on a normative level of advocacy. In this context, Strydom has argued collective responsibility should be understood in socio-cognitive terms as a development arising out of the cultural horizons of contemporary society in much the same way as the early discourse of rights emerged out of the cultural horizons of the previous two centuries (Strydom 1999a). This perspective has been heavily influenced by the discourse theories of Apel and Habermas and reflects a notion of global ethics as immanent transcendence and thus as socially rooted but having the capacity to bring about socio-cognitive change.

In a series of papers on discourse ethics and global ethics Karl-Otto Apel has argued that a global ethics must be conceived both in terms of an anti-foundational ethics and what he has called a discourse ethics, which corresponds to developments that are characterized primarily by communication and which are not constrained by national borders.[14] Apel believes that a global ethics is not rooted in specific cultural worldviews and is, like all kinds of ethics, procedural rather than substantive. In this sense, he argues that global ethics is 'thin', but this does not mean it is thinner than any other kind of ethics. Moreover, he argues a global ethics is empirically demonstrable in the growing volume of transnational debates, movements and politics; it is not then just idle speculation or a hopelessly utopian project but a real force in the world.

This is one of the most promising conceptions of global ethics and one that is capable of distinguishing between the different normative levels of the ethical, legal and political. What is distinctive about it is that it is primarily a discursive ethics: consensus is not the basis but the goal to be reached. This implies a constructive understanding of ethics; it is not a case of appealing to already existing beliefs, but attempting on the basis of past achievements to solve new challenges. For Apel, a discourse ethics that is global will be the basis of a binding international normative order. Where he differs from globalization theories is that in this approach a global ethics is the basis of an international normative order and not the result. In fact, he speaks of a 'second order' globalization, counteracting the economic or 'first order' globalization. In his view, then, globalization is a challenge for a global ethics, the aim of which is to bring global forces under morally binding values.

The version of a discourse ethics represented by Habermas departs only in one respect from Apel's. Where Apel sees the goal of a global ethics to be a legally binding order, for Habermas it is the nature of

---

[14] See Apel (1978, 1987, 1988, 1990, 1992, 1993, 1996, 2000, 2001).

discourse that it can never be concluded. The radical openness of the discourse ethics presupposes a degree of indeterminacy. Thus where Apel anticipates the closure of the discourse ethics, Habermas sees it as an ongoing dialogic rationality, the aim of which is not necessarily closure in a legal framework or political process. This is apparent, for example, in the different reactions of Apel and Habermas to the Kosovo war, with the latter taking a less strong position on the need for a political response in the absence of a legal framework (Apel 2001; Habermas 1999). In this view global ethics must be understood in terms of ongoing debates, the emergence of a global public sphere (as distinct from a global legal order) and socio-cognitive evolution. Whether on a national, local or global level, a discourse ethics is the ongoing raising of truth claims and which is realized in the communicative cultural logics of modernity, such as self-confrontation, reflexivity and the permanent critique of cultural values. For Habermas, all that is left of moral universalism today is precisely this capacity for critique. Although Habermas does not explicitly relate this post-universalistic morality to cosmopolitanism, it is not difficult to do so. Despite certain Eurocentric assumptions, his particular kind of moral universalism captures the cosmopolitan concern with the incorporation of the perspective of the Other and the mutual questioning of assumptions.

It is now widely accepted that ethics today must entail a largely procedural dimension and cannot be based on foundational principles. Substantive conceptions of ethics as rooted in particular cultural traditions are too restrictive in the context of culturally mixed societies and competing conceptions of the common good to be a basis for widespread acceptance. While ethics may be based on certain moral values, modern conceptions of ethics are almost entirely post-traditional and procedural. Substantive conceptions of ethics as rooted in particular cultural traditions are too restrictive in the context of culturally mixed societies and competing conceptions of the common good to be a basis for widespread acceptance. Deliberative theories of justice and ethics, such as Apel and Habermas's notion of a discourse ethics, are the strongest statement of this view of ethics, which is particularly relevant to global ethics. A global ethics is a non-foundational ethics which demands the recognition only of common ways of dealing with problems rather than an appeal to an underlying consensus. However, this does not mean that global ethics is purely procedural in the sense of a formal rationality. This would be to neglect the emotional dimension of commitment and solidarity.[15] It is certainly the case that the procedural model of global ethics proposed by Habermas places too much emphasis on a procedural rationality. The resulting 'thin' conception of cosmopolitanism that emerges from this fails to capture some of the 'thicker' aspects of global ethics, which do not conform to the model of a formal rationality. For instance, it is difficult to locate 'bottom up' global civil society movements or international humanitarianism in this model. Global ethics is best understood as a moral consciousness that is rooted in emotional responses to global issues. Without this dimension of affect it would not be possible to understand transnational forms of solidarity (see Connolly 2002).[16] This will now be considered with respect to the challenge of violence.

Violence today and the challenge of global ethics

Violence lies at the heart of modernity. Cosmopolitanism has been one response to the problem of violence in modernity (Beck 2000; Fine 2006). Eighteenth-century cosmopolitanism was a response to the revolutionary wars of the French Republic, and the rise of cosmopolitanism in the second half of the twentieth century can be seen as a response to the holocaust and the disasters of a century of two world wars. Modernity engendered many forms of violence – from wars to various kinds of ethnic cleansing – but it also brought about the search for peace based on a global ethics. As Fine argues: 'The cosmopolitan outlook is the attempt to keep both moments firmly in view: not only the experience of violence in the modern age but also the normativity of its non-acceptance' (Fine 2006: 51). In Chapter 2 it was noted how a new cosmopolitanism emerged in the aftermath of the Second World War with the foundation of the United Nations, the International Declaration of Human Rights and the legal category of Crimes Against Humanity. The current global situation in the post-Cold War era makes cosmopolitanism all the more urgent. The nature of war has changed in the last decades. In place of wars between states there is an increased incidence of wars against peoples. The holocaust marked the beginning of such forms of violence based on ethnic cleansing.

---

[15] The notion of solidarity does have a role in Habermas's work (see Habermas 1986), as Outhwaite (2007) argues.
[16] On affect theory, see also Clough and O'Malley (2007).

Recent wars, such as the Kosovo war, drew attention to the complex nature of political violence and the morality of intervention. From the perspective of global publics there were unavoidable issues of definition on exactly what constitutes violence and whether it is possible to use the very category of war (see Aijmer and Abbink 2000). The discourse of war around the Kosovo episode was one of uncertainty about the status of war and how it should be viewed in relation to other historical events of large-scale violence: was it a 'purge', a 'genocide', a 'war', a 'civil war', 'ethnic cleansing' or 'forced expulsion'? The use of these terms and the contestation over them was a striking aspect of the war which lacked a clear definition of violence as well as who were the victims and who were the perpetrators. Related to this was uncertainty over the 'we' – who is responsible or whether there was any responsibility for intervention. The point emerging from such controversies is that the subject of responsibility is discursively constituted.

What is particularly striking today is the opening up of a discourse of violence around a whole range of new issues: violence against children, violence against women, various kinds of rages, internet-based kinds of violence, violence against nature, torture. The question of violence is one of the central questions facing global ethics. War is becoming more and more of a cosmopolitan challenge since through media coverage people are more informed about war and violence throughout the world. Social reality is experienced through cultural forms which frame or construct reality. Distance is central to the experience of most kinds of reality. As Luc Boltanski has argued, images of suffering are becoming more common today as a result of media coverage, and consequently suffering is experienced as more distant (Boltanski 1999). This suggests that the discourse of suffering can become more open to multiple codifications and contested meanings. The frequency of images and information about suffering can lead to its normalization or can lead to moral outrage. How we think about violence today is changing as a result of many spectres of violence being drawn in global contexts and the assumptions of modernity can no longer be taken for granted, for instance, the assumption that the state has eradicated violence. In modern social and political thought violence has generally been conceived as primordial, as in Girard (1981), following Freud. From Hobbes to Carl Schmitt and Max Weber, violence was prior to the normative order of the state where legitimate authority resides. According to Weber, today the use of force is regarded as legitimate only in so far as it is either permitted by the state or prescribed by it. Thus the right of a father to discipline his children is recognized – a survival of the former independent authority of the head of a household, which in the right to use force has sometimes extended to a power of life and death over slaves. The claim of the modern state to monopolize the use of force is as essential to it as its character of compulsory jurisdiction and of continuous operation. (Weber 1998: 56)

The Weberian image was one of a political order that has progressively eradicated violence by the civilizing force of legitimate authority (Joas 1999). Examples of recent wars call this into question. What is called into question is a shared normative order underpinned by the state. Central to any normative order is the possibility of a negotiated resolution of conflict. Even in cases where there are deep divisions on values, there is generally a shared normative order that is underpinned by the legal and political order of a state. Negotiable conflict is likely to be easier to resolve in cases of conflicts within the same social group. This is so because these conflicts are less likely to be about fundamental issues of values and there is generally agreement on who the adversary is as well as on the goals to be achieved and means to be employed. In such cases there may be a shared value system. It is also the case that negotiable conflicts are likely to be found in cases where there is a high degree of interdependency among group ties, for instance industrial disputes. As Lewis Coser (1956: 75), following Simmel and Durkheim, has recognized, interdependency has been a major check on conflicts. In such cases violence is likely to be mostly latent or taking a symbolic form. Modern political violence has often been contained by the inter-state system and the prospect of negotiated resolution of conflict has in general been realistic, letting aside the two world wars when the international order collapsed. In cases where no resolution was possible, as in the Cold War, latent conflict was prevented from becoming an outright hostility. This is not surprising, for as Anton Blok (1998) has argued, major social conflicts erupting in violence have not been common in cases where the group differences are very great. Since Freud, it has been frequently noted that where cultural differences between groups are small and familiar due to the groups sharing a common social environment, there is likely to be a stronger hostility than in cases where cultural differences are great. In many cases the separation of Self and Other is precisely what the debate is about and many of the key features of negotiable conflict cannot be applied since there are only zero-sum options. This is frequently what happens when the conflict concerns moral, religious and certain kinds of cultural values such as euthanasia, abortion and vegetarianism. In such cases the possibility of a deliberated outcome is not possible. With regard to large-scale conflicts, the state has generally been the final arbitrator. Constitutionalism, though ill-equipped to deal with deeply rooted cultural conflicts for which it was never devised, is not quite as impotent as is often thought (Tully 1995).

But what happens when the state collapses and when there is no shared normative order based on legal and political institutions? This scenario of postmodern political violence has become all too common today as more and more conflicts are occurring in the increasingly volatile inter-state system (Bauman 2001; Munck and de Silva 2000). It is a feature of the present day that there are many conflicts merging which take place in the absence of both a shared normative order and a functioning state. The civil wars and genocides in Rwanda, Bosnia and Kosovo are examples of this situation which is one in which the state collapsed leading to the disintegration of a normative legal order. These conflicts were not only non-negotiable but any attempt to achieve a deliberated outcome would have exacerbated the extent of the violence. Such forms of violence may be termed postmodern in the sense of the absence of a clear political goal, normative framework or the assertion of a fundamental principle. Postmodern political violence is often conducted by the state against society or a people as opposed to being a conflict of one state against another in the name of national sovereignty. This kind of political violence, then, is about wars led by the state against society and resembles civil war, except that the belligerents are substantial proportions of the population and the state is merely an instrument in the hands of mobilized organizations or militarized cadres.

Given that there is little chance of these kinds of conflicts, because of their intensity and because of the collapse of a state-based normative order, evolving into negotiated conflicts, there is often a compelling case for the global community to intervene. This is where the challenge for cosmopolitanism arises and where global ethics becomes an issue. The cosmopolitan perspective cannot simply be content with a moral standpoint, as Habermas (1999) has argued. What is needed is a cosmopolitan framework so that political and military action will be legitimate and non-arbitrary. However, interpretations differ as to what might be the concrete form of this framework, whether for instance it should be based on the present inter-state system or based on a new and more global order of governance or simply placed in the hands of existing transnational normative orders, such as the EU.

This situation of normative uncertainty is underpinned by changing and competing definitions of the problem. The definition of war has become a problem as a result of the entry of many social actors in the definition of the problem. Since the Vietnam war, when the public for the first time became active in the justification of the war, there has been a growing contestation about war. Wars such as Kosovo and Iraq have had a major impact in the public spheres of many countries. In the former case the European liberal left was deeply divided over the question of intervention, with many well-known intellectuals associated with the left supporting it and others denouncing military intervention. This may be symptomatic of a collapse of a common political-critical stand-point based on underlying principles constitutive of a leftwing discourse. The problem of intervention is not an issue that can be answered by a straightforward recourse to a normative order, since one does not exist and the possibility for a consensus in specific cases is not easy to achieve. The justification for legitimate violence, as in intervention, has been complicated by the emergence of new discourses of justification, which do not rest on the conventional definition of political violence as involving a clear subject and object, a Self and an Other.

This is not surprising as wars have often been occasions of major shifts in the political and cultural models of societies. The end of the seventeenth-century wars of religion, the Napoleonic wars, and the Second World War, for example, have marked the emergence, respectively, of the Westphalian order of sovereign states, the republican order of constitutional states and the international order of nation-states. The international society, centred on the United Nations, was the basis of the normative system that existed over the latter half of the twentieth century and was designed to prevent major occurrences of war between sovereign nation-states. It was a conception of international society based on a tacit normative system resting on international law but in reality on the ability of individual states to uphold this framework. International law thus depended ultimately on its moral force and the existence of a normative order within states. It was embedded in a strong belief in the feasibility of negotiated conflict resolution rather than recourse to the exercise of force. The problem we are faced with today is that international society and its normative system is in crisis as a result of the emergence of forms of conflict which call into question the values and institutions of modernity, in particular the normative order resting on the state. In this negotiated conflict resolution is becoming more difficult given that its premises are being eroded. Nothing illustrates this better than the war in Iraq where the case for intervention has been comprehensively discredited and where there is no discernible resolution in sight. Indeed it may be the case that the Iraq war will transpire to be one of the turning points in world history. Despite the fact that there has been an increase in anti-Islamic currents in the Western world, there have also been cosmopolitan counter-tendencies. It is possible to speak of a cosmopolitan public sphere taking shape in many parts of the world. Violence can incapacitate a society, but it can also provoke solidarity both within and beyond.

Cosmopolitan public spheres and solidarity

One of the biggest problems for global ethics is the question of its social carriers. What is the evidence that a global ethics exists? Is it a purely utopian aspiration – at best, as Peter Singer believes, a response to its necessity – or is it a real force in the world? We can find some evidence that a global ethics actually exists, but it is important to stress that this exists only as an emergent process and is evident in the expression of new kinds of cosmopolitan community. A global ethics is not an ethics that exists exclusively on a particular dimension of globalization, such as a global legal normative order. While global forces and the spectre of global violence certainly have awakened a global ethics, it is rather to be found in the moral consciousness within all political communities throughout the world and consists of their capacity to look beyond the limited horizons of the local context. The subject of global ethics can thus be anyone and is not a particular globally mobile actor. A global ethics is the ultimate consequence of the dialogic rationality of modern ethics as something that operates below the level of legislative politics. Contemporary political communication in public spheres throughout the world provides evidence of global ethics as an emergent reality. Consciousness of global warming, ethical consumption that is responsive to fair trade and to environmental issues, support for humanitarian aid, and anti-war protests have entered into the public sphere, bringing about a significant shift in perceptions and in affect. Global issues are becoming increasingly important in domestic politics and many political issues are framed around global problems. McRobbie, follow-ing Butler (2004), argues for a cosmopolitan ethics that brings into political discussion 'mourning, vulnerability and ethical obligation to others'. Butler's cosmopolitanism is based on the human awareness of our own vulnerability. It is this that makes us responsive to the suffering of others. In order to minimize catastrophe and conflict a new way of thinking of global politics is required in which dependency on others and solidaristic and compassionate values play a role. Here the role of mourning is significant. As McRobbie suggests, one of the most impor-tant factors in the anti-Iraq war campaign was the mobilization of the parents who lost a child in UK and US armed forces. Such forms of mourning can be interpreted as a cosmopolitan bond with grieving parents in Iraq (McRobbie 2006: 84–5).

It is possible to see global ethics less as a system of rights and legal norms than as a medium of affective communication in which new concepts of morality are articulated. One of the key components of this is solidarity. Solidarity has been traditionally understood as a social bond that binds specific social groups together. As Honneth has argued, it is primarily a moral orientation to others and makes possible a form of social integration that is not based primarily on rights (Honneth 1996). Its roots lie, as Brunkhorst (2005) has demonstrated, in the classical idea of civic friendship and the Judeo-Christian notion of brother-hood, while its modern usage has been much influenced by the idea of Fraternity, as in the French Revolution's proclamation of Liberty, Equality and Fraternity. Since Durkheim, the notion of solidarity has been applied to whole societies. National traditions of solidarity have played a major role in shaping the collective identities of nations and in their traditions of citizenship. With the nation-state no longer the exclusive marker of identity, other forms of solidarity are coming to the fore. Karagiannis (2007a) argues that what Habermas (2001a) has termed 'solidarity among strangers' is possible since the idea of solidar-ity is a product of modernity and is meaningful only in a context of inequalities which it tries to overcome. Solidarity contributed to creat-ing and keeping the space of the city together, a way of instituting the social. However it is not confined to the nation-state, as Brunkhorst has argued. Rights are enforced both within and beyond state borders by well-established governmental and non-governmental organizations. Rights legislation is interwoven with national and supranational as well as with inter-state bodies (Brunkhorst 2005, 2007). It has been central to the international solidarity of the new social movements of the late twentieth century and has been at the centre of humanitarianism. More recently it has been given specific expression in the EU's Charter of Fundamental Rights (Ross 2007; see also Stevenson 2006) and has also entered into IR theory (Weber 2007).

Karagiannis (2007b) distinguishes between institutional forms of solidarity and solidarity expressed by social movements with the latter characterized by a stronger concern with a political project. In this vein, Kurasawa argues that the lived culture of an alternative globalization is constituting the ground of cosmopolitan forms of solidarity. The 'alternative globalization movement' is one such example of solidarity beyond national societies. 'A cosmopolitanism from below is taking shape through the creation of a relatively thick and rich bonds of global solidarity, which are sustaining a political culture of alternative globalization ordered around intersecting modes of thought and action, values, beliefs, narratives and symbols' (Kurasawa 2004: 247). This has been very successful in creating a global but decentred movement that has made a substantial impact on consumers who 'are sensing that they are bound to producers as co-participants in the circuits of global capitalism, and thus that all workers must enjoy certain rights and better working conditions' (Kurasawa 2004: 244). Such forms of solidarity can be seen in terms of a broadening of moral consciousness to incorporate an orientation to others beyond one's immediate community. On one level, this can be explained as a result of changes in experiences, shifts in perceptions of the world whereby the individual feels more connected with those far away; on an other level, it is a consequence of the impact of global issues on national societies and their forms of political communication. The expansion of the 'we' is very much shaped by the kinds of social struggles and problems the community of reference experiences. As Schwartz has commented: 'Just as the moral horizons of democratic polities have expanded only through the struggles of formerly excluded social groups, so will the transition from national to regional to international solidarity occur more through political contestation than by means of abstract philosophical argument' (Schwartz 2007: 132). This emphasis on conflict is also central to Honneth's conception of solidarity as a moral feeling of indignation against oppression and disrespect (Honneth 1996). It is an unavoidable feature of the present day that these are now being played out on a global level and are no longer experienced only on a national level. Pensky thus argues for a conception of solidarity 'as a process of inclusion into transnational deliberative bodies' that cannot be easily foreclosed, for it has indeterminate implications for both subjective motivations and social integration via institutions (Pensky 2007: 169).

Distinguishing between liberal and political cosmopolitanism, Jabri (2007) argues that a notion of solidarity can be related to the latter and differs from liberal conceptions in the way in which the question of solidarity is posed. Liberal cosmopolitanism is hierarchically consti-tuted in moral terms, whereby Western nations save others in the name of international norms and an undefined and depoliticized humanity at large. Political cosmopolitanism, in contrast, is not thought of in normative terms as such but is an arena in which contestation is constituted. In this case 'solidarity assumes a political agency that has the politics of mobilization at its core, where the case has to be made in a complex global arena wherein the universal is a contested space' (Jabri 2007: 724). In this vein Gould (2007) proposes a view of solidar-ity as a form of social empathy which is different from liberal notions of care when applied to the international or global context. This approach, which is influenced by feminist notions of empathy, takes the concept of solidarity beyond the Durkheimean tradition of a unity within a group or society, though retaining the dimension of differen-tiation characteristic of Durkheim's second sense of the term. This is different from affectional solidarity in inter-personal relations and conventional solidarity in group dynamics. Gould emphasizes how a discourse of overlapping solidarities takes shape in a situation of dissent and difference. Solidarity 'is not only a moral disposition but also requires social critique and attention to institutional structures, as well as to the opportunities that changes in such structures might afford for improving the lot of others' (Gould 2007: 158; see also Dean 1996). Solidarity is based on relations of reciprocity in which people are drawn into relations of obligation to each other. While being admittedly a weaker notion of solidarity than group solidarity, such as national solidarities, these new solidarities are implicitly reciprocal as opposed to being one-way communication. In this respect cosmopolitan solidarity differs from humanitarian aid and other forms of paternalistic forms of charity, which as normally understood do not require reciprocity. Solidarity in the global context complements empathy with a discursive relationship that is articulated in multiple networks of associations and individuals. Solidarity requires being in a moral relationship in which empathetic understanding does not just happen but requires active involvement with the Other (Harvey 2007: 35; see also Bartky 2002).

Communication is central to politics. Nation-states have been based on centralized systems of communication ranging from national systems of education and science, national newspapers and media such as television as well as national commemorations and popular culture in which national narratives and collective identities were codified, reproduced and legitimated. Most nation-states have been based on a national language, which was increasingly standardized over time. In addition, political parties have been at the centre of large-scale apparatuses of political communication which they have used for social influence. If the Enlightenment public was based on free discussion, the public today is based on professional political communication and mass persuasion through systematic advertising and lobbying: for Mayhew this amounts to a 'new public' (Mayhew 1997). However, as argued by Habermas (1989) in his major work on the public sphere, communication is an open site of political and cultural contestation and is never fully institutionalized by the state or entirely controlled by elites and their organs of political communication. The public sphere is the site of politics; it is not merely a spatial location but a process of discursive contestation (see Calhoun 1992; Crossley and Roberts 2004).

Until now this has been mostly conceived of as a national public sphere. Most of the examples taken by Habermas relate to national public spheres. Moreover the idea of the public sphere was theorized in terms of decline as a result of the rise of the commercial mass media. Although Habermas's (1996) later theory of discursive democracy revitalized the theory of the public sphere – which had in the meanwhile been complemented by alternative conceptions of the public sphere, including the notion of the 'proletarian public sphere', as opposed to the bourgeois public sphere (Negt and Kluge 2003) – this model remains still largely based on national societies. The new social theory of the public sphere has now moved into a wider view of the public sphere as cosmopolitan, with recent contributions noting the existence of non-Western public spheres (Hoexter *et al.* 2002) and global public spheres constituted by global civil society (see Eder 2005; Kögler 2005; Strydom 2002). To speak of a cosmopolitan public sphere is to draw attention to the transformation of all public spheres by global political communication. A cosmopolitan public sphere comes into existence as a result of a cross-fertilization of communication and the appearance of cross-national discourses as well as global ones. The public sphere has been transformed by global communication and it is hardly possible to speak of nationally cohesive public spheres anymore (Bohman 1998). As Calhoun has argued, public communication is itself a form of solidarity: 'It is often presumed people must be already joined in solidarity to form a public, but this seems wrong in so far as the very notion of public has to do with communication among those who are not bound to each other by private ties. Communication may take place among strangers and yet knit its participants into a sense of common undertaking' (Calhoun 2003b: 548).

While debates continue on the question of the global public sphere as a transnational space, what is more important then is the emergence of a global public discourse, which is less a spatially defined entity than a manifestation of a cosmopolitan discourse that is constitutive of global ethics. The public sphere is now pervaded by what, in the previous chapter, has been called a global public and is constitutive of new kinds of solidarity. The global public is the ever-present sphere of discourse that contextualizes political communication and public discourse today. The role of the public must be conceived as having a cosmopolitan dimension. The discursive construction of the social world takes place within the wider context of global communication in which the global public plays a key role. The global public has a major resonance in all of communication in the sense that it structures and contextualizes much of public discourse, as examples ranging from human rights, war and military intervention, environmental concerns, health and security illustrate.

The global is not outside the social world but is inside it in numerous ways. It is possible to see political communication in the public sphere as increasingly framed by global issues. This is due not least to global civil society which has greatly amplified global normative culture. However, global normative culture is diffused in many ways within public spheres and is carried by many different kinds of social agents, including states. Political globalization is most visible in terms of changes in political communication and in the wider transformation of the public sphere. It is possible to speak of a communicative kind of political globalization confronting economic globalization. This is different from global geopolitics, which as argued earlier has led to a transnationalization of the state in line with the rise of a global economy. An example of this is the impact of global events. Szersznski and Urry (2002: 120) refer to how in the early years of South Africa's move away from apartheid, Nelson Mandela would often refer to 'the people of South Africa and the world who are watching' on their television screens. This example and others – the fall of the Berlin Wall in 1989, 11 September 2001, the Asian tsunami on 26 December 2004, the destruction of New Orleans on 29 August 2005 – reveal that collective global events are key to the formation of a cosmopolitan culture. Szersznski and Urry (2002: 121) go on to argue that their empirical research leads to the conclusion that 'global imagery was starting to constitute an unremarked, all pervasive background to people's lives, one with a potential to reshape their sense of belonging'. It might be suggested that this sense of belonging can be understood in terms of an ethical sensibility shaped by the powers of affect entailing the interweaving of technology, feelings, mobility and consciousness.

Conclusion

Global ethics is more than the sum of individual ethics, but is not a collective ethics as such or a basis for a global order of governance. A global ethics is evident in ways of thinking, feelings, social movements and struggles, in soft laws as well as in international laws, tribunals and treaties. A global ethics is an emerging ethics and cannot be easily translated into legal and political forms since it is as yet largely a consequence of changes in moral consciousness and does not have a clearly specified subject or institutional form. It resides more in the domain of affect than in institutional or legislative arrangements.

Global ethics represents an important challenge for critical social theory. Habermas introduced a strong ethical dimension into critical theory, which previously had failed to connect the moral point of view with a conception of the political. By grounding ethics in communication as the context in which all normative models of society are formed, ethics becomes further tied to the cultural and political project of modernity. I have argued for a critical theory of communication that emphasizes the discursive construction of ethical and political models involving changes in subject formation. This approach suggests the salience of global ethics for an analysis of contemporary society based on immanent transcendence, for global ethical discourses are becoming increasingly embroiled in the shaping of the social world around affect and subjectivity. From the perspective of critical cosmopolitanism, global ethics can only occur in the plural and in ways that undergo transformation in the process of emergence. So rather than look at global ethics in terms of universal moral principles or in terms of common cultural values, from the perspective of a critical social theory it is best seen as a process of social construction in which communicative processes intertwine with moral and political standpoints. The discursive construction of the social world takes places within the wider context of global communication. Global ethics plays a major role in the discursive construction of the social world by structuring and contextualizing public discourse and collective identities, as examples ranging from human rights, environmental concerns, health and security, social justice and solidarity illustrate. It captures a process of inclusion that is in principle indeterminate and open to a continuous expansion of horizons.

Such processes of discursive transformation are open-ended due to the contingency that is the outcome of the public sphere. The upshot of this is that global ethics can take a huge variety of forms, from the micro-level of individual identities to global protest movements and inter-governmental policy-making as well as forms of consumption. It is likely to be one of the principal contexts for social identities in the future and a promising ground for sociological research on globalization.

4 | *Cosmopolitan citizenship and the post-sovereign state*

One of the most notable features of the current day is a shift from peoplehood to personhood. Throughout the world in recent times governments are forced to recognize the integrity of the person, not as an abstract individual as in liberal political theory, but as an embodied being shaped by social struggles. Personhood challenges the hitherto dominant notion of peoplehood that has been a feature of the era in which the modern national state determined the nature of political community. Peoplehood has mostly been defined in terms of nationhood, for the national community has been for the greater part the community of the national state. Current developments, which can be linked to the local–global nexus, suggest a reshaping of peoplehood along with political community more generally in the direction of personhood. This has been reflected in the growing importance of cosmopolitan politics: international law, the rights of minorities, global solidarities and global justice, and cultural rights of various kinds. What is implied by the turn to personhood is a conception of political community that avoids both communitarianism and individualism and which can be termed cosmopolitan. Cosmopolitanism indicates a transformative conception of belonging whereby the citizen is neither a passive entity nor a pre-political being but an active agent.

In the previous chapters a case was made for a view of cosmopolitanism as real, as opposed to an abstract ideal, and as such rooted in the practices of contemporary politics as well as socio-cultural processes. In this chapter an alternative and more inclusive notion of political community to nationhood will be discussed around the confluence of citizenship and cosmopolitanism in terms of local global links, and arising out of these relations new dispositions, capacities and virtues. This is view of cosmopolitanism that includes the poor – who in a sense are the universal class – as opposed to a transnational class or multiethnic social group, who are often taken to be the carriers of cosmopolitanism. Underlying the tremendous transformation in citizenship is a transformation in the nature of the nation-state, which is best understood today as a post-sovereign state. By this is meant a sovereign state that has had to compromise part of its sovereignty. Cosmopolitan citizenship is a mode of belonging that is most appropriate for the post-sovereign state. It captures one important way in which to conceptualize the expansion of capacities that can be related to cosmopolitanism. In Chapter 2, it was argued that these principally relate to the capacity for the relativization of one's own culture or identity, the capacity for the positive recognition of the Other, the capacity for a mutual evaluation of cultures or identities, and the capacity to create a shared normative culture. The concept of citizenship, with its emphasis on agency and participation, lies at the core of these capacities in so far as it concerns internal or immanent transformation of political community. Of particular relevance in this context is the question of shifts in the nature of hospitality. I begin with a critical examination of the dominant liberal, republican and communitarian traditions of citizenship. The second section of the chapter looks at the erosion of nationality in the post-sovereign state and the third section provides an account of the emergence of cosmopolitan citizenship.

Traditions of citizenship

As with many contested concepts in the social sciences, citizenship is not easy to define. The problem is due to the fact that the idea of citizenship has come to us from three different political traditions, namely the liberal, republican and communitarian ones. According to a commonly held view, republicanism is the characteristic European tradition of citizenship and can be seen as the political and philosophical basis for European citizenship. Another view states that European post-national citizenship is the expression of a variety of national traditions, which are all leading in the direction of a transnational citizenship. These are all questionable assumptions. Taking what can be held to be the three main traditions of citizenship – liberalism, republicanism and communitarianism – it can be shown that there is no clear-cut distinction between these as far as particular national contexts are concerned. Republicanism is itself a mixture of several components and it is difficult, if not impossible, to specify exactly what republicanism might consist of and whether there are differences between European and

American republicanism. Moreover, all these traditions are based on a notion of 'peoplehood' that is not easily applied to the transnational context.

The liberal idea sees citizenship largely as a legal condition based on rights. In this understanding of citizenship, which had its origins in English seventeenth-century political theory, citizenship concerns the rights of the citizen. The liberal heritage gave to the idea of citizenship a strong association with law, and a view of the citizen as the bearer of rights. In this view, citizenship is a legal status that defines the relation of the individual to the polity. Although it does entail duties, it is largely seen as one of rights. The traditional rights in liberal theory are the negative ones that specify the rights of the individual to be free of arbitrary violence and the positive rights to exercise political participation by voting. In the liberal tradition, citizenship participation has, overall, been limited to voting. This is because for liberal theory citizenship is just one dimension of democracy, the others being constitutionalism (or liberal democracy) and the representation of social interests (or parliamentary democracy). However, in the modern democracies, liberalism has mostly been modified by social democracy, at least as far as the theory of citizenship is concerned. T. H. Marshall (1992) reflected this tendency when he wrote his influential work on social citizenship. In this account, social rights complement the traditional liberal rights and, in Marshall's evolutionary theory, represent the end of the historical narrative of citizenship as a discourse. Social rights not only complement civic and political rights, but they are also enabling rights in that they compensate for some of the social disadvantages brought about by capitalism. It will suffice to mention here that this theory reduced citizenship to a passive condition whereby the citizen was a recipient of rights, and neglected the active dimension, ignoring for instance that many of these rights were the product of social struggles. Its evolutionary model cannot be so easily applied to many countries with different historical trajectories of rights. Finally, it failed to address other kinds of rights, such as cultural rights (Mann 1987).

In republican political theory – from classical thought to the Renaissance and Enlightenment – citizenship has been largely associated with the participation of the public in the political life of the community. This has given rise to a strong association of citizenship with civil society and, in general, with a definition of citizenship that stresses 'virtue' and the active membership of a political community.

Classical and modern republican theory differ from the rights discourse in stressing much more strongly the relation of citizenship to democracy. Where the rights discourse reduced this to a minimum, the republican tradition maximizes the democratic nature of citizenship by seeing it as a form of political participation in public life. With its origins in the classical Greek polis, the Roman *civitas* and the Renaissance city-state, the modern idea of republican citizenship was born with the Enlightenment and the ideas of the American and French Revolutions. In this tradition, the very idea of the republic is inextricably connected with citizenship (Pettit 1997). However, modern or civic republicanism has been a very backward-looking doctrine, seeing citizenship in decline in modern times. One of the most famous proponents of republican theory, Hannah Arendt, went so far as to see the republican ideal undermined by the social question. According to Robert Putnam (1999), modern individualism has eroded the ability of contemporary American society to generate social capital. Civic engagement, voluntarism, associational membership – epitomized in declining membership of bowling clubs, the quintessential feature of white Anglo-Saxon America – are in decline due to a nascent individualism, he argued, and consequently democracy is undermined. What makes democracy flourish according to Putnam, whether in Europe or America, is the stable core of a cultural tradition based on common values.

The communitarian conception of citizenship emphasizes duties and identity. In return for rights, the citizen had to perform certain duties, such as the duty to take up arms, to pay taxes, mandatory education, and the general duty to be a good citizen. In general, the communitarian tradition of citizenship has been tied to an organic notion of the people as an ethnic group based on blood ties and a shared cultural community. The people are defined less by civic and legal ties than by a common community of destiny. The communitarian tradition is one that is very difficult to disentangle from the liberal and republican models in that it is mostly presupposed in these traditions as the cultural basis of a civic or political community. One modern expression of it is in constitutional conservatism, which is closely linked to liberalism, giving a constitutional role to certain cultural traditions – a state church for instance – while anchoring the political culture in a principle of tolerance (see Chapter 6). The principle of tolerance is what marks it off from the more staunchly secular underpinning of republicanism, which demands a stronger separation of church and state. In this case, it is less a question of tolerance than of equality.

While it is possible to find examples of national traditions that are based on one citizenship tradition, according to a recent study, there is no single trajectory for the development of citizenship (Bellamy *et al.* 2004). The specific national forms that citizenship took have varied greatly as a result of the structure of the state, the nature of class relations, cultural and ideological divisions, contingent events such as war, and so on. It is out of the interaction of such factors that the different national citizenship traditions emerged. The implication of this approach is that some of the standard categories of citizenship regimes do not quite fit into most of the national traditions. Most countries exhibit instances of liberal, republican and communitarian forms of citizenship. Moreover, what counts as republicanism or liberalism also varies from country to country. Liberal principles are often indistinguishable from republican ones. What emerges out of this is a view of citizenship as highly mixed, instead of uniform or evolutionary. In Germany, France and Britain the respective models of communitarian, republican and liberal traditions do not quite hold. For example, as Ulrich Preuss (2004) argues with respect to Germany, contrary to many preconceptions, nationality and citizenship were differentiated in the German tradition. In the case of France, Cécile Laborde (2002) has argued that citizenship cannot be understood simply in terms of republican nationality as a *ius soli*, in that it also contains liberal and communitarian components. It has been noted that, in the case of Britain, contrary to Marshall's famous trajectory of citizenship culminating in social citizenship, social rights predated citizenship, which was a relatively recent innovation (Harris 2004). In many countries, most notably Portugal where the *ius soli* was established relatively early, the appeal to the principle of nationality had no connection with democratization (Ramos 2004). In Scandinavian countries, women's political integration led to a model of citizenship that did not correspond to the three dominant models (Siim and Skjeie 2004). In contrast, Italy may be an example of a country where the republican tradition has been more influential than other traditions. However, when we look more specifically at the republican tradition, what emerges is not a distinctive European political tradition but a variety of historical forms, all of which do not constitute a model of citizenship that can be claimed for the European heritage. Three problems emerge that can be briefly commented on.

First, as already indicated, republicanism took numerous forms in Europe, not all of which can be easily related to what today is called republicanism. Republicanism was primarily an early modern phenomenon. Italian city-states of the Renaissance period constitute one kind of, essentially city, government before the age of the nation-state. However, republicanism was not antithetical to nationalism. There is the early modern Protestant form of republicanism associated with the Puritan movement in England of the mid-1640s, when a republican commonwealth government was established by Cromwell in opposition to Catholic Royalists. This movement, despite its opposition to monarchy, was important in establishing the foundations of the modern nation-state in Britain. A different and more tolerant variant of republicanism emerged in the Netherlands where a commercial bourgeoisie was more central to politics (Blum 2002). There is a clear connection between Protestantism and republicanism. While the extreme example of this was the Puritan republic of Geneva in the seventeenth century, early modern republicanism was the political form in which non-conformist Protestantism developed. The tie with religion was broken with the rise of republicanism in revolutionary France where it was a far from democratic movement. Revolutionary republicanism was led by new elites whose pursuit of political power required state-based forms of violence. Republicanism in France, in any case, led to the establishment of a central nation-state based on republican principles.

The second problem with republicanism as the European political heritage thus is the fact that its connection with democracy, which we are led to believe must be integral to citizenship, is at best tenuous, if not entirely absent. One of the many criticisms made of Robert Putnam's attempt to rescue republicanism for the present day is that it is nostalgic for a bygone world of traditional cultural values. In his case, it is a world associated with the bowling clubs of Jeffersonian agrarian republicanism. Moreover, it was a view of culture that accepted the exclusion of large segments of the population – women and minorities – from a polity whose values were narrow, gendered and closed to the reality of diversity. Putnam's version of republicanism may be communitarian in inspiration, but the limits of the model also apply to Europe. It is certainly the case that republican ideas have been hugely influential in Europe, but these have not been inherently democratic and, what is more, have often been decidedly exclusionary. One only has to think of the controversy over the headscarf and veil in present-day France to recognize the limits of republican political values for multicultural societies. In this context, an interesting contrast can be found in different traditions of republicanism. Different conceptions of space play out in different models of citizenship in France and the Netherlands, in terms of different views of rights pertaining to the private and public domains (Stuurman 2004). This is ultimately a question of where the limits of the state lie. In the latter, a curious mixture of liberal and communitarian models led to a marked difference from France where the state has a far greater presence in people's lives.

One of the major limits of republicanism is the assumption that it makes about peoplehood. Republican thought emerged at a time when the polity in question was a relatively small one or, rather, when the polity was conceived as being based on a single conception of 'the people'. Thus, the French Revolution invoked a unitary notion of the people as a political entity. The subsequent republican state set about the goal of constituting the people as a national citizenry, defined in total by the state. As noted above, it entailed a view of the public realm under the jurisdiction of the state. Today, political thought and practice has moved beyond this conception of politics which requires a strict separation of private and public. Yet, the problem of how people-hood should be conceived remains.

Citizenship, properly understood, is separate from peoplehood. Citizenship can be understood to mean participation in political community and it is an essential aspect of democracy, which entails three dimensions: representation (i.e. majority decision-making through parliamentary democracy); constitutionalism (setting limits to what majorities can do); and citizenship, or public participation in civil society. Without citizenship, democracy would be minimal and lacking a public dimension. Citizenship thus gives to democracy a substantive dimension, linking it to individuals and to civil society. However, citizenship is itself both substantive and formal and although the substantive role has been important on the whole until the last few decades citizenship has been largely formal. In the famous definition of citizenship by T. H. Marshall, it is a formal status based on rights, which defines the relation of the individual to the state. This could be said to characterize liberal citizenship, the kind of citizenship fostered by the modern democratic state, but of course includes, as in Marshall's account, social rights. The modern liberal state was also a nation-state and as a result citizenship became indistinguishable from the bundle of rights associated with nationality. What we are witnessing today in our global age is, with the emergence of new kinds of citizenship, the growing importance of the substantive dimension and the dislocation of nationality and citizenship (see Delanty 2001; Isin 2002).

In formal terms, citizenship can be understood in terms of rights and duties. The classic rights of citizenship are political rights (the right to vote and stand for election), civic rights (which generally concern individual liberties) and social rights (rights to public goods, such as education and healthcare, and generally social protection from the free market). These rights are underpinned by duties, such as the duties of taxation, jury service, mandatory education, and in some cases conscription. In substantive terms, citizenship is expressed in active public participation, such as voluntary action – the virtuous citizen – and in collective identities, as in for example national identity and loyalty to the state and nation. While there is no reason why citizenship and democracy more generally has to be confined to the bounds of the nation-state, the reality is that citizenship developed alongside the nation-state: citizenship became indistinguishable from nationality and is often equated with the passport, which came into existence with the modern nation-state and the need to control large-scale and potentially mobile populations. So with the liberal nation-state, citizenship became defined in terms of the rights and duties of citizens to the state, which also defined the polity more generally, as well as civil society. This meant that citizenship was based on exclusion and was the means by which the state distinguished between members and nonmembers of the polity (Hindess 1998).

It is also the case that citizenship has been fairly apolitical in the sense that it has been largely a passive condition by which the individual was the recipient of rights bestowed by the benevolent surveillance state and for which the citizen had to perform duties. The historical experience has been that citizenship preceded mass democracy – seventeenth-century England is such an example – and there are many examples of citizenship having no connection with democracy, as in communist countries which had institutionalized social citizenship, and there are also cases of political citizenship existing without social citizenship. An example of a substantive kind of citizenship that has been connected with democratization is the republican heritage of citizen participation, which allegedly is the basis of social capital. However, this tradition, which has been influential in the United States, has often been criticized for being based on a highly exclusionary model of civil society rooted in localism and small-scale rural communities. It has been argued that this civic republican conception of citizenship is nostalgic for a kind of political community that is no longer pertinent for large-scale multi-ethnic societies.

Neither the republican, communitarian nor the classic liberal conception of citizenship is appropriate to the present day. As a result of the transformation of the state, the globalization of markets and communication, the rise of a global civil society, and new configurations of global and local connections, the assumptions of these conceptions of citizenship can be called into question. Radical pluralists have criticized these conceptions of citizenship for being apolitical and exclusionary. Despite their differences both kinds of citizenship saw only a limited connection with democratization and shared belief in the homogeneous nature of the political community as a relatively bounded and territorial national community. We can now consider the main aspects of the transformation of citizenship.

The erosion of nationality

It is possible to speak of an erosion of nationality today. The nation-state has been challenged from within and from outside by developments which oscillate around the encounter of the local with the global. In particular the relentless drive of globalizers and neoliberalism has challenged the nation-state, which should be understood as a post-sovereign state. The post-sovereign state is one that that has lost exclusive control of its sovereignty in a more globally connected world. The modern age was based on the state project and modern society was largely shaped by nation and class since the modern nation-state developed alongside industrial society. Today global capitalism and global markets are playing much the same role that industrial capitalism played in the formative phase in the making of the modern nation-state. The nation-state was highly successful in shaping political community and, in particular, in organizing citizenship into a formal framework, which was part of the wider process of democracy. Through the institution of citizenship the state was connected with civil society and anchored in private lives. Along with changes in the nature of statehood and the movement towards a global civil society, this connection has changed today. National politics can no longer be understood if we analyse it exclusively in the terms of national categories (Grande 2006).

The notion of the decline of the nation-state in a post-statist world of governance without government – or in a new medievalism of regional economies (Ohmae 1996) – should be replaced by the idea of the continued transformation of the nation-state. The idea of states disappearing in a global world of markets or replaced by global structures of governance, on the one side, or as in the neo-realist scenario the survival of the so-called Westphalian state as a sovereign actor, must be rejected. States continue to be powerful actors but exist in a more globally connected world that they do not fully control (see Sorensen 2004). The following arguments have been given with respect to the transformation of the nation-state under the conditions of largely economic globalization. According to Susan Strange (1996), in the most well-known formulation of this position, states have been usurped by global markets. With the transition from a world economy dominated by national economies to a global economy new economic forces come into play challenging the power of the nation-state. Instead of struggling to gain territorial power over other states most states are struggling to control firms that have become rivals to states. The result is that states have to share sovereignty with other global players. In other approaches, where the emphasis is more on the impact of global civil society the argument is that the nation-state must share sovereignty with non-governmental actors, leading to multi-governance. It is clear that in all these accounts the state is only one source of political power. Much of this revolves around the question of whether states are getting weaker or stronger as a result of global forces. In the case of Europeanization, which is a major area for the application of many of these arguments, at least two positions have emerged: the thesis that transnationalization enhances the power of the nation-state and the thesis of the rise of the regulatory state. According to Alan Milward (1993), European integration, as a movement that has led to the progressive erosion of national sovereignty, has paradoxically rescued the nation-state rather than undermined it. The movement towards transnational authority allows a more functional state system to operate since it is only those functions – for instance, regulation of finance markets and cross-border trade – that the solitary state is less well equipped to perform that are transferred upwards to the transnational level. But the result is an unavoidable loss of sovereignty, which does not necessarily translate into a loss of autonomy.

According to Majone (1996), the transnationalization of the state in Europe is best seen in terms of a regulatory kind of governance rather than the creation of a new state system that challenges the nation-state. The European Union possesses a large number of independent regulatory authorities, working in fields such as the environment, drugs and drug addiction, vocational training, health and safety at work, the internal market, racism and xenophobia, food safety and aviation safety. States have always had regulatory functions; what is different today is simply these functions are being performed at a transnational level through cooperation with other states. In the view of Robinson (2001) a transnational state has come into existence. This is a multi-layered and multi-centred, linking together on a transnational level many of the functions of statehood. The nation-state does not 'wither away' but becomes transformed by becoming a functional component of this transnational apparatus and a major agent of global capitalism. In this analysis, globalization reconfigures the state around global capitalism, making it impossible for nation-states to be independent.

It is evident that what is being discussed here is a transformation of the nation-state into a post-sovereign order rather than its demise. Moreover the European examples detract attention from the world context where the experience has been that the nation-state continues to be the principal political form of societal organization. Throughout Asia, Africa, Central and South America, nation-states are on the whole the main expressions of political mobilization and identity. Globalization has enhanced, not undermined, them. The two most powerful actors in the world today, the United States and China, are nation-states. Europe is undoubtedly an exception. However, even in Europe, since the most recent enlargement of the European Union, it is arguably the case that the introduction of several new countries in Central and Eastern Europe is enhancing rather than undermining the nation-state for the simple reason that for most of these countries entry into the European transnational order is a means of asserting rather than relinquishing national sovereignty. One only has to consider the results of the constitutional referenda on the ratification of the European constitution in 2005 in France and the Netherlands and in Ireland in 2008 to see how consequential national publics can be. However, the aspiration to national autonomy cannot hide the general movement towards the transnationalization of the state and the even more extensive movement towards a geopolitics of global power in which a global state is emerging around the global military–political unification of much of the world. As Martin Shaw has argued, after 1989 and the removal of the Iron Curtain, the bifurcation of global space ceased with the result that the Western state system has become a global power (Shaw 1997). In other words, the state has become more diffuse; it is less easily defined in terms of territory or in terms of political community.

The intervention of several Western governments in the crisis of finance capitalism in 2008, widely believed to be as significant as the Wall Street Crash of 1929, reveals that in the final analysis the state continues to rescue capitalism from its endemic crises. In view of the current turn to the partial nationalization of major banks it is difficult to conclude that the state has been rendered powerless by global capitalism. It is possible that we shall see a return of the state in the coming years, but this reassertion of the state against global finance capitalism will affirm rather than negate the context of post-sovereignty.

A distinction needs to be made between states and nation-states. While most states are nation-states there is a distinction which is particularly important in the context of political globalization. States, to follow Weber's definition, are centres of the monopoly of legitimate violence in a given territory while nation-states refer to the coincidence of the state with a defined political community. It is clearly the case that states are changing in response to globalization, as discussed in the foregoing. States are more flexible in responding to globalization than nations with the result that globalization has exercised tremendous pressure on nation-states, that is on the relationship between political community and exercise of legitimate violence. The resulting crisis of the nation-state is apparent in the transformation of nationality. Two kinds of decoupling processes are evident: the decoupling of nationality and citizenship and the decoupling of nationhood and statehood.

The decoupling of nationality and citizenship can be attributed to the impact of global normative culture which has led to a blurring of the boundary between national and international law. Especially in the countries of the European Union, it is now more difficult for states to resist international law, which has become progressively incorporated into national law. The result of this is that migrants can make direct appeal to international law. International legal tribunals are playing a growing role in national politics. The rights of citizenship no longer perfectly mirror the rights of nationality despite the efforts of states to create lines of exclusion based on nationality (Jacobsen 1996). The erosion of sovereignty has made a huge impact on nationality (Sassen 1996). In a similar way nationhood and statehood have experienced new lines of tension. The state does not perfectly mirror the nation with the result that the assertion of nationhood often takes on new and recalcitrant forms as reflected in the rise of the extreme right. The transnationalization of the state in the countries of the European Union has undermined the nation-state, leading to the rise of new nationalist movements (see Holmes 2005). The rise of nationalism since the early 1990s in Europe, which coincided with the fall of communism and the enhanced momentum towards European integration, has created the conditions for a new kind of populist nationalism that has as its central animus the claim to protect the nation from globalization of all kinds, ranging from the transnationalization of the state to global migration and global markets. The nation-state has thus become bifurcated: nation and state have become divorced, each following different logics. The state has become in part transnationalized, while the nation – seemingly in the view of many national publics – abandoned by the state has taken new forms and which can often be enhanced by globalization. Although this tendency towards a backlash of nationalism against transnationalism has been particularly pronounced in Western Europe as a result of Europeanization, it also emerges in the transition to market economies in the former communist countries and is also an aspect of new religious nationalisms. As Saskia Sassen (2002) and others have argued a further dimension to the global transformation of the nation-state is the rise of subnational politics. Global cities, for example, are products of the denationalization of the nation-state and the rise of non-territorial politics.

Thus many nations are now more shaped by globalization. Due to the conditions of globalization the nation-state has become dislocated from the state. The political community of the nation does not exercise sovereignty over the state and the state has lost much of its sovereignty. So with the rise of nationalism, on the one side, and on the other the growing power of global capitalism, the role of citizenship is particularly important. Its importance consists in the fact that it is reducible neither to nationhood nor statehood.

Post-national citizenship and cosmopolitanism

It is important to see that despite the equation of citizenship with nationality there is no necessary link. This means both new opportunities for citizenship, but it also means that some of the rights of citizenship as a condition underpinned by the nation-state dissolve. One of the features of the present day is the rise of new kinds of citizenship that go beyond the classic rights and duties associated with the nation-state, on the one side, and on the other the increasing recognition that the nation-state is unable to provide a framework for all aspects of citizenship. The current situation can be described as an uncoupling of nationality and citizenship. This is reflected in a number of developments such as the blurring of the difference between national rights and international human rights, the rise of cultural rights, the challenge of technological citizenship, the emergence of a global political community (see Stevenson 2002).

With regard to international human rights, the observation can be made that the traditional separation of national and international law is no longer valid. It is now more difficult for states to equate nationality and citizenship since many rights can be claimed on the basis of human rights. In short, membership rights are not exclusively defined in terms of a community of descent or of birth but of residence. Rights now extend unavoidably across borders (see Jacobsen 1996; Sassen 2007; Soysal 1994).

Cultural rights concern at least three areas. In place of the individual as the bearer of rights, they concern group-based rights, largely for minorities. In several countries, most notably Canada, Australia and New Zealand, rights for native or pre-colonial peoples have been central to the politics of citizenship. Such demands for special collective rights have introduced a distinction between the rights of migrant groups and the rights of aboriginal groups, with the latter having different claims from groups who settled as a result of migration (see Kymlicka 1995). Cultural rights concern some of the core issues in identity politics, in particular issues relating to women and to group-specific demands. The upshot of this is that citizenship can no longer be seen as formal equality between individuals, but must reflect group-specific concerns. It is now generally recognized that such concessions do not undermine the individual person as the bearer of rights, but are an essential dimension of democracy, which is enabled rather than hampered by cultural rights which can be seen in terms of a politics of recognition based on pluralism (Cowan *et al.* 2001). In short, citizenship has entered the domain of culture at a time when culture is being more and more seen in pluralist terms. Citizenship thus comes to reflect the pluralism of contemporary culture and the fact that there is no single national culture but contested sites of belonging (see Guttmann 2003).

Cultural pluralism has also impacted on citizenship in the area of lifestyle, with an important expression of rights now including consumer rights. In a world in which most people, at least in the developed Western world, are primarily consumers more so than producers, cultural citizenship is particularly important and includes rights related to mobility, since today people are more mobile. As a result of the tremendous transformation in temporality and space that has been a feature of the present day with global travel and informational capitalism, citizenship extends beyond the territorial limits of a given state to be a global condition. The global nature of consumption is, too, a reason to see the cultural face of citizenship in global terms.

In addition to cultural citizenship there are also additional rights relating to new technologies and environmental concerns. It is possible to speak of technological citizenship and environmental citizenship with respect to rights that pertain to concerns that did not exist in the era of the modern nation-state (Frankenfeld 1992; Zimmerman 1992). The characteristic feature of these rights is that they are not easily reduced to nationality and cannot be guaranteed by the nation-state. Because of new technologies, such as communication and information technologies, new reproductive technologies, the new genetics, biotechnologies, surveillance technologies, and new military technologies aimed at populations rather than states, technology has transformed the very meaning of citizenship, which can no longer be defined as a relation to the state. The new technologies differ from the old ones in that they have major implications for citizenship, given their capacity to refine the very nature of society, and in many case personhood. Citizens, in private and in public roles and as consumers, patients and university students are encountering the new technologies increasingly through the market. In the area of rights, we find issues of privacy, rights to information, victimization and new concerns, such as, for instance, global responsibility, responsibility to nature, to future generations, concerns that go beyond the traditional conceptions of the dutiful citizen. Social inclusion is now extended to technology, which is affecting citizenship, opening up more and more possibilities for personal lifestyles, consumption and culture.

These examples illustrate the rise of what can be called a cosmopolitan concept of citizenship, which in the new literature on citizenship varies from being a modification of the traditional understanding of citizenship in liberal political theory to an emphasis on global citizenship and post-national kinds of membership. The erosion of nationality is an undeniable feature of the present day. This situation does not result in the obsolescence of citizenship but rather leads to new expressions. The characteristic feature of the new face of citizenship could be described as cosmopolitanism. The argument advanced here is that there is an alternative to nationalism and to patriotism as a basis of political community. This entails establishing citizenship on a foundation separate from nationality. The cosmopolitan alternative is partly an expression of globalization, but it is not reducible to globalization.

The anti-cosmopolitan position, especially in its republican-communitarian form, assumes that the nation-state does not include cosmopolitanism. Liberals are less hostile to cosmopolitanism, but those liberals who argue that cosmopolitanism can be reconciled to liberalism generally see this as a concession and relevant only to a limited range of rights. In general, both liberals and communitarians place cosmopolitanism as outside the nation-state when in fact it can be argued that cosmopolitanism has been integral to the nation-state itself and that therefore the distinction between national and cosmopolitan community is a false one. As is suggested by Anderson's notion of the 'imagined community', the nation-state presupposes the very capacity of citizens to imagine a world beyond their immediate context. There is no reason why this cannot extend beyond the nation-state. Although Anderson (1983) did not extend his notion of 'imagined community' beyond the national community, his analysis is particularly applicable to all kinds of large-scale social groups (Phillips 2002). It was his thesis that a large-scale group such as the national community had to be imagined, since it could not be experienced by its members directly. For the nation-state in its formative period it was print-capitalism that made this possible, whereas today there are numerous technological means for a political community to be imagined.

In view of these considerations, the liberal and republican repudiation of cosmopolitanism can be questioned. Cosmopolitanism is not a straightforward product of globalization, but arises out of the encounter of the global with the local or national. In this sense, then, it exists in relations of tension and in transformative dynamics; it is not a given condition or goal to be reached. In other words, cosmopolitanism exists within all societies and can be seen as a transformative process of immanent transcendence (see Beck 2006). It is in reconciling the universalistic rights of the individual with the need to protect minorities that the cosmopolitan citizenship is most evident. In this context cosmopolitan citizenship is to be understood in terms of a cultural shift in collective identities to include the recognition of others. Cosmopolitan citizenship is marked by a decreased importance of territory, in particular as measured by the place of one's birth in the definition of citizenship rights. In addition, cosmopolitan citizenship entails a lesser salience on an underlying collective identity, for a cosmopolitan political community does not have to rest on an underlying cultural community. Cultural rights are thus possible in the space that has been created by multiple and overlapping identities. As Seyla Benhabib has argued: 'Cosmopolitanism, the concern for the world as if it were one's *polis*, is furthered by such multiple, overlapping allegiances which are sustained across communities of language, ethnicity, religion, and nationality' (Benhabib 2004: 174–5). Such developments have arisen as a result of cultural pluralization arising from migration, ethnic multiculturalism, cultural diversity of all kinds and the growing demands for the recognition of different life choices.

The upshot of this is that nationality has been eroded and citizenship has moved into the political space opened up by global civil society and by the internal transformation of the nation-state. Cosmopolitanism is the appropriate term to describe these developments since it includes within it the local and the global. The local is especially important in cosmopolitan citizenship since it is on this level that some of the major political struggles take place and it is the site of the voice of the global poor. We thus speak of cosmopolitan citizenship as opposed to global citizenship to capture this sense of the local global dimension.

Taking some of the main components of citizenship – rights, duties, participation and identity – the cosmopolitan turn is evident in a shift away from nationality and from a territorially bounded citizenship. This is most evident in the domain of rights, which, as a result of the growing incorporation of international law into national law, are no longer confined to rights acquired by birth. Increasingly states have to recognize the rights of others – migrants, political asylum seekers, indigenous groups – and in many cases have to grant special rights. In normative terms there is no reason why citizenship should be determined by one's country of birth. Carens and others argue that from a moral perspective the problem of immigration cannot be understood solely from the perspective of the Western world and will have to take into account the perspective of refugees, asylum seekers and immigrants (Beitz 1999; Carens 1995; Pogge 1992, 2002; Sassen 2007; Shabani 2007).

The duties of citizenship are also no longer confined to the duty to serve the state, but extend to cosmopolitan responsibilities beyond the state and even to future generations. The dimension of participation now covers a wider sphere than national civil society and extends into global civil society, which can be seen as encroaching on national civil society. Finally, as an identity the loyalties of citizenship are not confined to loyalty to the nation-state, but take cosmopolitan forms as in multicultural identities and loyalties shaped by concerns with global justice, as argued in Chapter 3.

Cosmopolitan citizenship shifts the focus of citizenship onto common experiences, learning processes and discourses of empowerment that make possible immanent transcendence. The power to name, create meaning, construct personal biographies and narratives by gaining control over the flow of information, goods and cultural processes is an important dimension of citizenship as an active process. In this regard, what needs to be stressed is the learning dimension of citizenship as a constructivist process. Such an approach would show how citizens learn citizenship, which mostly takes place in the informal context of everyday life and is also heavily influenced by critical and formative events in people's lives. Citizenship is not entirely about rights, but is a matter of participation in the political community and begins early in life. It concerns the learning of a capacity for action and for responsibility but, essentially, it is about the learning of the self and of the relationship of Self and Other. It is a learning process in that it is articulated in perceptions of the self as an active agency and a social actor shaped by relations with others. In this view, citizenship concerns identity and action; it entails both personal and cognitive dimensions that extend beyond the personal to the wider cultural level of society.

Examples of this deeper sense of citizenship as a cultural discourse are the confluence of the personal and the political. Adopting a psychoanalytical perspective, Stephen Frosh (2000) argues that a cultural understanding of citizenship entails looking at the emotional aspects of collective identity. The subjective dimension of citizenship is discussed by Elliott (2000) and Crossley (2000) for whom citizenship involves the capacity to take on the point of view of the 'Other'. As a learning process, citizenship takes place in communicative situations arising out of quite ordinary life experiences. It appears that an essential dimension of the experience of citizenship is the way in which individual life stories are connected with wider cultural discourses. What is interesting is this cultural dimension to citizenship, which goes beyond the institutional dimension of both rights and also participation. We need more information, as well as theoretical tools, for understanding the cultural dimension of citizenship. However, for present purposes it will suffice to note that one of the most important dimensions of citizenship concerns the styles and forms of language, cultural models, narratives, discourses that people use to make sense of their society, interpret their place in it, construct courses of action and thereby give rise to new demands for rights, which we may call cultural rights. It is important, too, to see the learning component of citizenship not just in individual terms, but also as a medium of social construction by which individual learning becomes translated and coordinated into collective learning and ultimately becomes realized in social institutions.

This discussion of cosmopolitan citizenship can be brought to a close with a few remarks on the virtues, or the qualities, of mind and character that might be associated with cosmopolitan citizenship (Smith 2007). This is to go beyond the dimension of rights to address the kinds of motivations and dispositions that shape the cosmopolitan sensibility. Bryan Turner has highlighted irony as a key feature of cosmopolitan virtue, that is the way in which one achieves distance from one's homeland. The capacity to achieve distance cultivates a sceptical attitude to claims that the native culture should be prioritized. For Turner such virtues are the basis of the cosmopolitan virtue of care and obligation to others (Turner 2001, 2002). In order to cultivate such obligations it is first of all necessary to achieve distance from one's own culture and tradition, without necessarily rejecting it. This requires irony, a capacity for self-reflexivity, and is the basis of dialogue with other cultures. Smith, in developing the notion of cosmopolitan virtue, draws from Hannah Arendt's notion of worldliness to argue that cosmopolitan virtue is based on the overriding significance of human plurality (Smith 2007). On this view, cosmopolitan virtue consists of adopting a self-reflexive mode of being in the world with others. This is the capacity to be able to gain distance from one's own culture in order to accommodate the perspective of the Other. To this virtue should be added the capacity to evaluate critically both the culture of the Other as well as one's own.

Conclusion

In view of arguments made in this chapter the limits of patriotism should be apparent. The nation-state is both too big and too small for citizenship. It is too big in that much of the actual practice of citizenship takes place on the local level rather than on the national level. National parliaments are generally felt by citizens to be remote and unconnected with local issues. On the other side, the nation-state is too small in that it is often felt to be inadequate when it comes to dealing with global challenges. However, it would be wrong to say that the state is no longer relevant and that all political problems can be addressed on the local or the global levels. The state is still vital to democracy and the failure of the state results in the collapse of civil society, as the examples of Rwanda, Bosnia and Kosovo illustrate. The state is still the main regulator of capitalism. Rather the argument advanced in this chapter is that citizenship operates on all levels, the local/national and the global and for this reason it is meaningful to speak in terms of cosmopolitan citizenship.

Rather than see global citizenship and national citizenship as exclusive, it makes more sense to see them as embodying different levels of citizenship. It is possible to identify at least three such levels: the subnational (that is, local or regional) level; the national level; and the global level. No account of citizenship can ignore the global dimension, although this does not mean that local forms of citizenship are redundant. This signals a view of citizenship as multi-levelled, rather than spatially confined to national societies. It also points to a flexible citizenship whereby citizens, especially migrants and those affected by transnational processes, negotiate more and more the different levels of governance. The citizen is a subject in flux and can alter their positionality, as Saskia Sassen argues (Sassen 2007). Under such conditions political community is more complex than multi-levelled governance, since the different levels interact producing new realities. This interactive process is a demonstration of the immanent nature of cosmopolitanism as a form of societal transcendence. Thus we find the gradual extension of a post-sovereign condition to all levels of the polity. For example, more and more countries are granting dual citizenship and the increasing prevalence of citizen's rights to sue governments.

Returning to a point made at the outset, the move towards cosmopolitan citizenship can be characterized in terms of a shift from a notion of citizenship determined by peoplehood to one based on personhood. The collective struggles and global solidarities that characterize much of the political landscape of democratic politics around issues of global solidarity and social justice are all based on the integrity of individual persons rather than the collective. Cosmopolitanism is also pertinent to the new cultural expressions of citizenship around issues of the environment, consumption, technology and corporate responsibility.

The cosmopolitan turn in citizenship draws attention to the existence of social relations that are not primarily shaped by the nation-state. It has been the aim of this chapter to outline some of the ways citizenship has undergone major transformation in recent times as a result of changed local–global links. The present situation as far as citizenship is concerned is very different from the contained world T. H. Marshall described in 1950: citizenship has ceased to be an instrument of social control and has become a site of social struggles and political contestation in which new visions of society are articulated.

5 | *Multiculturalism from a cosmopolitan perspective*

Throughout the world multiculturalism is entering a new and decisive phase. Traditionally associated with North America and Western Europe, multiculturalism can be applied to almost any multiethnic society. It is no longer possible to view it in the terms of any one tradition. Indeed, as will be discussed in detail in this chapter, there is no one tradition of multiculturalism and even the dominant Western models have changed over the past few decades. In the affluent societies of Western Europe it would appear that multiculturalism is under attack from the right while in central and Eastern Europe new discourses of ethnopluralism coincide with the belated discovery of Western multiculturalism. In many parts of the world there have been significant developments in the direction of multiculturalism. Yet there is little attention given to how non-Western societies have responded to the rise of multiculturalism which, having been internationalized, is now part of most societies throughout the world. In this chapter I argue that, despite their differences, all traditions of multiculturalism have been influenced by the Western liberal heritage and have come to rest on certain assumptions that are not always valid for the kind of challenges facing multiethnic societies today.

The discourse of multiculturalism must be brought in a different and, I argue, more cosmopolitan direction. There are three major dimensions to this. First, the distinction between the cultural and the social must be abandoned. The basis of this distinction is that ethnic groups are culturally defined in ways that distinguish them from the mainstream society of the natives. A cosmopolitan perspective is one of scepticism that an absolute distinction between natives and non-natives can be made. Second, multiculturalism must be reconceived in ways that directly address the wider society – such as institutional discrimination and everyday racism – as opposed to being reducible to measures for the management of minority groups. Third, the challenge of creating multicultural communities requires a wider and more globally oriented perspective than one that can be achieved by national policies alone. The objective reality of multiculturalism today is a world of global migration and the intermingling of populations. A cosmopolitan multiculturalism will thus require a wider dialogue with social groups beyond the immediate local and national community.

Underlying these three perspectives is a concern with reconciling diversity with the possibility of a shared public culture. Conventional forms of multiculturalism generally do not see multiculturalism as a basis of a shared public culture and radical approaches increasingly abandon the pursuit of a common culture. Against these positions, the cosmopolitan position advocated here places a strong emphasis on the possibility of a shared normative culture. However, this is something that requires a move beyond an understanding of multiculturalism as confined to the accommodation of the Other to a stronger critical engagement of both host and migrant cultures. In the terms of critical cosmopolitanism, a shared normative culture emerges only out of internal cultural transformation. This cosmopolitan conception of multicultural thus goes considerably beyond conventional liberal and communitarian approaches in that it opens up the possibility of the achievement of unity through diversity. I begin by looking at the various traditions of multiculturalism that emerged out of the liberal heritage. The second section attempts to advance a notion of cosmopolitan multiculturalism beyond liberal multiculturalism. The third section makes an argument for a notion of diversity as a condition of the possibility of a shared public culture. The next section looks at the problem of racism and the final section discusses the implications of non-Western forms of multiculturalism.

Multicultural traditions and the liberal legacy

There are four main traditions of multiculturalism, which can be termed egalitarian multiculturalism, liberal multiculturalism, ethnopluralism and radical multiculturalism. All of these – and other sub-themes that have emerged in recent times – are in different ways responses to the liberal legacy, which shaped the classic egalitarianism of early American multiculturalism. Liberalism, with its characteristic belief in the integrity and freedom of the individual, cultivated a strong belief in rights and in the virtue of tolerance. Central, too, to the liberal vision of modernity was the double separation of state and society and the separation of the private from the public. This was reflected in the rise of multiculturalism in twentieth-century United States, a society formed through European immigration. This classic kind of multiculturalism is best termed egalitarian multiculturalism to distinguish it from later developments. Although liberal in its fundamental orientations, it was primarily a process of nation-state building in that it was formative of the national character and self-understanding of the United States.

The basis of American multiculturalism was the equality of citizens in the shared public domain. A principle of public equality underlay it. This kind of multiculturalism gave its name to the so-called melting-pot model, which aimed at a certain degree of assimilation into a common public culture while accepting diversity on the level of the private domain and collective identities that lie outside the official public culture. In this way both unity and diversity were possible, with unity at a national and public level and diversity at an ethnic and private level. Arising from this essentially egalitarianism multiculturalism, which it can be termed, was a degree of civic integration into the public culture for all ethnic groups. Egalitarian multiculturalism does not recognize collective or group rights, but is based only on the recognition of individual rights in the public domain. Thus the state does not recognize minorities as such. In this way hyphenated identities – Irish-American, Italian-American – were possible and greatly contributed to the making of an inclusive American national identity.

In contrast, in Europe nation-state formation developed in a way that severely curtailed multiculturalism. In most European countries until the second half of the twentieth century the integration of minorities was achieved through policies of assimilation whereby minorities were compelled to integrate into the dominant national culture. This was most pronounced in the republican tradition in France where assimilation as opposed to integration has been for long the official public approach to cultural diversity. Unlike in the United States, assimilation oriented approaches to minorities have no place for the 'hyphen' that links the ethnic with the shared national or public culture. It was of course the case that the melting-pot model intended that in time a common citizenry would emerge with the hyphen giving way to identities that had been formed from a process of acculturation. But it was not primarily a state-led process of assimilation into a pre-established national culture as was the case in Europe. It was a case of a nation being formed out of the intermingling of cultures.

Egalitarian multiculturalism clearly had it limits. There was no place in it for collective rights or the recognition of injustice to pre-settler groups. It was not designed to overcome racism or discrimination of minorities and existed alongside the marginalization of large segments of the population. Moreover, the dominant social group, white Anglo-Saxons, remained in a culturally dominant position. In a certain sense it was not a model of multiculturalism in that it was not based on a coherent and organized policy for the integration of minorities and the pursuit of equality. The generalized principle of egalitarianism that was the basis of it was merely a modified version of nineteenth-century national acculturation.

Although best associated with the American tradition, multicultural-ism in time was an approach adopted, largely by default, in many European countries in the post-Second World War period when those countries became for the first time countries of immigration, as opposed to emigration as had been the case in the colonial period. The assumption that underlay multiculturalism as adopted from the 1960s onwards was that the mainstream society was homogeneous and that incoming groups, who were 'different', had to be managed to ensure, if not their assimilation, at least a degree of integration. In most cases there was no explicit commitment to equality or to acculturation. What emerged out of this was an uneasy mix of national assimilation, egalitarianism and the need to grant recognition to diverse groups, not all of whom were migrants but also included national minorities. Multiculturalism, properly understood, is a product of the second half of the twentieth century and is best termed liberal multiculturalism due to the new emphasis in it of rights for minorities. It goes beyond the appeal to egalitarianism to the recognition of difference.

Liberal multiculturalism is influenced by the view that minority groups, which also include large-scale national minorities, have to be given special rights to compensate for social disadvantages. In the case of regional or national minorities, the emphasis on rights was in part an acknowledgement that the older project of acculturation had to accom-modate diversity, including the demands for autonomy for minority nationalism. This modern kind of multiculturalism was essentially lib-eral in its understanding of how minorities should be integrated. The rise of communitarianism – with its emphasis on a social conception of the individual – has been much debated within political philosophy in normative terms. While its relation to multicultural policy is limited, it has drawn attention to the need for legal forms of recognition for minority cultures. It has also been generally acknowledged that communitarianism is a modification of liberalism rather than a departure from it. Within liberal theory several theorists have defended a limited conception of group rights on purely liberal grounds. Will Kymlicka (1995) argues that group rights can be defended for some kinds of national minorities such as indigenous groups, who at the time of their forced incorporation into the state possessed a distinct cultural way of life and territory. He does not think group rights can be generalized to all groups, such as those formed out of migration, since such groups, he argues, voluntarily gave up their cultural way of life to enter a new society. Kymlicka's position is compatible with a more broadly defined liberalism in that it is a qualified case for group rights.

Kymlicka's somewhat limited conception of liberal multiculturalism can be contrasted to a stronger version, which might be called 'communitarian' liberal multiculturalism. However, this is not essentially different from liberal multiculturalism and does not warrant being termed a different type. Charles Taylor (1994) has given a major intellectual justification of this in his argument for a politics of recognition understood in terms of the necessity for public recognition of large-scale national minorities. Against Kymlicka's preference for minority rights to be limited to pre-settler groups, Taylor has made a stronger case for minority rights to be extended to national minorities. In any case, in countries such as Canada, New Zealand and Australia multiculturalism has become a national imaginary and has significant implications for indigenous and other minority groups. As argued by Povinelli (2002), the confluence of liberalism and multiculturalism has led to a situation in which cultural identity must be mapped out in legal terms. The achievement of liberal multiculturalism is also its greatest limit: recognition can only be a legal recognition. Although it is not a mark of the failure of liberal multiculturalism, it means that indigenous alterity is forced to define itself in legal terms. The law thus becomes the site where local languages, indigenous ways of life and memories are diverted into juridical languages. This may mean a certain 'misrecognition' in that those groups can recognize themselves only in the language of the law. Nevertheless, despite the juridical nature of liberal multiculturalism, it has led to a situation of legal pluralism as is evidenced by the official recognition of alternative legal traditions associated with some indigenous peoples.

There is no doubt that liberal multiculturalism has been hugely influential in shaping multicultural policy in recent times. It has also coincided with the worldwide impact of human rights. It is also a way in which states have responded to the increase in worldwide migration. Liberal multiculturalism has also been influenced by the need to accommodate the demands for autonomy of large-scale national minorities, in many cases minority nationalisms. In the case of Europe, EU anti-discrimination legislation has forced countries to improve their record of discrimination. For all these reasons, liberal multiculturalism with its characteristic emphasis on minority rights has been the dominant expression of multiculturalism. Liberal multiculturalism places a stronger emphasis on a degree of political integration as opposed to cultural integration, and seeks less assimilation into a common culture than integration into the polity. As an essentially liberal philosophy, it is concerned with the removal of disadvantages rather than the positive or affirmative pursuit of diversity as a value. Unlike the older egalitarianism, it does not operate on the assumption of a neutral public domain, with diversity confined to the private sphere. Liberal multiculturalism allows for a limited degree of public recognition of cultural difference in order to make possible equality.

There have been two main routes out of and beyond liberal multiculturalism. The first is ethnopluralism and the second radical multiculturalism. Both can be considered to be post-liberal in that they are influenced by liberalism and at the same time signal a departure from liberalism. Ethnopluralism, which in effect is a communitarian multiculturalism, is a departure from the liberal multiculturalism in being primarily about the pursuit and accommodation of national minorities. It is relatively silent about other kinds of minorities, such as those formed through migration. While Western Europe has had a relatively long experience with cultural diversity, the situation in Central and Eastern Europe is less straightforward. On one side, it can be argued that the legacy of history has been one of greater cultural and political diversity and that this has never been successfully accommodated within the structures of the nation-state. This is a diversity that is primarily based on autochthonous minorities that have, in different ways, been associated with the former multiethnic empires (Habsburg, Ottoman, Russian) out of which the modern nation-states were created. The cultural heterogeneity of the old empires is to be found at the level of cross-national cultures and other kinds of overlapping affiliations. Although also a feature of Western Europe, it is a more pronounced feature of the cultural landscape of Central and Eastern Europe. However, on the other hand, the Central and Eastern Europe experience with diasporic minorities as a result of migration from outside Europe is limited with cultural diversity policies being generally aimed at autochthonous minorities to the relative neglect of other kinds of minorities. This is to the disadvantage of non-ethnic minorities such as refugees and asylum seekers. In addition, in the former communist countries, 'new minorities' are emerging as former majorities, or relatively large ethnic groups, become minorities (e.g. Russians in Latvia or Serbs in Croatia). Cultural policy in many cases is connected with nation-building exercises and there is a general interest in maintaining the old minorities as the crucial points of diversity and identity politics (Ellmeier and Radsky 2006: 29–33). As Robbins (2006) and Ellmeier and Radsky (2006) argue, in Central and Eastern Europe the language of diversity, with its source in liberal multiculturalism, is borrowed from the Western European experience, which has been heavily influenced by diasporic migration from former colonies, and is being applied to national minorities, so-called autochthonous groups. In the former case, diversity is predominantly postcolonial and diasporic and has been the basis of much of multiculturalism in Britain, Belgium, the Netherlands and France. The main difference, then, is that Western experiences with multiculturalism are predominantly based on postcolonial immigration while in Central and Eastern Europe, the main interest is in autochthonous minorities.

What we have here then are two different conceptions of diversity: one that is primarily based on multiculturalism and the rights of citizenship and one that is more ethnopluralist and is generally directly concerned with regional and ethnic autonomy. To an extent, the communitarian political philosophy of Charles Taylor falls within the ethnopluralist model. Though Taylor (1994) can also be easily located within liberal multiculturalism, he offers a strong defence for a politics of recognition that is primarily concerned with the recognition of national minorities.[17] This is in contrast, as noted above, to Kylimcka's concern with minority rights for indigenous groups. Whether a modification of liberalism in a communitarian

---

[17] This may be a simplification of Taylor's position. See Tong (2009).

direction or not, ethnopluralist multiculturalism is clearly a major influence on the politics of diversity in many parts of the world.

Radical multiculturalism, in contrast, is a rejection of the strong communitarianism of ethnopluralism and a move beyond the limited horizon of liberal multiculturalism. Many critics, most notably Marion Young (1990), have argued that group differentiated rights are more important than the collective rights of ethnic communities. This argument effectively undermines both ethnopluralism and liberal multiculturalism in shifting the focus away from cultures as holistic groups to specific groups as defined by social disadvantages. The aim of a more pluralistic multicultural society should be the reduction of such disadvantages rather than the pursuit of cultural autonomy. Moreover, radical multiculturalism is more attuned to the needs of migrants than of national minorities. In this view, the primary concern is not political integration or cultural autonomy, but social integration. Such forms of multiculturalism are reflected in policies of affirmative action and positive discrimination. Radical multiculturalism departs from liberal multiculturalism in being more affirmative of the desirability of diversity as a moral goal for society. Yet, like liberalism it is based on the centrality of rights as the mechanism of integration and differs only in its view of the extent and desirability of pluralization. Radical multiculturalism is of course a development of liberal multiculturalism, which it sees as too restrictive.

Radical multiculturalism has opened up multiculturalism to new conceptions that ultimately go beyond the liberal horizons of rights and tolerance. Postmodern conceptions of cultural diversity have influenced the view that diversity is more than liberal pluralism but suggests the ultimate relativity of values. In terms of multiculturalism it has led to the belief in the relativity of all values and that none should be privileged. With the growing recognition of the need for a global view of culture, this position has become a solution for many organizations, such as UNESCO, which has adopted such a view of culture as diverse (Eriksen 2001). Once the principle is adopted that all cultures are equal, the premises of liberalism are undermined, since liberalism holds only to a notion of the equality of persons but does not extend this to a principle of the equality of cultures. While, as argued above, liberalism can accommodate a notion of minority rights, this is limited in scope and generally takes for granted the existence of a mainstream national society.

It can also be noted that arising out of the turn to radical multi-culturalism the debate on diversity has also been influenced by post-modern conceptions of culture. It is possible to speak of postmodern multiculturalism. This is more than the equal recognition of all cultures for it entails scepticism of the possibility of any foundation for culture. A tension has thus arisen between the belief that all values are equally valid and scepticism of the capacity of culture itself to generate valid standpoints. Thus, for the postmodernist position, the admission of relativism must entail a scepticism of all of culture, including one's own. In this respect, the postmodern argument goes far beyond the assumptions of liberalism and all versions of communitarianism, which have been content with a politics of recognition. The kind of multiculturalism that corresponds to it will more likely be the reduction of multiculturalism to the expression of different points of view rather than the pursuit of an overall cultural goal or social inclusion. Its implications can point in the direction of Habermas's theory of discur-sively constituted public sphere, Rorty's postmodern liberal pragma-tism, or, as I argue in this chapter, a cosmopolitan conception of multiculturalism. The aim of multicultural policies that reflect this position will entail the view that multiculturalism is simply the promo-tion of diversity rather than the representation of different points of view or the reduction of inequalities. This is reflected in one of the main arenas of postmodern multiculturalism, the 'culture wars' over higher education, where the aim is often not confined to the presentation of the view of the marginalized voices but to promote their values in a re-politicization of cultural discourse. Cosmopolitan multiculturalism, however, entails an additional commitment, in the direction of a recov-ery of the possibility of a common public culture within the limits of a conception of culture based on unity and diversity.

So far I have tried to show that multiculturalism can mean quite different things depending on the conception of diversity that is invoked. Is the aim to reduce inequalities between different groups? Is the aim to promote diversity as a positive value? Is the aim the representation of different groups? Or is the aim to achieve integration or assimilation? These different goals reflect different views about the nature of diversity and the possibility of a common public culture; they also reflect different views on what constitutes a social group. The basis of much of the liberal conception of multiculturalism is the assumption that social groups are well-defined units characterized by a distinctive cultural way of life and that there is a tendential conflict built into the interrelations of social groups possessing different cultural forms of life. Multiculturalism is thus a method of managing differences.

Beyond liberal multiculturalism?

The presuppositions of liberal multiculturalism have been challenged by major societal transformations. Liberal multiculturalism emerged on the basis of economic and social stability in Western societies. In many of these countries today instability has become a reality that has undermined the prospects of multiculturalism. It was also a product of societies that did not experience major questioning of their national identities. In its inception, in the post-Second World War period in Europe, and earlier in the United States, it was formed out of societies that had to integrate, manage or accommodate exiles, immigrants, indigenous populations, and often displaced persons. It was based on the liberal principle of tolerance rather than in the extension of citizenship. It was constructed on the assumption that there was a dominant cultural identity to which the incoming groups had to adjust but to whom certain concessions could be made. It was never intended to be a model for pursuing social justice. Paradoxically, while there are more and more demands for group differences, it is more and more difficult to define exactly what constitutes a group.

Nor must it be forgot that at least on the cultural level, the boundaries between social groups are more diffuse than previously. Group boundaries are not easy to establish since they are constantly under negotiation and interpretation. The implication for multiculturalism is that it is more and more difficult to demarcate ethnic groups and the boundary between ethnic groups and the majority culture is not always so clearly defined. This is not unconnected to the fact that today many migrants are middle-class professionals and are transnational in the sense that they do not migrate to one country on a permanent basis, but may move to other countries or return to the home country (Ong 1999). Migration no longer takes the form of one-directional movement from a home to a host country, but is multidirectional.

The size and status of migrants has also changed. While many ethnic groups retain their language, this is not a marker of cultural

separation. The dominant groups in society have themselves been transformed by ethnic multiculturalism. Today cultural diversity rests less
on ethnic heterogeneity – the pluralism of 'cultural forms of life' – than
on the emergence of new subcultures based on class, gender, religion
and lifestyles shaped by consumption. That is, the notion of ethnic
diversity is no longer the primary basis of multiculturalism (Fisher
1999). Underlying the changed cultural context is a pronounced indi-
viduation in identity and values. As a result, it is less evident what
constitutes a social group.

The very term migrant is itself ambivalent. It is often used to cover
individuals whose parents immigrated to the country in which they
were born. Even though many such individuals may not have the
citizenship of their country of birth, they are not technically migrants
since they have not migrated. The category 'migrant' is closely linked
with ethnic groups, since patterns of migration are often connected
with the existence of an ethnic group that derives from the country of
origin. Clearly the complicated mosaic of migrant and ethnic groups
is different in every country. Germany has a large Turkish minority
(*c.*1.5 million) which includes second- and third-generation who cannot easily be termed migrants. This is also the case for France with its
large North African minority. Other countries such as the UK,
Belgium and the Netherlands have long established ethnic minority
groups.

According to the 'World Migration Report 2008' there were about
200 million migrants worldwide, or just under 3 per cent of the world
population. There are between 20–30 million unauthorized migrants
worldwide. In 2007 there were 26 million internally displaced persons
(IDPs) in at least 52 countries.[18] Migrants are a diverse group and
migrate for different reasons. While many migrants move for reasons
of work others migrate for family reasons or to study. Others such as
refugees and asylum seekers migrate for primarily political reasons.
For these reasons migrants cannot be said to constitute a homogeneous group and caution must be exercised when using the term
migrant. It should also be noted that migrants experience different
kinds of inequality and marginalization. Ethnicity (as defined by
nationality, language, religion) in combination with gender and class

---

[18] Figures cited in 'World Migration 2008' (www.iom.int).

produces many different kinds of exclusion. The implication of this may be that what is required today is a more differentiated notion of citizenship, an argument that Young (1990) has put forward in a well-known paper.

Western liberal multiculturalism rested on the assumption that diversity lay primarily on the level of cultural identity and that this was largely shaped by the ethnic values of relatively homogeneous groups of immigrants who were quite separate from the dominant national society. If we have reached the limits of liberal multicultural-ism today, it is because the assumption that ethnic groups are intern-ally homogeneous and therefore distinct from the national community is no longer tenable: cultural diversity has penetrated into the heart of the cultural ethos of society and has diluted the distinction between a pre-political cultural identity and a neutral or common public or political identity. Multiculturalism must reconcile itself to the reality of, what Hollinger has called, 'post-ethnicity' (Hollinger 1995). In short, the ethos of pluralization, to use William Connolly's term, has penetrated into the political domain, transforming the rela-tion between state and society (Connolly 1995). Rather than under-mining the possibility of a shared public culture, it may offer new possibilities for it to be formed on a different basis than before.

Diversity and the search for common ground

Multiculturalism, I have argued, has been shaped by the liberal notion of rights and equality. There has been a shift from equality to diversity and with this has come a new emphasis on minority rights and the questioning of the unity of a national culture. This has led to a certain crisis for multiculturalism, which has predominantly presupposed the existence of a dominant or mainstream national culture which guaran-teed common ground.

The first point to be noted is that diversity exists on several levels of which ethnicity is only one. It is possible to speak of civilizational diversities or major differences between worldviews, polynational diversity, regional diversity. Beyond these largely geopolitical diversi-ties, there are cultural diversities, of which ethnic ones are the most striking. In addition, there are other kinds of diversities, such as those relating to lifestyles and gender and related ways of life, and diversities associated with social class and generations. Finally, there are what might simply be called moral diversities, that is diverse conceptions of moral values, such as those relating to euthanasia, abortion, vegetarianism. It is questionable that ethnic diversities are the major expressions of diversities and that such diversities lead to conflict. It is arguably the case that there are other diversities that are more divisive, such as divisions over the limits of life and death. Indeed it may be suggested that conflict relating to genetic diversity may be the battlefield for politics in the future. Virtually every cleavage in modern society is accompanied by a diverse and culturally mediated life. The existence of such conflicts does not undermine the possibility of a shared public culture.

Thus to speak of diversity is to refer to the diversity of forms of life. But the notion of cultural diversity that has entered political discourse today has tended to make certain assumptions about the nature of social groups, who are the carriers of these diverse forms of life. Social groups, especially ethnic groups, are seen as coherent units that are defined by cultural values and packaged into symbolic wholes called 'collective identities' (Brubaker and Cooper 2000). Whether culture is ultimately what distinguishes a group is debatable, but what is problematic is the assumption that diversity refers to a fundamental divide between groups. This is to neglect the fact that diversity cuts into social groups and reflects the individualism of contemporary societies.

Diversity should not be confined to the relation between groups, but must take into account the deeper nature of difference and that many diversities in fact only refer to loosely defined cultural categories – many of which are linguistic – that are not underpinned by major cultural differences. In this sense, the postmodern approach to cultural diversity is correct in stressing that social groups are overlapping and diversity is a reality in itself and does necessarily presuppose an underlying unity since groups are connected in many ways. In the mosaic of group relations, diversity and unity are shifting terms referring to variable cultural reference points concerning power and inequality. If this is correct, the association of diversity with conflict must be re-examined. The border between diversity and divisiveness is increasingly discussed as if these terms were mutually implicated. In fact, we have little evidence that diversity leads to major cultural conflicts. Despite the continued existence of essentialistic myths of national unity, the cultural accommodation of diversity in many societies is mostly an accomplished fact today. Nor does cultural diversity lead to an extreme or destructive relativism, as some liberals fear. In actual practice, most cultures accommodate universalistic principles and, conversely, universalistic cultures are increasingly open to particularistic adaptations (Cowan *et al.* 2001). Ever since the anthropologist Ruth Benedict introduced the term in the 1930s, we have all become cultural relativists today (Benedict 1935).

Diversity is often exaggerated as a condition that undermines the possibility of any kind of unity. While liberalism maintains a basic commitment to the idea of a shared public culture domain, there is growing scepticism of this by critics of multiculturalism as well as by some of the radical kinds of multiculturalism. In place of unity there are only different forms of life or hybrid ones. While the postmodern position, and that of radical multiculturalism more generally, offers an important corrective to liberalism, along with other positions it is in danger of retreating into a myth of diversity as the only condition of cultural possibility. The result of this uncritical embracing of diversity is contemporary thought and practice, that we are in danger of having nothing left to resist the increasingly vociferous xenophobic arguments. The major division in contemporary society is not culture as such. There is more common ground that is often thought (Smelser and Alezander 1999). The idea of diversity has fed on notions of symbolic difference which are falsely premised on a view of culture as divisive. Whether diversity is positively embraced or regarded as a problem to be managed or overcome, we are still left with a challenge, namely the possibility of a unified society or of a variety of different social groups. If diversity is the dominant social reality, how can a shared public culture be possible?

It would appear that one answer is that community in the sense of common ground across different groups is possible in the construction of difference and in the un-ending capacity to transcend all boundaries. In an age of diversities, nothing is secure and enduring. This postmodernist argument is that belonging is transient, mobile and flexible and does not require locality or secure reference points. Identities, it is often held, are fluid and mobile, and cannot be endlessly reinvented by their carriers who are not constrained by space and localities. This may be the wrong response to the problem, since it exaggerates the other extreme, namely the capacity of cultural processes of invention to create forms of belonging and identity that can withstand the reality of social fragmentation. In making hybridity the norm, the perspective of the theorist and the perspective of the social actor are conflated. The reality is that social identities are relatively stable, despite their ongoing negotiation and interpretation, and the form groups take is very variable, depending on where they are located in the global processes of change. As Amit and Rapport (2003) have argued, what is often conflated here are personal networks with community and wider categorical identities. Undoubtedly the latter – Black, Irish, Chinese – can be imagined in many different and creative ways, but this is not easily translated into community as belonging. Networks are not made up of the same kind of relations of which communities are made. Networks are not groups. The danger is that diversity is becoming a legitimation of the social dislocations of globalization, as well as a justification of cultural incommensurability. On the one side, the idea of diversity runs the risk of being an argument for the flexibility of capitalism, the view that people can be moved about without loss of identity because they can always invent, or imagine, an identity. On the other side, there is the danger that the appeal to diversity strays into the xenophobic camp in which insiders are always to be distinguished from outsiders on the grounds of the latter's difference. Is there a way of avoiding these pitfalls to find an alternative foundation for multiculturalism? For reasons that have been much discussed, the retreat to a unitary national culture is no longer a viable option. However, a degree of common ground can be found in contemporary societies, notwithstanding their diverse constitution. Can people be equal and at the same time different? (Touraine 2000).

The most important goal for multicultural societies today is the creation of at least one mode of communication, if not more, for articulating an inclusive kind of community and one that is more than the recognition of difference. Community derives its force from its capacity to achieve belonging and belonging does not necessarily require cultural cohesiveness or a collective identity. The absence and even the denial of community is what sustains xenophobia. The new politics of xenophobia breeds on the absence of community in the sense of a shared public culture. The appeal to diversity alone will not be able to resist xenophobic currents, since it is now precisely the language of diversity that is used in the rhetoric of xenophobic discourse (Delanty *et al.* 2008).

Despite considerable discrimination and inequality, the reality in many countries, in particular in North America, is that there has been considerable social integration, and a lot of it has been unrecognized, as Steinberg has argued (Steinberg 1989). This thesis that the new radical multiculturalism has derived precisely from the success of older models has also been polemically stated by Russell Jacoby, who argues that a myth of cultural difference has been created by academics who have applied the curriculum debates and the 'all is culture' philosophy to society, thus distorting the reality of widespread integration (Jacoby 1999). In the view of many there is the danger that multiculturalism is a form of cultural separation and also fails to solve the problem of reconciling tolerance of group differences with the need to protect individuals who wish to dissent from the groups. Thus rather than speak of the total failure of multicultural integration, greater attention should be paid to successful integration.

From a cosmopolitan perspective, diversity is less a problem than a desirable condition and one that does not require either belief in a set of values or scepticism about the values of the Other. Diversity per se now becomes desirable in its own right and does not need to be managed by multicultural policies. Reflecting a more positive view of the virtues of diversity, the cosmopolitan position marks an exit out of liberalism and seeks to regain a strand of unity that has been rejected by many varieties of multiculturalism, and which might be summed up in the phrase 'unity in diversity'. In this view of diversity we are all different and what makes us different is not just our different ethnicities but our expanding horizons. To adopt James Tully's phrase, there are only 'strange multiplicities' rather than homogeneous societies consisting of cultural totalities (Tully 1995). This conception of diversity differs from the fixed categories of liberalism in recognizing that groups overlap and that there are multiple loyalties in an age of numerous and different kinds of mobilities. But it is more than this. The cosmopolitan position sees a certain unity emerging out of the interactions of groups, in particular ethnic and migrant groups, leading to the formation of a public culture formed out of mutually interconnected identities. The notion of a public culture that is suggested by this model is a communicative one in which a dialogue of all groups takes place. Common groups are ultimately possible and achievable in the ensuing discursive space that is made possible by communication.

The problem of racism for multiculturalism

The current situation, at least in Western multiethnic societies, is such that multiculturalism needs to be renewed in ways that address the changed social context today. The goal of achieving a multicultural society must be reconceived in ways that directly address problems in the wider society, such as institutional discrimination and everyday racism. In this respect the aims of liberal multiculturalism and other measures designed for the assimilation and management of minority groups are inadequate and must be complemented with additional measures. Liberal multiculturalism is inadequately prepared to combat systematic and structural forms of exclusion since it does not seek to change the mainstream society. To this end a cosmopolitan multiculturalism aims to transcend social fragmentation and create a common public culture in which all groups participate. Liberal multiculturalism, in contrast, has in fact only a limited commitment to the creation of a common public culture.

In Europe multiculturalism has remained in a time warp. It is unable to move beyond the older models, which were based on smaller and more nationally specific kinds of migration. Migration presents a challenge for European societies for several reasons. Several decades of migration have transformed European societies. In the post-war period which saw the foundation of the European Union and the consolidation of national welfare states, most if not all European societies were relatively homogeneous. The 100 years of nation-state building from the middle of the nineteenth to the middle of the twentieth century had the effect that by 1950 in the aftermath of the Second World War national societies had considerably reduced the size of their minorities either through forced assimilation, popular exchange or had simply exterminated them. From about 1950 to the late 1970s the main cleavages in Western European societies were associated with class. From the 1970s this gradually changed as a result of labour shortages resulting in guest workers coming in substantial numbers but also as a consequence of decolonization. Several decades later we are in a different situation. The scale of migration has increased and European societies have experienced varying degrees of assimilation as a result of multicultural policies in education, changing patterns of consumption and intermarriage. While many migrants retained their distinctive culture, others adopted the culture of the host country and many evolved multiple identities.

European societies are ageing. The birth rate in many countries is lower than the mortality rate. In 1901, just over 6 per cent of the population were at or over current pension age, this figure rose steadily to reach 18 per cent in 2001 (Powell 2005). Migrants offer the best chance for European societies to increase the fertility rate. Many Western European countries have labour shortages, especially for skilled workers. In several Western European countries the service sector depends on labour from Central and Eastern Europe.

Migrants are now more effectively organized than they were a few decades ago and have a greater capacity to mobilize. Migrants are more likely to be educated and many are less inclined to give up their ethnicity and take on the culture of the majority population. The phenomenon of the veil is a pertinent example of a cultural development that points to a change in identities. It is often educated and relatively independent women who choose to wear it for reasons that cannot be explained by reference to the force of tradition. It is in short a product of individuated life choices. This represents a challenge and a possibility for societies to adapt to new realities of migration.

The question has been posed as to where the limits of tolerance lie: does tolerance have to translate into solidarity across culturally defined groups or does it breed indifference? Does tolerance amount to accepting others who are different and possibly intolerant? In France there has recently been a reversal of the liberal discourse through the protection of diverse cultures through the separation of different groups. Another example of late-liberal anxiety is the discourse of liberal xenophobia that appears to have gained some popularity in the Netherlands in recent years. According to this, liberal values are antithetical to migrants who must be excluded in order to protect the liberalism of the majority. This protects the majority from becoming intolerant. Thus, multiculturalism becomes a defence of the 'national' culture, and 'tolerance' becomes a way to keep communities separate. For this reason the liberal emphasis on 'tolerance' needs to be modified in the direction of 'acceptance', 'recognition' or 'respect' instead.

The general point emerging from this is that the challenge presented by ethnic diversity and the cultural pluralism that several decades of migration has brought is one that goes to the heart of European integration. It is not something that can be reduced to migration policy alone since the issues it brings to the fore are inseparable from wider social, cultural and political processes. Racism is not marginal but is integral to institutions.

Liberal multiculturalism has fostered a soft cosmopolitanism around anti-racism, anti-discrimination legislation, tolerance, and limited group rights. But anti-racism, which was based on countering ignorance and prejudice, alone is inadequate in creating genuinely multicultural societies. Ineffective, too, is an appeal to a universalized notion of humanity, since the problems facing minorities and especially migrants are often quite specific ones related to institutional discrimination. Traditional anti-racism is based on a limited strategy around basic civic rights and does not address wider issues of citizenship and social inclusion. For the same reason strategies based on improving individual access to opportunity also prove to be inadequate in face of structural discrimination and the more deeply rooted practices of social exclusion and discrimination within institutional practices in work, education, housing and health. The problem with traditional liberal multiculturalism is that is lacks the two key elements essential for a genuine multicultural society: solidarities and recognition. It is now more essential than ever for multiculturalism to be redefined in terms of recognition and respect, not as tolerance. The obstacles to multiculturalism are not in fact cultural incompatibilities between mainstream groups and migrant and minority groups, but very often social obstacles. It is essential that multiculturalism goes beyond this level of anti-racism. While the extreme right represent a danger, they are not the primary problem in perpetuating racial discrimination. There is enough evidence to suggest that it is the more deeply ingrained practices of everyday life and institutional structures that present the greatest obstacles for the creation of a multicultural society.[19] This is why rights alone are insufficient.

Unlike liberal conceptions of political community – which do not go beyond the view that we are all different and requires only a toler-ance of difference – cosmopolitan political community is based on a politics of recognition. This entails a positive recognition of difference. Cosmopolitan multiculturalism is not merely about the plurality of cultures but more about the embracing of difference and the search for an alternative political order. In this respect it differs from the liberal

---

[19] This has been one of the main conclusions of a cross-national research project. See Delanty *et al.* (2008).

emphasis on tolerance and the tendency found in much of communitarian multiculturalism to relinquish common ground in an exaggeration of cultural differences. This is not to say liberal multiculturalism is redundant, but that it alone does not offer a viable foundation to combat structural racism. There are two kinds of cosmopolitan recognition that need to be addressed separately: internal and external differences (see Beck and Grande 2007). Of these, external recognition is simpler to achieve in that it is easier to recognize others who are far away than those within. Internal cosmopolitanism, as argued in Chapter 2, requires a form of recognition that entails self-transformation. Cosmopolitan multiculturalism is a condition of self-problematization and requires the transformation of society as a whole.

Multiculturalism beyond the West

The previous discussion has drawn attention to the diversity of traditions of multiculturalism and its contested nature. When we take the wider global context this becomes much more evident. Within Europe there are already major differences between East and West and within Western Europe there are significant differences between, for instance, France, the Netherlands, Germany and the UK. Western multiculturalism has been very much shaped around postcolonial migration. In the case of countries such as Canada, Australia and New Zealand migration has been a key dynamic in the creation of a multicultural conception of the nation. In Europe, despite considerable pluralization, it is not possible to speak of a multicultural conception of the nation. This is not the case for much of the rest of the non-Western world, though there are exceptions of which India is a notable example.

One of the most important challenges for multiculturalism is the way in which Western multiculturalism has made an impact in societies beyond Europe and North America. There has been surprising little literature on multiculturalism in non-Western societies (Kymlicka and He 2005). Yet the discourse of Western multiculturalism has become increasingly influential worldwide. Even in countries where democratization is limited, the impact on international discourses of human rights has been huge, as is evidenced by the worldwide opposition to China over the Tibet question in 2008. The non-Western world has seen the rise of identity politics and demands for autonomy relating to various kinds of minority nationalism.

However, there are clearly limits and obstacles. He and Kymlicka (2005) mention a number of difficulties. The colonial context has created a different situation than in the West where it has been traditionally minorities who have experienced injustice, while in many countries in Asia and Africa it is the majority who have experienced injustice. This has led to a situation in which minority rights have been secondary to other and more national forms of injustice. There has also been a legacy of pre-colonial hierarchies leading to oppressed minorities supporting colonial rulers. Following independence many countries saw a reassertion of the pre-colonial hierarchies whereby the margins were controlled by the centres. In addition, unlike in the West where minorities are no longer regarded as potential collaborators with an enemy state, this fear continues to be a problem in non-Western countries leading to an association of minority rights with geopolitical instability. Democratization is also a factor since in many countries beyond the West multiculturalism has emerged alongside democratization, whereas in the Western world democratization preceded multiculturalism. In many ways, the pursuit of difference and demands for equality is sharper in Asia than it is in the West due to incomplete democratization. In the West a politics of equality was bound up with democratization and institutionalized in welfare systems. Moreover, the adoption of multinational federalism has been less difficult, due presumably to a relatively advanced degree of democratization. This is not the case in many non-Western countries, where multinational federalism has generally been resisted. However, it needs to be considered that, as the example of Central and Eastern Europe suggests, the transition to democracy and the introduction of rights-based political cultures is not incompatible. Finally He and Kymlicka (2005) point out that the three main types of groups – indigenous peoples, national minorities and immigrant groups – who are the basis of Western models of multiculturalism and minority rights do not always easily translate into non-Western contexts or if they do, they may obscure as much as they reveal about the groups and their aspirations.

This is also where a cosmopolitan perspective becomes particularly pertinent. The great cultural and linguistic diversity of Asia is not something that can be easily understood in the language of Western multiculturalism, which in ethnic terms is less diverse. While Kymlicka (2005) sees only the adoption of liberal multiculturalism, a case can be made for a more differentiated picture. While Western discourses of

multiculturalism have clearly had an impact in shaping multiculturalism in many parts of the world, the ways these discourses have been
imported has also reflected the quite different cultural and historical
context of those societies. In many cases the colonial context has played
a role, as have different and more traditional ways of accommodating
diversity. While the non-Western world has been influenced by
Western concepts, experiences and approaches to multiculturalism,
there is little to suggest that the non-Western world has had a similar
impact. A cosmopolitan perspective suggests that in a world of global
migration there is a need to address multicultural challenges through
inter-cultural dialogue. Multiculturalism and cosmopolitan inter-
cultural dialogue until now have been separated, with the former confined to national policies relating to the integration of minorities
and the latter a cross-national dialogue that has had relatively little
impact on issues of migration and minority rights. In this view liberal
multiculturalism, with its emphasis on rights, is only one dimension
of a broader picture of democratic transformation and cultural
pluralization.

There are at least two major considerations. As pointed out by He
and Kymlicka (2005), notwithstanding the differences between Western
and non-Western experiences, it is not possible to speak of a clash of
values with a Western rights-based civilization and oppressive anti-
rights cultures in the non-Western world. The impact of the international concept of justice has been very significant for most countries
throughout the rest of the world. It is equally wrong to dismiss rights
discourse as simply Western ideological strategies as is too often the
case. This would be to neglect the adoption of such discourses which
have been a central feature of democratization everywhere. Moreover,
we cannot distinguish between a rights- or civic-based Western tradition and ethnic- or culture-based traditions elsewhere in the world,
since in the West ethnic and cultural definitions of the national community have played a central role and, as argued above, multiculturalism
has been predominantly seen as a way to accommodate minorities
within a predefined cultural definition of the political community.

Second, the non-Western context offers an interesting and important
example of how multiculturalism must be conceived in terms of a
cosmopolitan model of mutual learning. Asian experiences show how
Western notions of multiculturalism have often been combined with
native traditions for dealing with diversity. The cultural traditions

associated with Islam, Hinduism, Buddhism and Confucianism, for instance, have all articulated different ways of accommodating diversity. The creative synthesis of these traditions with modern Western notions of human rights and multiculturalism is a characteristic feature of multiculturalism in many parts of the world. To an extent it is possible to understand this, as Kymlicka (2005) argues, as an internationalization of Western liberal multiculturalism. Minority nationalism is a universal phenomenon having spread throughout the world in much the same way it spread through the West in the nineteenth century. There is little doubt that the liberal discourse of rights has been very prominent and that it is has provided an influential framework for understanding and for evaluating minority rights. Kymlicka's framework is ultimately a limited one in its rigorous adherence to a Western conception of minority rights. The reality in much of Asia is closer to ethnopluralism than to liberal multiculturalism, where the former is primarily about recognition demands for national minorities. As several contributors to a cross-national study of multiculturalism in Asia have shown, there is a need to take into account conceptions of diversity that cannot be so easily conceptualized in terms of a Western understanding of rights. Mika Toyota has put this succinctly:

Kymlicka's argument is based on the idea that the term 'cultural community' can be used synonymously with a 'group of people', without taking into consideration the shifting nature of its boundary and or its multilayered character. Kymlicka seems to perceive a minority group and its culture as a primordially bounded entity through their 'sharing a distinct language and history', and hence he assumes that it is possible to define and separate one cultural community from another, and that such 'difference' has remained the same from one generation to the next, in spite of the fact that culture is in practice multifaced, dynamic, essentially overlapping, interactive, and internally negotiated. (Toyota 2005: 134–5)

The point being made here is that the very category of a minority is problematic since what needs to be considered is the fact that such categories, especially in non-Western contexts, have been forged in situations of power and inequality and are contested. It is possible for a minority group to shift to become a majority group and an indigenous people does not always mean what it means in Western countries such as Canada, New Zealand and Australia which have pre-settler peoples.

He (2005) draws attention to the Confucian heritage which has a notion of *ronghe* (intermingling) and which can be contrasted to *tonghua*, which corresponds to assimilation and which might be related to sinicization. The former suggests a dialogic relation in contrast to the hierarchical relation indicated by the latter. *Ronghe* is to be understood in terms of harmonization by which minorities are encouraged to retain their uniqueness so long as they do not constitute a threat to the state. He believes that this notion offers an alternative not only to national assimilation but also to national separatism and thus may be a viable foundation for a multicultural society. In context where there is a high degree of multiethnicity, as is the case in many Asian regions and countries, the terms ethnic and autonomy lose their specificity. It is possible to understand *ronghe* as cosmopolitan in the additional sense of being influenced by Western notions of rights. However this remains unclear, but it can be speculated that the combination of traditional notions of diversity with Western ideas is increasingly becoming the reality in much of Asia as well as the wider non-Western world.

The upshot of this is normative pluralism as opposed to straightforward normative convergence around a common framework of norms. As Bowan (2005) argues with respect to Indonesia, three distinct kinds of claims have shaped deliberations about diversity. The first is when a claim is made on the basis of a group whose existence preceded the state. This roughly corresponds to the notion of an indigenous group, but it is not necessarily a minority for it can in many cases be a majority. A second and related case is where a claim, for instance for self-government, is made on the basis of a local tradition. Finally claims can be made on the basis of Islamic norms and where the basis of the legitimacy is a religious principle. Now, normative pluralism does not mean cultural or legal incommensurability. As Bowan points out, 'distinct sets of norms may be irreconcilable on an abstract and metanormative level, but be subject to reconciliation and convergence through processes of reinterpretation. Hermeneutically speaking, the one set of norms provides the ground for the other. Politically speaking, each set of norm advocates can play to its own audience while engaged in serious negotiations with the other camp(s)' (Bowan 2005: 167).

From a cosmopolitan perspective, then, normative convergence may be seen as occurring through different normative systems – religious doctrines, local customs, claims of indigenous peoplehood, Western liberal notions of rights – rather than through the obsolescence of any of these as a result of the adoption of Western liberalism. Normative pluralism can simply be a case of coexisting if not overlapping moral worlds, but it is more than this. The different normative orders are forced to address each other and as they do so they undergo change as a result. In so far as this happens, it is possible to speak of a certain process of convergence, but one that is not necessarily occurring in the direction of a universal order of liberal multiculturalism.

Conclusion

Generalizations on multiculturalism are difficult due to the great variety of approaches and conceptions that broadly fall under the heading of cultural diversity, but also because of the diversity of social and historical experiences. Liberal multiculturalism is without doubt the most influential model. The argument advanced in this chapter is that multiculturalism needs to be reconceived in a cosmopolitan direction in order to compensate for some of the shortcomings of the liberal conception. One of the key aspects of this is the creation of a common public culture achieved through communicative deliberation. In this conception of public culture, unity is neither presupposed nor reduced to a purely procedural normative system of rights. It is possible to conceive of a multicultural society based less on difference than on the discursive negotiation of difference. Thus, instead of presupposing discreet cultural groups, as in liberal multiculturalism, a cosmopolitan perspective requires the internal transformation of all groups in a process of ongoing deliberation and interpretation. Unlike postmodern or radical multiculturalism, cosmopolitan multiculturalism does not jettison the possibility of creating a common public culture. However, this is not a pre-existing normative system, but an ongoing deliberative process that is created through the active contribution of all groups. Cosmopolitan multiculturalism thus entails an emphasis on deliberative public communication through which all groups, including the mainstream society, undergo transformation in their self-understanding. While for the present time this can be best conceived on a national basis, there is no reason why it cannot also be developed on a wider and more global scale whereby a fusion of the horizons of collective identities occurs.

6 | Religion in a cosmopolitan society

The question of the place and role of religion in modern secular societies has been a subject of much discussion in scholarly debates. Sociologists of religion have noted the increasing secularization of modern societies in terms of the separation of church and state and have noted the overall declining importance of religious belief and practice. Although the so-called secularization thesis has been much debated, since much of the decline of religion in fact amounted to the privatization of religious belief, there does appear to be widespread agreement that modernity entails the overall decline of religion (Bruce 1996; Norris and Inglehart 2004). This is not the place to enter into a detailed discussion of the secularization thesis, but it can be noted that the secularization of religion does not amount to the disappearance of religion. To take an obvious example, the United States is a highly secular society in terms of the role of religion in the state and the Constitution of the United States of America is one of the most secular constitutional documents in existence. However, US society is highly religious and there is in addition a certain cultural stream commonly referred to as civil religion, a sense of nationhood that has many features of religious worship (Casanova 1994, 2001; Madsen *et al.* 2002). In much of Asia and in most parts of Africa, religion has become highly important to rapidly modernizing post-industrial countries that did not undergo a European-style reformation where major doctrinal change occurred before industrialization. The resurgence of religion is not in spite of modernity, but because of modernity and is not easily explained in term of the traditional secularization thesis, which for the greater part was concerned with the role of religion in the passage from pre-industrial to industrial societies. Secularization was once a vehicle of democratization while today popular democratic movements throughout the world have been allied to religion in many different ways (Castells 1997).

Europe is a different case and is the main focus of this chapter. In comparison to other parts of the world, and especially the United States,

Europe is highly secular (Davis 2000; Remond 1999). Virtually every indicator – belief, church attendance, church–state relations – suggests an overall decline in religion and the tendency too has been towards the increasing separation of church and state. Most of the details of this will be examined later in this chapter, but it can be established that the general trend in European political modernity has been secular and that the privatization of religion has not led to a religious society within the bounds of a secular state, as has been the experience of the United States. It is not the aim of this chapter to doubt this but rather my aim is to raise new questions about the nature of secularism in Europe today, not least given the multiethnic nature of European societies. The central question to be addressed is whether Europe can move from a secular to a post-secular conception of religion. There are several reasons why such considerations are timely and relevant to a critical cosmopolitan analysis of contemporary society.

First, while there can be no doubt that although secularism played a decisive role in democratization, Europe is now experiencing certain problems with the integration of ethnic minorities for whom the secularization of societies has resulted in degrees of marginalization. The issue here is the complicated relation of secularism to pluralism, for it cannot be automatically assumed that secularism leads directly to pluralism. Secularism concerns church–state relations; pluralism concerns the co-existence of culturally distinct social groups. Secularism of course too has often been linked with dogmatism and with intolerance of non-Christian religions (Keane 2000; Connolly 1999). As will be discussed in this chapter, there are different kinds of secularism in terms of church–state relations. One of the key challenges for Europe will be to devise secular relations that foster rather than undermine pluralism. Secularism was a development that preceded the democratization of European societies and while it was to become an important means of democratization it was not itself a democratic institution. Its roots lie deep in the history of Europe and in one tradition it was connected with anti-clericalism, or anti-Catholicism. With the democratization of societies that are now multiethnic, secularism does not always lend itself easily to democratic pluralism. In short, a key question is the degree to which religion can be permitted in the public sphere.

Second, in the wider global public sphere religion has a greater presence than has been the case for much of the recent past. Religion was marginal to the social movements of the industrial and post-industrial age, but has become considerably more central to the social movements of the global information age. It has also become increasingly linked to nationalism (Juergensmeyer 2006). The post-9/11 environment of security has been couched in the language of global anxieties about religious inspired terrorism. Along with popular notions of a 'clash of civilizations' by which the major world religions allegedly collide in a new age of cultural warfare, the global increase in Pentecostalism and various kinds of evangelical Protestantism, which has now spread into China, the growth of orthodoxy in Eastern Europe and in particular in Russia, religion has become a significant part of politics. The funeral of John Paul II in 2005 was a global mega media event in which the Catholic Church demonstrated its relevance for people throughout the world.

Third, specifically with regard to Europe there is the question of whether the cultural identity of Europe can be plausibly described as Christian. In this debate the Christian nature of Europe is often invoked as a part of the identity of Europe. Human rights, as in the debate over the Human Rights Charter are held to be the universal products of the Judeo-Christian heritage. In this case there is the uncomfortable paradox of Europe being Christian but also secular. It is undoubtedly a problem that the global anxieties about religion are occurring at precisely the same time that multiculturalism has entered a critical period in Europe. In Europe religion has entered the public sphere around the question of Islam, which has witnessed global mobilization and, in many countries where Muslims live as large minorities, there has been a process of Islamization (Esposito and Burgat 2003). In several countries there is controversy over headscarves and religious symbols associated with Islam and since 2002 there has been ongoing debate about whether Turkey can join the European Union.[20] These anxieties have been fuelled by the terrorist bombings in Madrid in 2004 and London in 2005. The riots that occurred in French cities in 2005 are also a reminder of the degree of marginalization of Muslim minorities. But the reality is that Islam has become an integral part of Europe although this is not yet recognized on the level of cultural identity (Al Sayyad and Castells 2002; Goody 2004; Husain and O'Brien 2000; Vertovec and Rogers 1998). Although Islam has now become the main focus of hostility, much of European religious intolerance has

---

[20] Although the prospects for early membership are not strong, Turkey is formally a candidate country to join the EU.

been exercised against the Jews and there has been an increase in cultural anti-Semitism – that is violence against symbols of Judaism – as well as in more physical forms in recent years, a situation that has of course been complicated by the consequences of the war in Iraq. Despite secularization, or possibly because of it, religious conflicts continue to play a major role in many European societies. The controversy in 2006 around the publication of satirical cartoons relating to Mohammed is one such example.

Thus it has come about that the veil and the headscarf have become the embattled concerns of European identity in an age of global anxieties about religion. This chapter will address some of these issues in order to clarify the nature of secularism and its relation to pluralism. The chapter begins with a discussion of the historical context of secularism in modernity. On the basis of the analysis in this section, the next section develops the historical contextualization in a critical assessment of the extent to which Europe is actually secular. Here the main emphasis is on the different meanings of secularism and church–state relations in European countries, for European secularism does not take one form but many. The section discusses the different relations between secularism and pluralism where the argument is made that secularism does not necessarily entail pluralism. In the final section the notion of pluralism is developed around the idea of cosmopolitanism, which is in turn related to a different expression of cultural negotiation. The upshot of these considerations is that in normative terms secularism, modified by cosmopolitan pluralism, does not have to preclude the presence of religion from the public culture.

Modernity and the forms of secularism

It is helpful to begin with some consideration of the origins of secularism within the context of European political modernity since the legacy of this tradition has shaped the current situation presenting both opportunities and disadvantages for cosmopolitan pluralism. The history of church–state relations in Europe was a struggle between two forms of authority, one religious and one political. This was one of the defining features of European history prior to the modern period. Neither church nor state ever succeeded in dominating the other. With few exceptions, and then only for short periods, European states were confessional states, but the principle of statehood was never subordinated to ecclesiastical authority, with the possible exception of some bishoprics in the Holy Roman Empire of the German Nation, but even in these cases theocracy never took root in Europe. In addition, the history of Christianity in Europe has been a history of its divisions. While many churches did gain considerable political and social influence, no church actually gained power over the state for long. This was due in part to the nature of the state but also to civil society as well as to divisions within the elites.

It was not until the principle of *cujus regio, ejus religio*, whereby the ruler decided the religion of the population, that political authority established its final superiority over clerical authority, though this did not eliminate religious strife and even caused wars of religion. Since the Peace of Westphalia in 1648 when the European states finally agreed not to wage war on another state on behalf of their co-religionists the inter-state system has become anchored in secular politics. Thus the peculiar feature of European secularism is that the state, in establishing its superiority over ecclesiastical authorities, itself became the arbitrator of religion, for the ruler effectively decided the religion of the population. The history of Europe in the early modern period until 1648 was shaped by the conflicts and upheavals that resulted in changes in the religions of the elites and masses. Since 1054 there was no pan-European religion but three major religions: Catholicism, Orthodoxy and Lutherism. In addition, Judaism can be mentioned, although this was not a confessional geopolitical bloc. Today, it is possible to add Islam to the list of European religions (Goody 2004). Against this background of a religiously divided continent, the only unity that emerged was that established by the national traditions of the individual states, which for the greater part effectively imposed secularism understood as a relation between state and church in which the former established its political superiority.

It would be a mistake to believe that Europe entered a post-religious age since 1648 with progressive secularization. For centuries it was the state that established religion, thus beginning the age of established churches, that is official state churches supported by state subsidies. Those countries shaped by the political modernity that arose from the French Revolution rejected established churches, but almost exclusively gave a privileged role to the religion of the majority of the population. On the whole it was the Protestant states that established a state church, while the largely Catholic countries embarked on a more radical separation of church and state. Thus it came about that two models of secularism were established from the late seventeenth century. The first, the constitutional conservative tradition, whereby secularism entailed an official church established by the state and thus controlled by the state. The second, associated with the republican tradition, whereby the state separated the church from the public domain, in effect privatizing religion. European secularism is a product of these two traditions.

In both cases religion did not disappear from society, but was institutionalized in the first case as an official religion and in both cases in the privatistic domains of family, education and other social institutions, such as health. Indeed, by keeping religion out of the domain of the state, the more it survived the transition to modernity. Churches also played a key role as charitable institutions. The Enlightenment itself was for the greater part fostered by the reformed Protestant churches in Western Europe. It was only in France of the Catholic *ancien régime* that it took an anti-clerical form. Although it was to be one of the signatures of the Enlightenment movement, the anti-Catholicism of the French Enlightenment intellectuals was an exception. It was not long after the French Revolution that Napoleon re-established Catholicism as a state religion. The Enlightenment along with the movement we now call modernity in which science and law were separated, or secularized, from religion, occurred precisely in order to preserve faith from the critique of science. Virtually all the major Enlightenment philosophers sought to place religious faith on a separate level from scientific reason or knowledge. This was encapsulated in the philosophy of Immanuel Kant, who argued that religious belief and ideas could not be justified on the basis of reason and had to be separated, or in other words secularized. The consequence of this was that faith was protected from the critique of rationalists such as Voltaire, who argued only reason was a criterion of belief.

The two pillars of modernity – belief based on faith and belief based on evidence-supported knowledge – have not always been equally acknowledged by the critics and defenders of modernity. Jürgen Habermas and Joseph Ratzinger, now Pope Benedict XVI, in a dialogue in Frankfurt in 2002 commented on this feature of modernity, which they both agreed could not be reduced to the culture of rational science. However, it would be wrong to see religion and reason as separate and thus assume modernity has simply two faces that never interact. Max Weber discussed the mutual implication of religion and rationality in what he called the 'paradox of modernity', the paradox that the very rationalization or disenchantment that eventually eroded religion from society was actually produced by the tendency within Christianity, in particular in its Protestant forms, to intellectualize religious belief of all traces of magic (Weber 1948). The progressive rationalization of religious belief as a result of the belief in salvation by a personal God who rewards worldly deeds cultivated a rationalistic work ethic and a methodic approach to life that finally brought religion close to the capitalistic ethnic. In Weber's view rationalism was present in all domains of life – religion, law, economic activity, culture – religion was not exempt from it. Hans Blumenberg offered a related argument, claiming that secularization operated within religious doctrine in a growing intellectualization and rationalization (Blumenberg 1983). In this sense, one direction of religious secularization is its progressive intellectualization.

A further example of the religious origins of European political modernity is the somewhat extreme thesis, generally associated with Karl Löwith, that modernity is itself a secularization of Christianity (Löwith 1949). This is the view that modern Western democracy derives from Christian ideas. Thus the liberty of the individual derives from the belief that all people stand equal before the eyes of God. This is questionable in so far as the claim is that there has been a direct transformation of a religious principle into a political one. More plausible is the view put forward by Max Weber that an inner rationalization is present in different spheres of life. Undoubtedly the values of solidarity and individual responsibility have a certain resonance in Christian ideas, but this does not mean that Christianity is the explanation. Many of these values can be related to pre-Christian traditions, such as the Roman and Greek traditions and have been transformed in the course of history (Brague 2002). Indeed, S. N. Eisenstadt has made the claim that the key impulse of modernity – the notion that the world can be fashioned by human agency – was born with the great religions in the Axial Age with the discovery of transcendence and the desire to bring the kingdom of God onto Earth (Eisenstadt 1986). All modern political movements, he has argued, have been driven by the numerous ways in which this antinomy can be worked out.

Finally, as regards the religious origins of European political modernity a different argument can be proposed, one which avoids some of the difficulties of the secularization thesis. There is much evidence to suggest that the modern quest for liberty was facilitated by – although not necessarily caused by – religious struggles. The political demands of dissenters and much of the Protestant reformation for freedom of worship provided the conditions for the recognition of other kinds of liberty, although largely only for Christian churches. While this took many forms – in England leading to an established Church – the position that emerged from the end of the seventeenth century, while being very far from late modern pluralism, was part of the movement towards the democratization of state power. Eventually, too, it led to the removal of the social and political exclusion of the Jews.

In sum, secularization means different things: it refers to the separation of the legal foundations of the state from religion, but it can also mean the separation of science and knowledge from faith, and it can mean the decline or rationalization of religious belief in terms of the erosion of the difference between the sacred and profane.

The previous remarks serve as a background to the current situation in Europe. It has been argued that European political modernity to a very large degree has been greatly influenced by religion and, as will be claimed below, the different forms of secularization – those associated with the constitutional conservative and republican traditions – did not eradicate religion from society but granted it a particular place and set conditions to its existence in the public domain. The separation of public and private was never complete and final in the way that it was in the United States and, as will be argued below, religion did exist within the public domain in most European countries. The result was that European secularism has been highly ambivalent; on the one side, the existence of either established churches or socially privileged churches often led to discrimination of members of other faiths, in particular Jews, while, on the other hand, European secularism has been such that there is no fundamental obstacle to a limited presence of religion in the public sphere and there has been a long tradition of the freedom of worship. This is one of the paradoxes of European secularism, which should be understood as the containment of religion. The main thesis of the chapter is that secularism is no longer adequate and instead a post-secular society needs to be created.

How secular is Europe today?

There has never been an American-style secularization of church and state in Europe. Contrary to a commonly held view, France did not separate church and state until 1905 in the wake of the Dreyfus Affair, although there was a gradual movement towards secularization from the late nineteenth century. Although the French Revolution was anti-clerical, following the Concordat with the Vatican in 1801 Napoleon established Catholicism as the state religion. Only the communist countries were atheistic, in the sense of actively discouraging religion. The general European trend is one of neutrality, but this has been ambiguous since there has mostly not been a total separation of church and state and there are different interpretations as to the meaning of neutrality, ranging from non-recognition, to a principle of equality of all churches, to a position of privatization. In Ireland, for example, state neutrality was a means of maintaining the power of the Catholic Church, especially in social policy, while in the Netherlands it has been a means of giving equal support to the main churches.

Many states support the main Christian churches and do so in different ways, even if it is only in the official recognition of religious funerals. Several states support the main churches with large subsidies, granting tax exemptions or, as in Germany, collecting taxes for the churches (see Madeley 2003a, 2003b; Madeley and Enyedi 2003). This is also the case in Belgium, Denmark and the Scandinavian countries. Sweden has only recently disestablished its church and Germany is moving towards a position of greater neutrality. Austria, the Netherlands and France remain strictly neutral. But this strict neutrality is relative. France, possibly the best example of republican secularism, provides limited subsidies for churches, including synagogues, tax exemptions for the clergy, allocation of television time for religious broadcasts, and various minor concessions for religious education and the recognition of religious funerals (Safran 2003: 59). The French commitment to *laïcité* is not as inflexible as is often thought, and allows for a certain degree of religious symbols in schools (see Kastoryano 2002). In the case of the Netherlands, as noted above, state neutrality is intended to be supportive of all the major churches as opposed to non-recognition.

Although many countries such as the UK, Norway and Denmark have state churches, these generally have a weak function. Greece in contrast is a country where religion has a strongly official function. The Orthodox Church is the official established church, with the salaries and pensions of the clergy paid by the state, which appoints bishops and gives exception to the clergy from military service (Pollis 2005:

158). It plays a leading role in Greek national identity comparable to the role of Catholicism in Croatia and Poland. In Poland however, Catholicism was rooted in civil society, while in Greece it is firmly embedded in the state. There has been a general upsurge in religion in the former communist societies, which have moved from being atheistic to a position of neutrality, with many giving partial support for religion. Hungary is an exception in this regard. In particular there has been an increase in Orthodoxy in Romania and in Russia, although less so in Bulgaria. In these countries the Orthodox Church has been successful in recovering property confiscated by the communist state. However, it should be noted that the increase in religious activity in post-communist countries is not greater than the extent of religious worship in Western Europe (see Norris and Inglehart 2004).

The United Kingdom is an example of a country with an ambivalent tradition of secularism based on an established church the head of which is the reigning monarch and a constitutional arrangement enshrined in the Act of Settlement of 1713 which determined a line of succession that was designed to prevent a Catholic becoming the head of state. Yet the UK cannot be considered to be anything but secular in practise since the influence of the Anglican Church has diminished to a largely ceremonial role and there is widespread recognition of the multi-ethnic nature of British society. Yet, the secularism of British society has also been accompanied by a dogmatism and intolerance that may be precisely a product of secularism, as the controversy over *The Satanic Verses* in 1989 illustrates. Further examples can be found in hostility to Muslims in the wake of the bombings in London in 2005. However, the different reaction of the British press to what has been widely regarded as a provocative decision by several European-wide presses to publish satirical cartoons depicting the prophet Mohammed as a terrorist suggests that there has been a learning process in coping with the politicization of Islam.

How secular is Europe then? It can be established that Europe does have different religious cultures with different degrees of secularization. There is no Christian unity to Europe, but there is evidence of a residual Christianity. Many countries have Christian parties, and several have state churches, but throughout Europe there are Christian commemorations and festivities, which are all a reminder of the Christian background to European modernity. Most Europeans are affiliated to a church while being otherwise unreligious. The decline in religion in

Europe is partly demographic in that the more traditionally staunch Catholic countries, Ireland, Spain and Italy, have lower birth rates than the Lutheran countries (Crouch 2000). Religious practice is predominantly a matter of formal affiliation around birth, marriage and death, but is relatively unimportant for identity for the vast majority of Europeans. Formal affiliation does not amount to identity or strong attachment of ideological conviction. There are also differences in terms of religious practices and religious beliefs, making general conclusions difficult (Halman and Draulans 2006).

The privatization and disappearance of religion from the domain of the state has not led to the total disappearance of religion. Many of the Christian churches have become increasingly tolerant of dissent and have to varying degrees embraced the idea of a multi-faith society, often more so than political leaders. For this reason the resistance to religion that has been a feature of much of political modernity is less prevalent today and may even explain the religious revival in many parts of the world. The adaptability of religion in the information age is one of the striking features of religion today. It has been often noted that John Paul II created more saints than any previous pope, suggesting that modernity and religion are not irreconcilable (Madsen *et al.* 2002).

The question of Christianity has recently become an issue for the European Union. In order to articulate a European identity, a view has gained currency in recent years that Europe is rooted in Christianity and this is the basis of its identity (Seidentop 2000). Although attempts to place a special emphasis on Christianity in the proposed European Constitution were abandoned, this is an influential position (Schlesinger and Foret 2006). Joseph Weiler has argued in favour of the official acknowledgement of the Christian heritage for the EU since, in his view, this would enhance the ideal of religious pluralism (Weiler 2003, see also Menendez 2004). The document 'The Spiritual and Cultural Dimension of Europe', although not an official statement of the EU, was commissioned by the President of European Commission and argued that the public role of European religions is particularly important and that this includes Islam (Biedenkopf *et al.* 2004). There is also of course the role Christian values have played in shaping the EU. Douglas Holmes has commented that Christian social values have played a significant role in the making of the EU, in particular the tradition of Catholic social modernism (Holmes 2000).

The notion of a European Christian heritage has not been unconnected with the prospect of Turkey joining the EU and wider concern
over the relation of Islam to Europe. With the waning of the Kemalist
project in present-day Turkey, the strictly secular state created by
Atakurk has reduced hostility towards Islam in the public domain
(Özbudun and Keyman 2002). The decisive development was the election of the Islamic-based Justice and Development Party, a moderate
Islamist party which has been an agent of Europeanization, in the
historic election of 2002 when it won two-thirds of parliamentary
seats. It is clearly the case that the notion that Europe is Christian is
invoked in order to express hostility to Turkey with its predominantly
Muslim population. In this there is the interesting paradox of a
Christian heritage defining a Europe that has become, we are led to
believe, secular.

One of the questions that this all raises is how does secularism relate
to the existence of a multi-faith Europe? Until recently, the challenge of
religious tolerance was largely an issue that concerned the Christian
religions and their relation to the state. It concerned issues such as the
presence of religion in the public domain, the question of state churches,
and where the limits of the public domain lie etc. The major exception
to this was Judaism, which lay outside the secular politics of modernity.
Today, in an age when non-Christian religions are becoming more
important some of the assumptions of secularism need to be revisited.
Islam is having a growing impact on Europe (see Bontempi 2005). The
EU area has a Muslim population of 2.4 per cent of the entire population.
In France 6 per cent of the population is Muslim, while in many other
countries it is around 3 per cent. The religious denominations within
Islam also differ greatly. In the UK there is a wide variety of Muslim
minorities while in France most are predominantly North African, while
Germany's large Muslim ethnic group is almost entirely Turkish. In
addition to Islam there are many other ethnic minorities, many of
whom are defined by religion. This does not mean that all these groups
are fervently religious in a way that the Christian population is not.
It does appear to be the case that two trends are in evidence, especially
with respect to Islam. There is a clear tendency towards the same kind
of secularism within Islamic groups, who it must be stressed are not
uniform, while on the other hand there is a marginal group within
Islam, who range from young Muslims who have rediscovered strict
Islamic teaching, to groups who are receptive to political radicalism.

Secularism and pluralism

Having outlined and discussed the historical and contemporary context concerning religion in Europe, we can now consider the actual mechanisms of secularism and their relation to the wider goal of pluralism in the context of multiethnicity. There are essentially three models of secularism operating in Europe, all of which are related to different conceptions of political community discussed in the previous chapter: the republican, liberal or constitutionalist conservative and liberal communitarian models.

The republican model has been central to church–state relations in many states and has also defined multicultural relations. The basic approach is a view of religion as a private matter. In the French variant religion cannot encroach on the public domain and there is no official recognition of ethnic groups or religious categories. The state recognizes individuals as citizens, not as members of a social group. Although as noted above in actual practice most republican states are flexible when it comes to specific problems resulting from the exclusion of religion from the state, the republican model of secularism is not designed for multi-faith societies (see Kastoryano 2002). It derived from a historical context in which religion had to be banished from the state in order to reform the *ancien régime*. The republican mode of secularism related to the religion of the majority, but in the multicultural and multi-faith societies of today, the policy of strict legal neutrality and recognition only on the basis of the individual citizen is not compatible with pluralism, which requires an enabling approach by which the state must actively promote social inclusion. As a model for Europe it has its limits in that a strict secularism does not accommodate many of the needs of minorities.

The republican model can be contrasted to the liberal tradition in which the attitude to religion has been shaped by constitutional conservatism. The kernel of this is not the separation of religion from the state, but the principle of tolerance. The liberal tradition itself has been closely related to the Protestant tradition and the emphasis on the freedom of worship, while the republican tradition has been mostly influenced by the belief in the sovereignty of the people. Tolerance was not central to the republican tradition, which was often opposed to religious tolerance and, in the European state tradition, came to stand for a religiously neutral legal identity. If France is the paradigmatic example

of the republican tradition, Britain is the classic example of constitutional conservatism. Other countries, such as the Netherlands and
Germany, embody to different degrees a similar approach to religion
but also include elements of the republican tradition. The private–public
separation is common to most countries, even those that have official
churches. The relation tends to be flexible and functional rather than
being rigid. Possibly more significant than the principle of neutrality and
the demarcation of public and private is the question where the lines
are drawn. Simply put, there are different notions as to the definition of
the private and the public. In the Netherlands the general understanding
of the private domain is that it consists of a larger space than in France
where a good deal of the domain of the state includes what in other
countries would be the private domain.

There is much to suggest that the liberal/constitutional conservative
approach to religion offers more scope for pluralism than the strict
republican adherence to the principle of neutrality. This does not suggest that there are no problems with the notion of tolerance that underlies it. Tolerance can mean different things and does not necessarily
entail pluralism. While the liberal understanding of tolerance is a largely
negative view of liberty as the removal of unreasonable constraints, the
version that has been influential in official policies towards religion is
one that, on the one side, accepts the freedom of worship for all and
does not require that this be confined to the private domain and, on the
other side, recognizes official churches. This recognition varies from
official state churches to the Dutch practice of recognizing the main
churches in the policy known as pillarization. In these cases the principle
of state neutrality effectively amounts to a policy of equal treatment.
The Dutch case is a good example of the limits of this kind of liberalism
which was designed to accommodate the mainstream churches and was
not intended to be applied to minority religions, such as those associated
with migrant or ethnic groups.

There are two problems with the liberal approach to the creation
of a secular society. The underlying notion of tolerance can mean
different things and does not at all necessarily lead to pluralism.
Tolerance is not the equivalent of acceptance and can simply mean
indifference, but it can also mean the right to be different. In recent
times, many questions are being asked about the meaning and limits of
tolerance, such as the question whether intolerance should be tolerated.
Is it merely a matter of 'we are all different'? A second problem with

liberalism is the assumption of integration into a dominant, cohesive culture as the goal. Those who do not fit into this culture can be 'tolerated' within limits. The result is only a limited kind of pluralism.

Liberal communitarianism is another model of religious secularization which has become an important aspect of multiculturalism and in many ways it constitutes multiculturalism as opposed to the traditional republican and liberal conceptions of political community. Communitarianism, as used here to refer to the modification of liberalism proposed by a range of largely North American political theorists, is based on a stronger notion of community than in the liberal tradition, where the emphasis is on the individual. Liberal communitarians demand that democracy requires the empowering of minorities as a positive act, as opposed to a limited notion of liberal tolerance for difference. There are broadly two positions on this. One is the position associated with Will Kymlicka and discussed in the previous chapter that only certain social groups should be empowered through special rights. The other position is one that is often termed radical pluralism and demands a more general application of positive recognition of all social groups. Liberal communitarianism, for the purpose of this discussion, refers simply to the view that official state recognition of minority religion is an essential part of a pluralist democracy and is very strongly based on the belief in diversity in the public sphere itself. Some pluralists, such as radical multiculturalists, see diversity itself as the goal (Young 2000).

Liberal communitarianism offers an important alternative to the traditional secular practices of modern Europe in so far as it is explicitly addressed to the current reality of multicultural societies. Is this the alternative for Europe? The suggestion made in this chapter is that liberal communitarianism is not the ideal solution for the problems discussed above with secularism in that the move towards pluralism requires a further development. The communitarian turn in liberal and republican theory is primarily based on the pursuit of diversity and has been particularly shaped by North American experiences. The US and Canada are societies formed out of successive waves of migration and in addition have pre-settler populations, whose concerns are quite different from migrant groups. Europe, on the other hand, is composed of societies that have far fewer migrants and a more complex mosaic of class and ethnic relations than is the case in North America, and there is the more or less total absence of pre-settler populations. The different colonial histories of European societies have led to different ethnic patterns of migration. However, the principal problem with liberal communitarianism as a multicultural practice is that it does not problematize religious/ethnic identities or recognize their hybrid nature. Religions and ethnic identities are largely accepted at their face value and the goal is simply the pursuit of diversity. This results in the abandonment of common ground and can also lead to an exaggeration of cultural differences between groups. For example, it does not accommodate the many Asian groups in Britain whose identity can be defined as British Muslim. The reality is that many ethnic groups have evolved identities that are not easily defined in terms of religion or a single ethnicity but are overlapping.

What has not received adequate attention is the process by which value systems, such as religion, change as a result of encounters with other value systems and as a consequence too of the inevitable contestation that results from the public sphere. The modified position this suggests can be termed cosmopolitanism.

Cosmopolitanism and the prospect of a post-secular society

Cosmopolitanism is not merely about diversity or about the separation of the private from the public. Although cosmopolitanism is certainly concerned with secularism, it is not the main or only aspect: cosmopolitanism is not a generalized version of multiculturalism where plurality is simply the goal or a modernist drive to eliminate ethnic, religious and other markers of identity from the public sphere and the domain of the state. The concept of culture underlying cosmopolitanism is different from that in liberalism and republicanism and its communitarian alternatives. Culture must be seen as a learning process; it is a developmental process entailing self-problematization and the discursive examination of all claims. This also pertains to ethnic groups and to religions. So this is not just a matter of liberal tolerance or the communitarian pursuit of diversity and is also stronger than soft cosmopolitanism in the sense of the promotion of the awareness of otherness. As argued in the previous chapter, a cosmopolitan approach differs from the established approaches, which are all based on keeping cultures separate, in promoting openness and public contestation. Cosmopolitanism is not often related to questions concerning religion, but is highly pertinent to the predicament about religion in Europe today (see Turner 2001). Cosmopolitanism is compatible with secularism without accepting all the assumptions of secularism, such as the policy of an official faith or established church. Secularism in cosmopolitan terms does not require the exclusion of religion from the public domain, which should be seen in more flexible terms in its relation to the private realm. A cosmopolitan approach suggests that all religions should be allowed in the public sphere but does not accept the constitutional conservative position that one religion be granted constitutional protection over others. Above all, it is the basic tenet of cosmopolitanism that religion should not be protected from contestation in the public sphere and that cultural value systems undergo transformation as a result of dialogue and self-problematization. It is fundamentally opposed to the privatistic containment of religion that has been a feature of the republican tradition wherein religion is banished to the pre-political private domain. It is also in marked contrast to the implicit dogmatism in much of liberal and republican attitudes to religion. Cosmopolitanism is a position that is compatible with a view of the public culture as an ongoing site of contestation.

So rather than separate private and public, what is needed is a multi-culturalism of mutual learning. This can include religion if the mode of communication is compatible with public discourse. No religion or church can separate itself from modernity and the need to justify through argument. Thus, as Habermas has argued, the condition of entry into the public sphere should be a willingness to engage in public discourse (Habermas 2005, 2006). However, this does not mean that more extreme religious groups should be excluded, as Habermas suggests. The discussion about Islamic extremist groups that has come to fore, especially since the bombings in London in 2005, suggests the importance of public dialogue of all groups. The isolation that secular-ism demands in banishing religion from the public domain can create the conditions of militancy. Although many Muslim militants have been far from isolated in terms of education and isolation alone does not explain radical political mobilization, cultural isolation in conjunction with other facts, such as access to a global web of Islamic communica-tion, can create the conditions for a counter-consciousness.

A pertinent example of the cosmopolitanism of the public culture in practice is the peace process that arose out of the Good Friday Agreement in Northern Ireland. What is illustrated by this is the dis-solution of fixed identities rooted in primordial religious traditions and the cultivation of negotiated identities. While the peace process still has

a long way to go before significant progress will be evident, the fact that
such a process is underway is an indication of the institutionalization
of pluralism and the public recognition of the need to move beyond
forms of identity based on exclusivist notions of statehood, religion
and territory. To be sure, it is evident that the emerging pluralism is
highly limited, confined as it is to the reconciliation of the dominant
confessional groups and there has been no attempt to extend the politics
of recognition to other contexts. Although what is at issue here is not
the recognition of minorities, but the accommodation of the dominant
confessional groups, it is clearly the case that a significant dissolution
of hegemonic national identities has occurred and with it a growing
transgression in borders and the intellectual discreditation of confessional politics.

The presence of religion in the public domain does not amount to
its acceptance. To varying degrees religion plays a role in people's lives,
be it on the level of formal affiliation, which is the case for the vast
majority of Europeans, or it may play a more central role, as it may do
so for many migrant groups. Although by no means most of Europe's
some 15 million Muslims are believers, a significant number are and this
is the case too of other migrant groups as it is of many Christians. The
very terms inherited from an earlier modernity may be inadequate in
comprehending religion today, since it is neither a question of churches
nor sects. The famous thesis of Ernst Troeltsch in the *Social Teachings
of the Christian Churches*, one of the major works in the classical
sociology of religion, that the conflict between church and sect that
had been a feature of European history has given way to the collapse of
a universal church needs to be looked at in a new light (Troeltsch 1931;
Turner 2005). The very category of the church, like that of the state,
while far from irrelevant, does not explain the complex nature of
cultural transformation in meaning, memory and identity that is a
feature of the present day. The contemporary expressions of religious
revivalism do not correspond to the model of the sect revolting against
the institutionalized orthodoxy of a church; they are the products of a
culture of individualized identities and the fulfilment of the impulse
within modernity towards emancipation. Far from traditional, religious
movements have become central to the global information economy,
providing meaning, self-expression and orientation to many people
(see Hellas 1998). Such movements are likely to be particularly attractive to young migrants and members of ethnic groups, many of whom

may be poorly integrated into local communities while highly integrated into global communication communities. As has been frequently noted, fundamentalist movements can occur within Christianity as much as in Islam, although the European experience of Christianity has not been in the direction of Christian fundamentalism (Buruma and Marglit 2004). However, the nascent Islamic fundamentalism in Europe, like all fundamentalist movements, is opposed to the traditional teachings of the past and is modernist in the pursuit of a personal liberation.

Secularism in its conventional forms is inadequate when it comes to responding to the challenges of religion. Whether it is the presence of headscarves in schools, state support for minority schools, the fine line between free speech, blasphemy and incitement to hatred, tax exceptions for churches, religious education in schools, the exclusion of religion from the public sphere or the pursuit of policies aimed at the public neutralization of religion, they are doomed to failure and are ultimately contrary to the goal of democratic pluralism. This does not mean that a secular society is not possible; rather it means that the public culture must be able to address all kinds of cultural challenges (see Benhabib 2002; Gutmann 2003). It is in this sense that the term cosmopolitan pluralism can be used.

Conclusion

The argument outlined in this chapter is that secularism is not an irreversible or clear-cut fact of European political culture (see also Eder 2002). It is rather a process and one that is expressed in many different forms.[21] While it is often argued that the secularization of modern society has led to a situation that is incompatible with the presence or recognition of religion in the public domain, the reality is that the European experience has been in theory as well as in practice more flexible when it comes to the public role of religion. European secularism has been characterized by dogmatism when it comes to non-Christian religions, but the inherent ambivalence in the policies on neutrality relating to church–state relations is an indication of the mutual intertwining of religion and politics in European political modernity.

---

[21] See also Asad (2003) and Scott and Hirschkind (2006) for a wider interpretation of the complex nature of secularism.

The challenge now for Europe is to articulate what in this chapter has been called cosmopolitanism. This involves moving from a secular understanding of the polity to a post-secular society. Europe is neither Christian nor simply secular, but post-secular. Islam has become an integral part of late European modernity. Islam is now more visible in Europe due to the presence of Muslim minorities and the Islamization of political discourse. It is possible to speak of a European Islam but this is as yet one that lacks a specific identity. Rigid adherence to a secularism that does not recognize the presence of religion in the public sphere cannot be the European solution to some of the problems of multiethnic societies. The argument advanced here in normative terms goes beyond communitarian and multiculturalist policies that simply demand the recognition and pursuit of diversity. It has been argued that a pluralist and cosmopolitan public culture can, and indeed must, include the contributions of religion provided that religious traditions can engage in self-problematization. The myth of secularism is often an obstacle in the path of creating a pluralist multiethnic society. This chapter has attempted to dispel some of the myths of secularism.

7 | Cosmopolitanism, modernity and global history

Introduction

Cosmopolitanism is a condition or orientation that has taken a huge variety of shapes and forms. In the previous chapters it was argued that cosmopolitanism can be related to a new expressions of multiculturalism where collective identities interact as opposed to being discrete units. This dynamic, which is both interactive and transformative, captures the key to the contemporary significance of cosmopolitanism. The cosmopolitan moment occurs when cultures or collective identities interact and undergo transformation as a result. Without the transformative moment it is meaningless to speak of cosmopolitanism. But it must also be demonstrated that something has been learnt from the encounter of cultures.

Until now the context for looking at such cosmopolitan processes has been the national culture. As argued in the previous chapters with respect to global ethics, citizenship and multiculturalism, it is no longer possible to confine cosmopolitanism to the national context and, as also argued, to the West. Viewed in broader societal terms, the cosmopolitan moment occurs not only in the encounter of one culture with another, but also when the local and global interact. Although such encounters can be related to the earliest expressions of civilizational formation, it was only with modernity that this dynamic really took on an enhanced momentum and significance. Cosmopolitanism, of course, precedes the formation of modernity, but without being a product of modernity as such, it is inseparable from the cultural and political dimensions of modernity. For this reason, the focus of this chapter is on modernity and developments within historical sociology and global history that are concerned with conceptualizing modernity in ways that do not presuppose a Eurocentric understanding of the world.

The case has already been made for a post-universalistic conception of cosmopolitanism, which while not rejecting universal normative principles does not accept universalism as a given. Nor does it accept the equation of universalism with Western concepts and principles. A post-universal cosmopolitanism, accordingly, is a universalism that is genuinely universal in not taking for granted Western normative principles or values and is formed out of the encounter of different universalistic value systems. Later in this chapter this problem will be discussed around the question of the translatability of concepts and it will be argued that cosmopolitanism is best understood as a form of cultural translation in which new horizons open up in the creative dialogue of cultures. But first the case for a cosmopolitan conception of modernity must be established. This is less than straightforward since modernity and its offshoots – post-modernity and late modernity – have generally been related to the Western historical experience. Through a critical reading of notions of multiple modernity and the emerging field of global history, I argue for a conception of non-Eurocentric modernity that emphasizes the open-ended nature of modernity as a site of tensions between different forces, such as the local and the global and inter-civilizational encounters. In short, new approaches to modernity offer a very promising way in which to contextualize cosmopolitanism as a post-universal condition that is of global significance.

The chapter begins with a discussion of the problem of Eurocentrism with a view to clarifying what a non-Eurocentric approach could be. The next section concerns the notion of modernity and, in the third section, I move onto a focus on the notion of multiple modernities and global history where the aim is to clarify the nature of a pluralized concept of modernity. The final section develops this notion of a pluralized conception of modernity in terms of a cosmopolitan theory of cultural translation where the emphasis is placed on major societal processes of civilizational interaction.

Problems of Eurocentrism

Avoiding the charge of Eurocentrism is not easy since the term lacks specificity and Eurocentrism is often an all-embracing category that covers virtually the entirety of scholarship. The notion of Eurocentrism has often been related to arguments or assumptions, implicit or explicit, that argue the West is superior to the rest of the world or the tendency to take Western experiences as the norm by which the rest of the world should be judged (Amin 1989; Bhambra 2007; Blaut 1993; Latouch

1996; Wallerstein 1996; Young 1991). The first sense is now largely discredited, as few argue for the superiority of the West over the rest of the world. This position, which was a product of the nineteenth century and the Enlightenment legacy, at most lives on in the second sense whereby western experiences are the norm to judge the rest of the world. A famous example of this is Max Weber's much quoted opening sentence to the *Protestant Ethic and the Spirit of Capitalism*: 'A product of modern European civilization, studying any problem of universal history, is bound to ask himself to what combination of circumstances the fact should be attributed that in Western civilization, and in Western civilization only, cultural phenomena have appeared which (as we like to think) lie in a line of development having universal significance and value' (Weber 1978: 13). In this case Weber was not declaring the superiority of the West, as is so often thought, but he believed as a matter of empirical fact that the Western route to modernity was different in that capitalism became the dominant force and was to assume global significance. So, for example, capitalism, which is now universal, did not develop in China in the way that it did in the West and the ascetic personality associated with Western Christianity came to have a universal significance in giving to modernity an ethos that cultivated a certain kind of rationality. It was Weber's conviction that modern instrumental rationality as expressed in capitalism and legal rationality took on the universal significance that they acquired because of the specific circumstances in the West where economic rationality and the ethical and religious modes of conduct formed a mutual unity of purpose. However while it would appear Weber used the term universal significance in the sense of global magnitude, he was not very clear on what he meant by universal significance. Since he was a critic of Western rationality, it is hard to see how he was claiming it had normative significance.

Habermas is another such example of a Eurocentric universalism that presupposes a conception of modernity as the completion of the Enlightenment project and an 'occidental understanding of the world' (Delanty 1997). Although Habermas has established the foundations of a post-universalistic conception of rationality as dialogic and critical, he has continued to adhere to a European conception of modernity and a model of discourse that does not break from a particular interpretation of European modernity as developed by Kant and Weber, who are his main references. In this understanding of modernity, rationality split into the differentiated spheres of art, morality and science out of which were laid the foundations for emancipation and the critique of power. Weber's Eurocentrism consisted of his tendency to view the rest of the world in terms of deficiencies. Moreover, it was Eurocentric methodologically as opposed to normative terms in that Western experiences were the reference point for all comparisons. Habermas's Eurocentrism, in contrast, is more normative than methodological in that he defines universalism in terms that are largely derived from the European historical experience. However, there is no reason why the discursive model of reason that is the basis of his philosophical approach cannot be extended to a wider sphere of application and to issues of cross-cultural communication where the differences between cultures are very great and underpinned by different models of modernity.

A non-Eurocentric approach would thus aim to identify those features of modernity than can be found in non-Western parts of the world and where the explanation of the phenomenon in question does lie not in Western influences, but in autonomous logics of development. Thus, for example, democracy and capitalism are in different ways universal phenomena and while the influence of the West is difficult to deny, it is possible to examine them in terms of local adaptations. Indeed, even in the Western world there are many varieties of capitalism and democracy. This is one of the most promising developments in recent scholarship. A non-Eurocentric social science would seek to identify those features of all civilizations and society that display internal logics of development without taking Western experiences as the normative standard. This is roughly what global history sets out to achieve and it is also implicit in some postcolonial approaches, as in Chakrabarty's aim 'to provencialize Europe' (Chakrabarty 2000). In other words, a non-Eurocentric approach will have at least two options. One is to take concepts which are generally associated largely with the Western world and, rather than assess the deficiency of the rest of world with respect to the degree to which they exhibit such experiences or characteristics, examine their different logic of development. Thus, the notion of civil society or the public sphere, which can be clearly located in the history of Western societies can be related to non-Western societies. The aim of such an approach would be confined to demonstrating the varieties of historical experience without proclaiming Western varieties as having universal significance. Universalistic conclusions would have to be limited. This approach, however, suffers from the disadvantage that concepts derived from the Western historical experience – democracy, human rights, civil society – are used to make sense of non-Western societies. This difficulty exists only if one assumes that non-Western societies exist, for a case can be made that all societies have been influenced by such concepts which have lost their Western specificity. A second option, which is the postcolonial preference, is to have a stronger emphasis on entirely different experiences in non-Western societies. This may require developing a new theoretical language that does not presuppose the terms of Western historical analysis. Given the interconnected nature of modernity and global history, it is difficult to see how this latter option could be executed in practice. Thus much of postcolonial theory rarely amounts to more than a self-critique of Western modernity.

The argument developed in this chapter brings an additional perspective to bear on the prospect of a non-Eurocentric approach to historical experience and one in which the cosmopolitan dimension is more strongly present. Rather than abandon all concepts as Eurocentric or simply confine global analysis to the identification of a plurality of experiences, a cosmopolitan approach gives greater centrality to the creative interaction of different historical experiences. In this view, what is more important is the ways in which societies interpret and transform themselves through the encounter with the external context. Historical experiences are always subject to interpretation and to adaptation. This is as true of the Western world as it is of the non-Western world.

This argument refutes the orientalist thesis that Western interpretations of Otherness are always limited by the fact that the Other is from the beginning a construction in which the West seeks to gain mastery over the Other which can only be known as a construction reflecting Western power (Said 1978). Said's critique of orientalism is without doubt an important corrective of Eurocentric assumptions, but it has a limited range of application. Even if extended beyond English and French literary accounts of the orient in the late nineteenth-century colonial period, which was his primary focus, the orientalist critique does not offer an adequate account of the complexity of inter-cultural relations in general or even of East–West encounters. As pointed out in Chapter 1, much of the Enlightenment's preoccupation with the orient cannot be understood in Said's terms. This would be to neglect the complex interaction, including mutual learning that has been a feature of East–West relations. In order to advance the argument beyond the terms of orientalism versus Eurocentrism, what is clearly needed is a new conceptualization of modernity that takes into account different civilizational models and their interaction.

Conceptualizing modernity

In the most general sense, modernity is what Johann Arnason has aptly termed a 'field of tensions' (Arnason 1991). It is not a particular era or time-bound phenomenon, but a particular mode of historical experience and interpretation, as Koselleck (1984) has argued in a classic work. In his historical semantics approach, modernity is the constantly changing interpretation of the present by reference to the past and the open horizon of the future. The modern sensibility arises with the consciousness that the present is radically different from past. The 'modern', or *modus*, literally meaning now. As such it signals rupture and has been famously defined by Baudelaire (1964: 13) as 'the transitory, the fugitive, the contingent'. Agnes Heller defines the central animus of modernity to be the view that: 'Everything is open to query and to testing: everything is subject to rational scrutiny and refuted by argument' (Heller 1999: 41). Modernity could thus be described as the loss of markers of certainty and the realization that certainty can never be established for once and for all.

This position differs from the argument made by Toulmin (1992) who has identified modernity with what he calls 'cosmopolis', the creation of a rationally organized society reflecting the Newtonian concept of nature and the modern nation-state. The end of modernity coincides with the end of that epistemological and political order. However, Toulmin detects a counter-movement to the dominant tradition and which has as its origin less the seventeenth-century than the preceding one with the humanistic Renaissance. Toulmin's argument that modernity has two distinct starting points, a humanistic one grounded in classical literature and a scientific one rooted in seventeenth-century natural philosophy, is in one sense correct but is also misleading. The doubled-edged nature of modernity has been commented on by several theorists who see modernity as a site of tensions rather than something that can be defined by a single tradition. However, Toulmin's double vision of modernity gives a more central place to the vision of a universalizing rationality and moreover is an overly historicist interpretation that is defined in terms specific to the European historical experience.

As a site of tensions, to follow Arnason's proposal, modernity is neither a particular historical condition with its origin in the sixteenth or seventeenth century nor a single mode of interpretation. Thus for Habermas, the project of modernity in one of its dimensions entails the progressive extension of a potentially emancipatory communicative rationality to all parts of society (Habermas 1984, 1987a, 1987b). This leads to a fundamental tension at the heart of modernity between communicative rationality and instrumental rationality. So modernity cannot be reduced to one particular structure or rationality, but it is a condition formed out of the ongoing contestation of societies as they find communicative solutions to problems, in particular those deriving from systemic forms of integration. In some of his work, Habermas, like Toulmin, has tended to define modernity in terms that relate it to the Enlightenment. However, his more general insight that modernity has been forged through the conflict of communicative rationality versus instrumental rationality whereby social forms of integration clash with systemic forms of integration, suggests a vision of modernity as a dynamic force and which recalls the famous motif of the *Communist Manifesto* where modernity is described as a condition in which 'all that is solid melts into air'. Another useful way to conceptualize modernity in terms of a tension between contrary orientations is Castoriadis's characterization of modernity as a radical imaginary confronting the institutional imaginary, which tries to domesticate it (Castoriadis 1987). For Castoriadis the self-articulation of society is made possible by the radical imaginary which projects an image of an alternative society. This is such a constitutive feature of modern society that even the tendency towards domination and instrumental mastery does not eliminate it. According to Castoriadis, all societies possess an imaginary dimension, since they must answer certain symbolic questions as to their basic identity, their goals and limits. The imaginary in this sense is not in contrast to reality, since it itself is something real. The imaginary asserts the desire for autonomy against the instrumentalizing logic of capitalism.

Castoriadis's concept of modernity as a dual logic has been influential, and is reflected in the work of several social theorists, including Arnason, Heller, Lefort and Wagner. Common to their various contextualizations of modernity is the attempt to give prominence to the creative dynamics and tensions in modernity which result from the pursuit of the goal of autonomy, on the one side, and on the other the pursuit of power and material accumulation. This approach avoids the reduction of modernity to a single logic of instrumental reason, as is reflected in the theories of Adorno and Horkheimer as well as Foucault. It also avoids the Eurocentric bias of relating modernity to the European historical experience. Instead of conceiving modernity as a historical period or era, modernity can be described, as Peter Wagner has outlined, as a relation between liberty and discipline (Wagner 1994). In different terms, this can also be expressed as in Touraine's theory of modernity as a struggle between Reason and the Subject (Touraine 1995). Another illustration of the tension within modernity is Adam Seligman's characterization of modernity in terms of a 'wager' over the nature of authority: modernity staked everything on reason and the individual as opposed to the sacred. There is some evidence to suggest that this bet has not been won, given the return of ethnic and religious identities (Seligman 2000: 32–3). Claude Lefort (1986) has also argued in a similar vein that modernity contains within it emancipatory possibilities in that no political order has fully captured the modern social space, which has remained radically open to new interpretations. The tension that characterizes this – which can be seen as one of openness and closure – is one of the defining features of modernity and the basis of the impulse within modernity towards immanent transcendence.

A theory of modernity will have to take into account both logics, not just one. Thus, for example, in the European context, various forms of openness were established by the republican, the liberal and the cosmopolitan project only to be brought to closure by other dynamics. Both the liberal idea of freedom and the republican vision of a self-governing political community opened modernity to new possibilities, but, following Marx, Weber and Foucault, we can see how these projects also established closure on the openness of modernity's first major transformation in the early modern period. Nonetheless, this did not eradicate openness, not least because of the multitude of projects within liberal modernity. The previous remarks on the central conflict at the heart of modernity should not neglect the multiple forms of modernity, to be considered shortly, and the multiplicity of tensions, which extend beyond particular societies and also extend beyond a given civilization. While in the most general sense modernity is shaped by a tension between freedom/autonomy, on the one side, and power, discipline and instrumental reason on the other, this tension is played out in social and political dynamics through the interaction of state, market and civil society within geopolitical units which have generally been national societies. The diversity of forms of modernity as a social formation – from nation-states to empires – will depend on the specific forms of interaction between state formation, markets/capitalist accumulation and modes of accumulation, and civil society and social movements. In many cases these forms of interaction can be related to specific national patterns, but the notion of modernity draws attention to a wider pattern that may include more than one nation-state.

A qualification can be made with respect to one aspect of the debate on modernity. The notion of a break between modernity and postmodernity must be rejected. The idea that modernity has come to an end in a new age of postmodernity is a misappropriation of the latter, which is primarily a term relating to certain aspects of cultural analysis which do not translate into social and political analysis without severe distortion. Scott Lash, for instance, argues that postmodernist categories are less relevant to the new kinds of information power today (Lash 2002: 3). Postmodernism in one way has some relevance to the re-conceptualization of modernity as a relation between rupture and continuity. A theme in much of postmodern thought, in particular in the aesthetic sphere, is the creative combination of modernity and tradition. Where one school of thought that gave rise to modernism stood for the rupture of present from past, the rise of postmodernism in the 1970s sought to recapture tradition in an emphasis on mixed styles and the intertwining of rupture with continuity. In this sense postmodernism opened a route to cosmopolitanism as radical plurality and against the modernist reduction of form to functionality. In this view, then, postmodernity is best seen as a moment within modernity whereby the mix of tradition and modernity, the old and the new, entails the formation of new cultural forms that are neither new nor old. The postmodernist tendency towards hybrid cultural forms is not far removed from cosmopolitanism, but has constrained cosmopolitanism to a movement within the largely Western tradition of postmodernism.

The cosmopolitan dimension in a different and more globally oriented sense, comes into play only by moving beyond the terms of the Western discourse of modernity and postmoderntity. As a site of tensions the development of modernity takes shape – in principle anywhere and at any time – through the interaction of the local with the global. The field of conflicts that defines the modern project cannot be reduced to a limited spatial context, such as a national sphere of influence or Western post-modern culture. The national or local context is interlinked with global forces. This perspective suggests a move beyond the terms of postmodern analysis, which has remained largely concerned with the notion of cultural modernity and expressed in its major forms in Western cultural developments arising out of the transformation of Western modernism. The rise of the idea of 'varieties of modernity' has brought about a change in the understanding of the idea of postmodernity (Gaonkar 2001).

Multiple modernities and global history

The notion of alternative modernities has opened a new and more cosmopolitan conception of modernity that takes it beyond a purely Western focus. The notion of an alternative has been an important basis of a critical perspective on modernity (Eder 1985). One way of looking at this notion of alternative modernity is to see counter-movements, such as fascism and communism, to Western modernity as anti-modern (Furet 1999). However as Arnason (1993) has argued, it is questionable that these movements are not modern and should be seen as different versions of modernity, albeit ones which ultimately failed. Communism and fascism were modernist projects, animated as they were by some of the most captivating of modern ideas, for example the belief that it is possible for elites to reconstruct society in the image of the state and bring about a new order, a vision close to Toulmin's notion of a total cosmopolis. Alternative and unsuccessful modernities they may have been, this should not lead to the conclusion that there is one single and successful modernity or one that can be summed up in the term Western modernity. As Mouzelis (1999) has argued, modernity is not merely a question of Westernization for its key processes and dynamics can be found in all societies.

This suggests a view of modernity as a plural condition. Instead of a singular Western modernity the notion of multiple modernities has gained increased attention in recent scholarship in historical sociology and social theory. This is a position advocated by a very broad range of approaches which in different ways seek to offer an alternative conceptualization of modernity viewed from the margins (Al-Azmeh 1993; Eisenstadt 2003; Gaonkar 2001; Kamali 2005; Kaya 2003; Taylor 1999). The idea of multiple modernities points to an epistemic break from a conception of modernity as a historical condition that with some delays and modifications has been generalized to the rest of the world. One of the leading proponents of the idea of multiple modernities is

S. N. Eisenstadt, who in a large number of publications has been at the forefront in the reformulation of modernity as plural. Following in the footsteps of the comparative sociology of Max Weber and Benjamin Nelson, Eisenstadt (1986, 2001, 2003) has traced the origins of modernity to the 'axial' civilizations of antiquity whose universalistic cultures the revolutions of the modern period took over and transformed. European civilization provided the major entry point into modernity, which has now become a global condition. Modernity has become global, but is appropriated in different ways: 'The actual developments in modern or – as they were then designated – modernizing societies have gone far beyond the homogenizing and hegemonic assumptions of the original European or Western programme of modernity' (Eisenstadt 2001: 329). His thesis is that the 'multiple and divergent modernities' crystallized during the nineteenth and twentieth centuries; modernity was a process of continued revolution and upheaval arising out of units, contradictions and antinomies. Eisenstadt remains convinced that modernity is not just global, but is a new civilization and one that has been shaped by the initial impetus of Western modernity.

This work offers a fruitful basis for a new conceptualization of modernity beyond the modernity versus tradition dichotomy that has been the basis of modernization theory. It offers an important corrective of the traditional Eurocentric bias in the Enlightenment narrative of modernity as a continuous march of civilization and progress. However his notion of multiple modernity also has some drawbacks. Eisenstadt's own approach entails an over-emphasis on the Axial Age civilization as providing the basic animus for modernity. This leads to a certain difficulty when it comes to non-Axial Age civilizations, which include Japanese civilization, and much of Africa. Moreover, Eisenstadt holds too strongly to a view of a primary European modernity that, through colonialism or due to its worldwide significance, became the basis of all subsequent modernities. Whether or not European modernity was the primary motor of modernity is an empirical matter, rather than as would appear to be in Eisenstadt an ontological claim. One of the main problems is that in correcting the unitary sense of modernity, the result has been an over-pluralization leading to a lack of clarity. Thus we have an African modernity, a Japanese modernity, an Islamic modernity, a Turkish modernity. It is easy to conclude that modernity takes varied forms, but if the concept becomes a numerical matter it loses its specificity and becomes ultimately reducible to national models of modernity. The danger here is over-pluralization. Eisenstadt does attempt to correct this tendency, arguing that modernity refers to the features common to its diverse forms. Nonetheless, the debate on multiple modernities does not appear to have advanced beyond a general recognition that modernity takes more than one form. It is clearly the case that modernity cannot be reduced to national contexts without rendering the notion meaningless, but further progress needs to be made. The thesis advanced in this chapter is that rather than over-pluralize modernity in an attempt to correct the universalistic and Eurocentric value-ladenness of the term, modernity should rather be theorized in terms of processes of self-transformation that occur in different forms and ones that are shaped by a constant widening of networks, spheres of social exchange and communication. Thus the most influential forms of modernity were those that possessed the cultural versatility and technological means to become globally significance.

The concern with multiple modernities, without this interactive dimension, can lead to the mistaken view of different modernities isolated from each other. Whatever the solution to this problem is, it will have to entail a theory of how modernizing cultures interact and why modernity is present to varying degrees. This is where global history enters the picture. Global history has arisen in the movement from world history to global history. Global history takes the contemporary world as the perspective and differs from world history in not assuming either a teleology or a universal civilization, as in classic approaches of Spengler and Toynbee. There is no single global history, only histories. It is based on multidirectionality and interconnectivity. It is concerned with the interactions of different cultures and civilizations; it is transnational and focused on processes of interaction rather than autonomous national trajectories (Bentley 2002; Buultjens and Mazlish 1993). This historiographical turn has inadvertly opened up a cosmopolitan perspective on the formation of modernity as a condition of interconnections and consciousness of globality. Recent scholarship has drawn attention to earlier expressions of globalization in history and the emergence of a consciousness of globality, which Robertson has highlighted in a seminal work on the cultural dimensions of globalization (Bayly 2004; Hopkins 2002; Robertson 1992).

In this context, the notion of 'entangled modernities' has been proposed to capture the enmeshed, interconnected nature of modernities and that there are not just multiple but overlapping ones (Arnason

2003; Therborn 2003). This has the advantage of capturing the ways in which Western and non-Western modernities are linked and the co-existence of different modernities within one national tradition. The suggestion that modernity exists not just in multiple forms, but in overlapping, entangled forms points to transformative processes and, as Arnason (2003) argues, interconnections. No account of modernity in global perspective can neglect the interactive mechanisms and processes that lie at the root of modernity as a transformative process. Modernities do not simply exist as coherent or stable, well-defined units, but are in a constant process of change and this is due to the nature of the particular forms of interpenetration, selection, combination, adaptation and processing of cultural codes, resources, imaginaries etc. This is reflected in recent studies on global trade and cultural encounters, which suggests a more explicit connection with cosmopolitanism (Bayly 2004; Bentley 1993; Curtin 1984). The key to this is the interaction of modernities. This is one of the central insights of global historians such as Hodgson (1993) and McNeil (1963, 1980) whose revisions of the rise of the West thesis have given a central place to the interaction of East and West. Their work builds upon the earlier pioneering work of Benjamin Nelson, who introduced the notion of civilizational encounters and the idea of a civilizational complex (Nelson 1976, 1981). Influenced by Weber's comparative sociology of civilizations, Nelson went beyond Weber's conception of civilization as holistic entities to emphasize the importance of cultural interaction between civilizations in the shaping of civilizational forms of consciousness.

Arnason's contribution to the debate on multiple modernity extends the hermeneutical dimension that was implicit but undeveloped in the work of Nelson. As with Eisenstadt and Nelson, he approaches modernity from a civilizational perspective (Arnason 2003). His starting point is Castoriadis's theory of the imaginary, which is a central feature of the self-constitution of every society (Castoriadis 1987). For Arnason, Castoriadis broke new ground with his notion of a radical social imaginary, which for Arnason can be seen as the mechanism that lies at the core of civilizations and civilizational encounters. His civilizational analysis holds that civilizations are contested grounds in which different visions of the world emerge and undergo transformation, central to which are dynamics of encounters and syntheses. Civilizations are internally plural and exist within a plurality of civilizations; they are

all based on frameworks of meaning that can be interpreted in different ways within and beyond the contours of a given civilization. Such
frameworks constitute fields of interpretation for more or less radical
interpretations of the world. Modernity, he argues, is the major example of internal conflict and contested identity and as such it bears the
imprint of the fundamental tension of the imaginary significations of
civilizations. The divergent patterns of modernity should thus be seen
as combinations of civilizational complexes. His aim is 'to link
the civilizational perspective to an important but under-developed
theme in the theory of modernity: the dynamics of tensions and conflicts, between basic orientations (such as the cumulative pursuit of
power and the more ambiguous moves towards autonomy) as well
as between divergent institutional spheres – economic, political and
cultural – with corresponding interpretative frameworks' (Arnason
2003: 49–50). In other words, the self-transformative capacity of
societies is thus grounded in a pluralistic vision of civilizations and
of modernity.

In addition to the plural and overlapping nature of modernity, the
global nature of modernity must be noted. Modernity, while not globally uniform, is nonetheless a globalizing process. This does not mean
one single modernity, but rather a uniformity in forms of consciousness,
modes of cognition, interpretation and orientations. Modernity is necessarily global in outlook, while it first emerged in Western Europe and
North America it is not Western. This can be clarified further by an
argument Therborn (1994) has made concerning the global nature of
modernity. Rather than begin with a premise of diversity, he argues
for a notion of modernity as global but which expresses itself in major
macro-regional variations, of which he lists four: the European route
of revolution or reform; the American route of independence; a route
represented by Iran, Thailand and Japan based on external threat and
selective imports; the route of conquest experienced by much of Africa
and Asia. In addition to avoiding an over-pluralization and reduction
of modernity to national trajectories, it places globalization at the core
of modernity without reducing modernity to globalization as such. As
Dirlik (2003) has also argued, the notion of non-global modernities
makes little sense. Moreover, it also avoids a purely culturally oriented
view of modernity.

The global dimension to modernity is most evident in the relation
of the local to globality. Globalization can be seen as a process that

intensifies connections, enhances possibilities for borrowing, translation, transformation. As such, it can be found in many historical
contexts. The forms, interrelations and dynamics of modernity are
varied and uneven, but underlying them is the most basic impetus
towards self-transformation, the belief that human agency can transform the present in the image of an imagined future. This view of
modernity as a break from the past seems to accord with the major
philosophical and cultural understandings of modernity as a dynamic
process that has made change itself the defining feature of modernity.
Modernity is thus a particular kind of time consciousness that defines
the present in its relation to the past, which must be continuously
recreated. Modernity is not a historical epoch that can be periodized,
but a mode of experiencing and interpreting time. Modernity unfolds
in different ways, according to different paces and can take different
societal forms depending on the configurations of state, the capitalist
market and civil society.

Modernity is thus not exclusively Western but can emerge anywhere.
It is therefore possible to speak of multiple modernities without pluralizing the notion to the extent that it becomes meaningless. Viewed
from the lens of global history there are at least three ways to approach
a cosmopolitan conception of modernity. The first and minimal approach is simply to demonstrate through empirical examples how concepts
that ordinarily relate to Western societies can be generalized to all kinds
of society. Thus, the notion of civil society, generally associated with
European modernity, is a relevant term of analysis for non-Western
society. Indeed, the very notion of modernity can be universalized to
include, for example, an Islamic modernity, an African modernity, a
Chinese modernity etc. The disadvantage with this approach is that it
seeks only to find non-Western examples of concepts that have a largely
Western applicability. A second approach is a modified version of the
previous. Rather than generalize Western experiences to the rest of the
world or take Western concepts as a point of departure, a radicalized
global history would posit universalizable concepts that take multiple
civilizational forms. In this case the objective will be to examine, for
example, the global diversity of concepts rather than posit a universally
valid framework of concepts. In this case there is a plurality of civilizational forms and concepts. Pollock's argument discussed in Chapter 1
of a vernacular cosmopolitanism would be an example of such an
approach to global history. A third approach would shift the emphasis

from plurality towards modes of interaction, such as cross-cultural encounters and interactions. In this case the cosmopolitan moment occurs when two or more cultures interact as a result of global forces, for example, trade or even as a consequence of war or large-scale migration. Approaching the problem of multiple modernities in this way avoids the limits of internal and external accounts of modernity. The rise of the West and European modernity, for instance, cannot be explained without taking into account how the West interacted with the East and with other parts of the world. However, reducing the relation to a one-way account of colonial appropriation, as reflected in recent revisions of the rise of the West (Frank 1998; Hobson 2004) neglects the complex nature of the interaction, seeing it only in terms of appropriation. In an assessment of the internal and external accounts of the rise of the West, Arnason (2006) concludes that the latter perspective is best seen as a corrective of the traditional account that would explain the rise of the West with respect to factors internal to the West. Implicit, but underdeveloped in Arnason's account, is the recognition of a third position, which is neither internalist nor externalist but interactionist. An interactionist account of the rise of modernity would place the emphasis on the dynamics and modes of interaction whereby different parts of the world become linked through the expansion and diffusion of systems of exchange, networks of communication, and various forms of third culture. Thus it was not the case that modernity was European per se or that different models of modernity emerged spontaneously on their own, but the rise of modernity was determined by the extent to which in a given part of the world the capacity existed for the expansion of local cultures into a globally oriented third culture. It was consequential that this happened in Europe, and only in certain parts of Europe, but this does not mean that modernity was European per se.

Approaching the problem of modernity from the perspective of global history offers, then, a corrective to the received view of modernity as a Western condition that was transported to the rest of the world. Moreover, it also avoids some of the problems of an appeal to a non-Western modernity or multiple modernity. The notion of modernity divested of its Eurocentric assumptions has a direct relevance to cosmopolitan analysis if it is accepted that it is a transformative condition that arises out of multiplicity and interaction. It is a concept that cannot be confined to national patterns of development, but has a wider application including, importantly, civilizational influences.

Cosmopolitanism and cultural translation

The shift towards global history and the related emphasis on multiple modernity as discussed in the foregoing can be complemented with an additional argument that may go some way towards correcting a weakness in the global history perspective. The major revision that global history has brought about in the approach to modernity is that it corrects the Eurocentric bias that was an integral aspect of the older comparative history with its characteristic emphasis on Western civilization as the norm and nations as self-contained entities. From a cosmopolitan perspective, this has not gone far enough in that the emphasis on multiplicity and interaction alone does not sufficiently capture all aspects relevant to the cosmopolitan dimension of modernity. The main weakness is that the emphasis on encounters and borrowings is not strong enough to capture fully the transformative dynamics of modernity. One of the major impulses in modernity is the striving towards an alternative society and the genesis of universalistic principles. The central impulse of modernity – the belief that the world can be reshaped by human agency – has entailed a commitment to normative frameworks that offer a means of imagining an alternative social world. This has been expressed in modern political ideologies – nationalism, republicanism, socialism, communism – which, in their various ways, have responded to the modern condition of perpetual renewal and a future orientation. The turn to post-Eurocentric global history may have opened up new perspectives of a cosmopolitan nature, but what needs further development is the normative, critical dimension. As argued in Chapter 2, cosmopolitan normative critique concerns changes in self-understanding arising out of the encounter with another culture whereby, to varying degrees, a relativization of values occurs and eventually the movement towards a shared normative culture emerges.

Civilization analysis, as in the impressive body of work by Eisenstadt and Arnason, is not normally associated with cosmopolitanism since there is not an explicit attempt to connect global historical analysis with normative critique, though in the case of the latter the connection with immanent transcendence is more evident.[22] An additional problem is that civilizational analysis is primarily focused on Europe and Asia and

---

[22] Neither Eisenstadt nor Arnason make any such attempt to connect their theory of modernity with cosmopolitanism.

would appear to exclude non-Eurasian civilizations. Furthermore the emphasis on civilizational analysis may be too limiting when it comes to understanding the nature of modernity. The problems with normative critique in empirical analysis have been raised in Chapter 2 and can only be briefly commented on in the present context. The key issue to be highlighted is that normative cosmopolitan critique and empirical social and historical analysis of cosmopolitanism can be integrated around a focus on immanent transcendence. To develop this the idea of cultural translation can be adopted, for the problem is essentially a matter of how one culture interprets itself in light of the encounter with the other and constantly undergoes change as a result. This involves more than the relativization of universality or the emphasis on interaction, but a logic of transcendence.

The notion of cultural translation draws attention to immanent processes of transformation determined by modes of interpretation in which an evaluation occurs. Global history does not give adequate attention to the genesis of the new and to interpretative frameworks in which cultures undergo transformation arising out of the re-evaluation of standpoints. The emphasis tends to be more on global histories than a developmental logic in which subject formation occurs. Viewing modernity in terms of the model of translation offers a way to conceptualize the cosmopolitan current in modernity as one that has normative significance as well as cultural specificity. The significant consideration here is the tendency within modernity for translation to become the very form of culture. The universalizing feature of modernity is the drive to make all of culture translatable. This does not mean the obliteration of cultural differences or the creation of a universal language but a condition of universal translatability. As a condition of universal translatability, modernity arises when cultures become embroiled in the logic of translation. The key feature of this is the communicative relation of cultures to each other by means of a third culture. This third culture – globality, world culture – does not necessarily exist as an overarching culture or a global lingua franca, but is a medium of translation and one that is embedded in local cultures. Throughout history the world religions and universalistic languages – Latin, Sanskrit, English – served this purpose which is today being carried forward by the Internet and other media of communication as well as by new discourses such as democracy and human rights which provide cognitive models by which cultures interpret themselves. The result is that cultures are becoming more and more translatable. As they do so, changes in self-understanding occur and a certain cosmopolitanism enters the interpretative system. If, as Ricouer has argued, cosmopolitanism entails the capacity to view oneself from the eyes of the Other, then cultural translation might be the medium in which one views one's own culture as foreign (Ricoeur 1995, 1996). The resulting universality is more one of pluralization than a singular rationality.

The notion of translation has increasingly been applied to the analysis of a broader concept of culture than the purely textual (Assmann 1997; Bassnett and Lefevere 1990; Budick and Iser 1996; Cronin 1998). A developed use of the notion of translation has existed for sometime in philosophy since Wittgenstein (Benjamin 1989) and has been implicit in anthropology (Asad 1986). Translation has been proposed as a general methodology for the social sciences (Callon *et al.* 1986) where it refers to the process whereby one thing represents another thing so well that the voice of the represented is effectively silenced. New perspectives on translation have been opened by Gadamer's *Truth and Method* and MacIntyre's signal essay, 'Tradition and Translation' (Gadamer 1975; MacIntyre 1984). Walter Benjamin's classic 1923 essay, 'The Task of the Translator', is now a key work in rethinking the contemporary relevance of translation from a cosmopolitan perspective (Benjamin 1982). The essay introduced the idea that in translation an element of foreignness is brought into one's own culture. The idea of cultural translation has been an important focus for Homi Bhabha (1994) who has argued for a concept of translation as the performative function of communication and which comes into play in the discursive constitution and contestation of cultural phenomena. James Clifford (1997) has extended the notion to various kinds of localization, hybridization and vernacularization (see also Ang 2003). This is not the place to review this diverse literature, but it can be noted that it offers a fruitful approach to global modernity and cosmopolitan analysis. What is suggested by these diverse approaches is that translation is more than interpretation and the transmission of meaning; it is also about the transformation of meaning and the creation of something new, for culture is never translated neutrally. The logic of translation is inherent in culture, which is not static or the expression of authorial meaning but is dynamic and transformative.

The cultural logic of modernity can thus be seen as a mode of translation that is constitutive of modernity and its forms of communication in which otherness is constantly transformed. The capacity

for translation – of languages, memories, narratives, experiences, knowledge – is the basis of communication, tradition and cultural possibility
and entails a continuous process of social construction. Translation as a
cultural process is a mode of cultural transmission wherein the process of
transmission is transformative. It has been widely recognized that translation is not a simple act of replication. As Gadamer has argued, 'every
translation is at the same time an interpretation' (Gadamer 1975: 346).
Translation refers to something that transcends both Self and Other. In
Gadamer's words: 'The horizon of understanding cannot be limited
either by what the writer has originally in mind, or by the horizon of
the person to whom the text was originally addressed' (Gadamer
1975: 356). Translation can never overcome the gulf between two
languages, he argued in this seminal work on truth, tradition and
interpretation. Translation arises because of a need to bridge this
gap but it cannot overcome it. While Gadamer makes the point that
translation is never the norm in 'ordinary communication', which is
based on a shared language, or even when the speaker is speaking a
foreign language, it is increasingly becoming the space in which many
forms of communication are played out. Migration, globalization,
new information and communication technologies have changed the
nature of communication to a point that cultural translation has
become a central category in all of communication.

The terms of Gadamer's approach also need to be expanded in the need
to take account of the critical moment in which newness is created.
Cultural translation is a process of mutations, transferences, innovations,
appropriations, borrowings, re-combinations and substitution. It concerns the symbolic and cognitive processes by which cultural aspects of a
given collective identity are appropriated by a different one, which will
variously adapt, transfigure it, subvert it. In the resulting re-codification
of culture, new meanings and structures are created. Bhabha has hinted at
a critical normative interpretation that is lacking in Gadamer's account:

> it is not simply appropriation or adaptation; it is a process through which
> cultures are required to revise their own systems of reference, norms and
> values by departing from their habitual or 'inbred' rules of transformation.
> Ambivalence and antagonism accompany any act of cultural translation
> because negotiating with the 'difference of the other' reveals the radical
> insufficiency of our own systems of meaning and signification. (Bhabha 1994)

This is the cosmopolitan condition of living in translation.

The question of power and inequality cannot be neglected since translation is not only never neutral but frequently involves violence. This is particularly the case in multicultural encounters where there can be significant questions of power at stake in those cases where one cultural form as opposed to another is privileged (Asad 1986). Forms of translation can be devised which reduce the inequality of positions. For example, law, which is itself a form of translation, is the major way in which modern societies have created a universal language to translate differences. But not all translation takes this form. When cultures meet, dislocations and even pathologies can result. Cultural translation can have a destructive moment producing reifications, racism, misunderstandings. It this therefore necessary to address the 'failures of translation and whether the result will be changes in self-understanding, in acts of resistance and empowerment' (Clifford 1997: 182–3). How to achieve reciprocity is the cosmopolitan challenge in cultural translation.

On the basis of the foregoing three kinds of cultural translation can be identified: translation of the Self and Other, local and global translations, and translations of the past and present. Translations of the first kind can be simply a matter of the translation of one culture into another; they may take the form of an adaptation or a partial or a wholesale borrowing. Such forms of translation in undifferentiated pre-modern societies generally assume a degree of sameness in the cultural and social presuppositions of the two cultures. With the advancement of civilization and the resulting encounter of cultures that are very different, a new mode of translation emerges based on a shared system of exchange based on a third language. Examples of this syncretism vary from a lingua franca to a common system of exchange to universalistic religions. In this case the integrity of the local culture is not necessarily in question and can even be protected since the native culture does not have to translate itself into the categories of the Other (see Assmann 1997; MacIntyre 1984). In the case of the second type of translation, the local culture is translated onto an overarching global or universal culture, which also functions as a third culture. Examples of this tendency towards universalization range from money and cartography to nationalizing projects to science and law. While this can lead to hegemonic forms of translation in which the local is obliterated or becoming unrecognizably transformed, the reverse can also happen in that the global can be translated into the local. This localization can take many forms, ranging from vernacularization to hybridization and indigenization. Finally, translations of past and present are a perpetual feature of all societies since the present is always defined by its relation to the past. Such translations may take the form of an 'invention' of the past, they may also take the form of a renunciation by which the past is translated into a new symbolic form. The nature of the translation – which may be nostalgic or revolutionary – will depend on the understanding of the present. The past can be translated into the shared present time of a given culture or into a globalized present.

The nature of translation thus entails a relation to otherness, to the universal, and to an origin which are all experienced in terms of distance and loss. Translation arises in the first instance because of the reality of cultural distance and plurality. Translations have existed since the beginning of civilization when the need to communicate with others arose but became intensified with modernity, which has brought about a culture of translatability in which all of culture has become translatable. In this translation is more than a medium of communication; it is the form in which communication takes place and expresses the modern condition of culture as communication. Rather than define modernity as a singular or a multiple condition it can be defined as a condition of translatability. Modernity is a condition that can arise within cultures as a cognitive form or structure in which the various parts of a culture are translated not into each other but also into a third language. The multiple forms of modernity are simply the diverse expressions of this orientation towards universal communicatability. Modernity is thus always in process depending on the nature of the particular forms of interaction, selection, combination, adaptation and processing of culture codes, frames of meaning, symbolic structures. While the capacity for translation has existed since the beginning of writing, it is only with modernity that it has become the dominant cultural form. Prior to modernity, translation served the function of communication and was not the basis of a given culture. The movement to multiplicity has become a more pronounced current in modernity today as the logic of translation has extended beyond the simple belief that everything can be translated into a universal or global culture to the recognition that every culture can translate itself and others.

Conclusion

The main thesis of this chapter has been that the concept of modernity must be related to the self-transformative capacity of society. I have related this to a radicalized notion of cultural translation. The argument is that what is often called multiple modernities is best seen as different modes of cultural translation. Modernity can arise anywhere; it is not a specific historical condition, but a mode of processing, or translating, culture. Modernity is a particular way of transmitting culture that transforms that which it takes over; it is not a culture of its own and therefore can take root anywhere at any time; this is because every translation is a transformation of both the subject and the object. Viewed in these terms there is a cosmopolitan dynamic to the project of modernity. This goes beyond arguments concerning the multiple nature of modernity and also the global diversity of cosmopolitan cultures to a position that places at the centre of historical awareness the interconnectivity of the world.

8 | Cosmopolitanism and European political community

Introduction

As noted in Chapters 3 and 4 there are cosmopolitan dimensions to the contemporary political community as reflected in a growing concern with global ethics, post-national expressions of citizenship and solidarity. The European transnationalization of the nation-state is one of the most important contexts for the crystallization of cosmopolitanism as a political reality. This is not to say that the European Union represents a cosmopolitan order, but that European integration in establishing the foundations of a new kind of polity, which can be roughly described as a post-sovereign state, is without doubt one of the most significant examples of what Ulrich Beck and Edgar Grande (2007) have called a 'cosmopolitanization' of social reality in Europe. The theoretical approach to cosmopolitanism in this book, as outlined in Chapter 2, stressed the processual nature of cosmopolitanism, which is not an end state or complete condition but a developmental logic. On this basis, the argument is not that the EU is a cosmopolitan polity, but that certain elements in the Europeanization of the nation-state have established preconditions for cosmopolitanism to be a significant dimension to contemporary European society.

In the terms of the four-fold conceptualization of cosmopolitanism discussed in Chapter 2, elements of all four are present to varying degrees: the relativization of national identity, the beginnings of a politics of recognition, critical and deliberative forms of culture, and signs of the emergence of a normative public culture. This is ultimately an empirical matter and needs to be examined in terms of, for instance, the increased degree to which people identify with, and express solidarity towards, people beyond the local and national to the wider world; changes in rights as a result of demands for the recognition of others; the impact of cosmopolitan values of care and hospitality on national politics; the impact of global events on national politics; the expansion of the global civil society movement and movements towards global co-operation.

It has been recognized for some time that the project of European integration has moved beyond purely market-based objectives. The social and cultural dimensions have now come to play an additional role beyond economic forms of integration. With this has come a new emphasis on diversity leading to a rethinking of the limits and possibility of European unity. The notion of unity has been challenged both on the political as well as on the cultural level as a result of increasing pluralization. Indeed, it appears to be the case that Europeanization is leading towards greater pluralization rather than a straightforward kind of unity such as that indicated by the notion of European integration.

Virtually every political order has had to deal with the problem of diversity. The existence of different groups with their own claims to political autonomy has been a challenge for many states and some have been more successful than others in recognizing the claims of competing groups. This has been particularly a problem for the European Union, which was initially an intergovernmental organization aimed at fostering the national interests of its members and pursuing limited economic integration. With its transformation into a post-sovereign political order, there have been unavoidable tensions between the pursuit of the national interests and the enhanced dynamic of the transnationalization of the nation-state. Until recently the EU has been relatively successful in achieving a balance between national interests and European integration. A kind of unity in diversity was reached as far as the relations between the individual states and the EU is concerned. Despite the failure to develop the Union into a fully fledged constitutional order, the existing level of integration may for the time being solve the problem of political diversity, but it leaves unresolved the problem of cultural diversity and political community. Is culture merely a matter of recognizing diversity or can there be also a shared public culture of a cosmopolitan nature? This is the topic of this chapter. My argument is that the European project needs to respond to new kinds of diversity which were largely absent in its foundation. Such forms of diversity extend beyond the older national communities to include social groups of all kinds, but specifically ethnic and minority groups. European societies today are being transformed by migration and from changed relations of cores and peripheries. As I argued in Chapter 5, this is a diversity that is not primarily cultural, but it is also social and one that has major political implications. The political or national diversity of Europe was easier to handle than these new kinds of diversity, which are intermeshed with inequality. It was a diversity that was primarily state or nation based. The new challenge of diversity is different. It is bound up with issues of social integration and citizenship and cannot be easily solved on an intergovernmental level. To this extent it is inextricably bound up with questions of rights and values and with anti-systemic challenges. The implications of cultural diversity go beyond purely cultural questions to pose entirely new political questions about the nature of political community, especially in times of increased civil unrest.

Conflicting visions of Europe

After five decades following its foundation we are witnessing a fundamental transformation in the European project. The implications of this are as yet not fully clear, but there are indications that the assumptions about the nature of political community that have prevailed until now are becoming increasingly inadequate. The EU was once a project aimed at the integration of states, but became in time a project aimed at the integration of peoples. The current situation of a much enlarged polity has opened the European political community to new interpretations. My argument is that the European project needs to be relaunched around a new idea in which political community is more central than market-based objectives. I will term this new conception a European cosmopolitan commonwealth. The main feature of this is a more inclusive conception of the European polity based on recognition and solidarity. I argue that there are two major challenges to be addressed: the recognition of diverse identities and the advancement of solidarity. Connecting both of these is an essentially social project addressed to the problem of social justice. The idea of a European cosmopolitan commonwealth is based on a social conception of the European project and one that recognizes that Europe today is not just multinational but also multiethnic. The overall implication of this is that there needs to be a stronger emphasis on Europe as a social and cultural project as opposed to an exclusively market-led project. A strengthening of the social basis of the EU will be an essential foundation for the strengthening of the EU as a political actor that can influence global politics in a cosmopolitan direction.

It is not unreasonable to conclude that the project of the transnationalization of the European nation-state has reached its limits. While the foreseeable future will probably see a consolidation of the legal framework of the EU, the rationale of European integration in terms of its identity and legitimacy can no longer be based on the existing models and modes of justification. In many ways the current crisis is a result of the fact that the EU has achieved its earlier systemic objectives without setting new ones. On the one side, the EU seeks to have a democratic mandate from its member states and from citizens and, on the other side, it aims to strengthen the supranational level of political governance and become an influential global player. The current situation, as illustrated by problems in democratic ratification to the Nice and Lisbon treaties, points to a contradiction in these goals and to the growing presence of anti-systemic forces.

At the present time there are three competing models of the European project. It would not be an exaggeration to speak of a clash of cultures, in the sense of a clash of different visions of what Europe is and where it is going. First there is a vision of Europe as a transnational suprastate; second, a vision of Europe as a post-national political community of rights; and third, in opposition to the previous two, a vision of Europe based on core values of peoplehood as embodied in both national and European traditions. By far the dominant vision of Europe is that associated with what might be called the official EU ideology: a vision of Europe that is primarily based on the political level of the state. In this dominant discourse Europe is a matter of the transnationalization of the nation-state by a post-sovereign suprastate whose main legitimation is that it is able to solve the problems that have beset the nation-state in an age of globalization. The EU is thus able to integrate the economies of its member states while protecting them from the wider global context. This is primarily a functional, if not a technocratic, legitimation and one that has been the principal focus of support among electorates. So long as it delivers the goods and achieves legitimacy through efficiency, it has the support of citizens. This concept of Europe has considerable appeal and can even command a degree of loyalty and identity. But its support basis, which is nationally variable, is relatively limited due to the predominance of domestic politics.

Competing with this official vision of Europe as an emerging transnational state are two other visions. One of these is a largely leftist position that sees Europe in terms of a political community based on rights within a post-national constitutional order. As best exemplified in the writings of Jürgen Habermas, the European project exhibits some signs of a post-national democracy based on the rights of the individual and a republican constitutional order (Habermas 2001a, 2001b). Rather than see Europeanization in terms of a transnationalization of the nation-state in the direction of a supranational state, an essentially civic conception of Europe is posited as the ideal. This vision of Europe is based on rights as opposed to efficiency. For Habermas a constitution is the expression of the political will of a people. Given the diversity of Europe, political community cannot be based on a substantive community of fate. What Europe therefore needs is a higher principle of identification beyond the national and which at the same time would be a framework for democracy to develop. This is a vision of Europe that is clearly highly pertinent to the challenges facing European societies in integrating diverse groups of peoples. Given the scale of human mobility within the EU, a rights-based conception of the political has a huge relevance (Eriksen 2005). While not entirely in opposition to the technocratic model of Europe, it does point to a democratization of the EU in the direction of a greater role for civil society. As a strongly normative model, it is not a vision of Europe that has found strong support among electorates. It has not succeeded in articulating a model of identity, other than the relatively thin identity of what Habermas (1998) has called a constitutional patriotism, that is an identity focused on the abstract principals of the constitution as opposed to substantive values of a people. The problem with this vision of Europe is that constitutions are not normally the basis of identification. The idea of a constitutional patriotism may not in fact be a genuinely European consciousness, but one that is largely based on German experience (Turner 2004). It is not self-evident that all European countries have renounced their national past in favour of a post-national identity.

In opposition to both the efficiency and rights-based visions of Europe is an alternative and more explicitly anti-systemic one that has considerable support among electorates. This is a vision of Europe based less on rights than on the core values of peoplehood. Such values are generally seen as embodied in national traditions, but it can also be embodied in the very idea of a European political heritage. In this view, which is often expressed in anti-European sentiments, the European project has lost its ability to connect with the core values of peoplehood, which include rights but also include a wider sphere of values such as those of solidarity and social justice. While often taking a nationalist and populist form, this defensive stance with regard to Europeanization can claim to represent an important tradition within the European political heritage. At the core of this is a social conception of society based on the values of solidarity and redistributive justice. This is generally associated with culturally specific conceptions of peoplehood, as defined in largely national categories.

These three competing visions of Europe with their respective emphasis on efficiency, rights and values are often overlapping. The rights-based model of Europe associated with Habermas makes certain assumptions about the nature of peoplehood. The official discourse of European identity associated with the EU often makes appeals to a vaguely defined notion of a European people based on a unity in diversity. But as visions of Europe they embody fairly distinct modes of legitimation and understandings of political community. None of these models is capable of providing a solution to the demands of the present day.

Efficiency can no longer be the only justification for the EU, which must devise different kinds of legitimation, which also cannot derive from the principle of subsidiary or purely regulatory policy-making. The expansion in the competences of the EU has unavoidably led to its politicization and to a questioning of its democratic basis. There is a widespread perceived lack of accountability, whether justified or not. In addition, there is a nascent fear of the social consequences of the liberalization of markets, a fear that is now increasingly associated with global markets. It is this that is more significant than the issue of the so-called democratic deficit. My thesis is that the social question is becoming more and more important and as it does there will be a deepening crisis of the European project. The three dominant visions of Europe will be unable to address this challenge due to their limited horizons and the failure to see that the social question of solidarity and social justice cannot be solved without the creation of an entirely new vision of a European society in the sense of a social conception of Europe. The three dominant visions tend to avoid this. The model of Europe favoured by the EU is one of political coordination of functions and has relatively little to say on questions of identity and solidarity. It is often associated, whether rightly or wrongly, with a neoliberal agenda. The rights model suffers from a more or less total neglect of issues of social justice, operating with a narrow rights-based view of the polity as a civic order. The social contextualization of political community is thus neglected. While more explicitly addressed to issues of social justice, a values-based defence of peoplehood fails to offer a robust vision for the future.

Four examples of the deepening crisis of European integration can be mentioned to illustrate these considerations: the 2005 constitutional crisis and the 2008 crisis of the ratification of the Lisbon Treaty, the rise of the extreme right, the French riots in 2005, and the continued controversy over Turkey's bid for EU membership. Lying at the core of these crises are major issues about social justice and which point to problems that are far-reaching and cannot be easily accommodated within the existing models and visions of Europe.

The momentous no votes in May 2005 when the French and Dutch voters overwhelmingly rejected the draft constitutional treaty marked a fundamental turning point in the history of the EU. It was the first hard choice to test the desirability of a post-national Europe. It was also the first major example of the masses revolting against the elites. It would be a mistake to see this as a straightforward endorsement of the nation-state and a rejection of the European project since the no vote was a product of a diverse coalition of interests that had little unity to it. Opposition to the draft constitution was the means for diverse interests to pursue their different goals and which even included the means to bring about the destruction of each other. Some of the main concerns that led to the no vote were social concerns relating to a perceived liberalization of markets and fears of large-scale immigration. A strong EU and a weaker role for national governments is simply not an attractive proposition for electorates accustomed to a long tradition of social securities and the stability of a strong national state. The appeal to legitimacy through efficiency is not enough when it comes to such choices. The Irish no vote on the ratification of the Lisbon treaty in 2008 further reinforced the unpopularity of a strengthening of central European authority and precipitated a major crisis of the efficiency model of Europeanization.

The rise of the extreme right throughout Europe, with some exceptions, is a product of social fears being channelled into political support for right-wing parties, whose support derives from social anxieties and fears. The extreme right have a foothold in many of the small Western European countries – Denmark, Belgium, Austria, the

Netherlands, Sweden and Norway – whose social models have been challenged by the wider cultural transformation of Europe, on the one side, and on the other by the steady decline of social democracy. Immigrants have been the obvious targets for these parties who have frequently been able to combine fears of immigration with anxieties over jobs and welfare. The Europe-wide trend to Third Way style politics has created space for such parties to exploit social fears. Such anxieties, combined with the perceived loss of national sovereignty and the changes in the nature of employment, are fertile ground for xenophobic currents. In other words, the transnationalization of the nation-state is occurring at the same time as the state is retreating from the social commitments it has been associated with. The proposed European constitution did little to address such concerns and seemingly was a continuation of the transnationalization of the nation-state. The consequence was the affirmation of nation and statehood.

Further examples of the social malaise of Europe are the riots in France in November 2005, when ethnic minority groups, mostly of North African background, reacted to the death of two Muslim youths in a French suburb. This was the event that provoked violent clashes with the police and involved burnings of some 9,000 cars and several public buildings. Widespread anger and resentment against poverty and marginalization against the circumstances in deprived working-class suburbs was the background to these events, which were quickly repeated in several other European countries. Although on a smaller scale than in France where a state of emergency was declared, in Germany, Spain, Belgium and the Netherlands there were also riots involving the burning of cars and buildings. It was not only resentment at high employment and social deprivation that played a role in the riots. The negative image of Islam in France and the popular view of the middle class that the French Muslin ghettos are hotbeds of Islamic militancy was an important factor in politicizing the Muslim youths to rebel against their social and cultural marginalization. The riots can be seen as symptomatic of a social malaise in Western European countries where a new kind of poverty and social marginalization is developing and in which migrants and ethnic communities are most likely to be based. It may be an exaggeration to say that the traditional class conflict has been replaced by a conflict of migrants versus citizens, but there is some truth to it as far as the most visible cleavages today are concerned.

The controversy over Turkey's bid for EU membership is a further illustration of the growing anxiety and uncertainty that has arisen around the European project. The resistance to Turkey is clearly linked to fears of immigration of large numbers of Turks. Already there are some 3.5 million Turks in EU countries, with the largest number in Germany. With a population of 70 million, many people fear the capacity of the EU in its current form to absorb such a large country which shares borders with some of the least stable parts of the Middle East.

These crises are linked. The marginalization of minorities, the growing appeal of the extreme right and the popular rejection of the draft constitution are linked. The mobilization of migrants and ethnic groups in France in 2005 was driven by the same underlying social forces that has led to the rise of the extreme right, namely the undermining of the social bonds by capitalism and the retreat of the state from the social. Turkey's bid for EU membership has been linked with the spectre of an Islamification of Europe, but the dominant fear is less this than the economic sustainability of a union that might be extended to include a significantly larger country with a different economic and demographic structure.

To appreciate the current situation attention must be given to the wider societal context. Two related factors can be commented on: the global context and the decline of the social democratic project. Although open markets for labour and capital are confined only to the EU area, the wider context of global markets is increasingly impacting on Europeanization, which is a process that interacts not only with the national but also with the global. It is possible to see Europeanization as an expression of globalization in the sense of a movement towards transnationalization. The success of the EU has been partly due to its ability to offer protection against global markets for its member states organized into a 'Fortress Europe'. The price of this has been a relatively small group of countries. The enlargement of the EU to 27, the uncertainty as to Turkey's eventual membership and the inclusion of other countries as well as the implications of the neighbourhood association relationships have led not just to a bigger EU but one that has less clear-cut borders. The EU itself is becoming more important as a global actor in what is becoming a multipolar world. The relation with Asia is already becoming more important. The UK government favours a larger EU with as much trade liberalization as possible. A likely scenario for the future is that this pragmatic vision of Europe as a free trade zone will prevail. If this is the case there is likely to be a deepening of the crisis discussed above, with popular opposition against the transnationalization of the nation-state and growing hostility to migrants and Islam in particular. But it is not inconceivable that the EU in its current form will be able to build a Fortress Europe, without undergoing major structural transformation. The draft constitutional treaty was itself an attempt to modify and clarify existing practices without any major change in direction. It was an attempt to reconcile the demands of the transnationalization of the state with the attempts to build a Fortress Europe offering minimal protection against globalization.

Already the European project is bereft of what it most needs, namely a social dimension. This has been increasingly apparent with the gradual turn to Third Way-style politics, on the one side, and on the other the transformation of capitalism into new and more flexible forms of work. The EU in its early decades was built on the foundations of industrial society and the forms of social solidarity it produced: trade unionism, social democratic parties, the traditional loyalties of class and nation. In combination with long-term demographic change, leading to a demographically older Europe and a more multiethnic Europe, changes to the nature of capitalism have far-reaching consequences. Against this background, it can be argued that the apparent crisis of the European project must address the double challenge of the rise of the extreme right and the marginalization of ethnic groups and migrants, for underlying both of these problems is a social malaise and crisis of values. This will require a new emphasis on solidarity which needs to be attached to an inclusive and more cosmopolitan vision of political community.

The problem of solidarity and social justice

Solidarity and social justice has not been fully recognized to be a new political context for the European project, which until now has been mostly bound up with economic and political integration. The challenge that migration and ethnic pluralism presents is not only a cultural problem, but a social one. Cultural integration without social integration does not produce lasting results.

It is of course true that European integration had a social dimension, but this has been limited to societal cohesion. The EU has not been very successful in creating a social model. The Social Charter, promoted by Jacques Delors, aimed to reflect the interests of workers as opposed to employers. In that sense it reflected a concern with social justice. In 1991 all EU member states, with the exception of the UK, signed the Charter of Fundamental Rights for Workers, which was the foundation of what has become known as the European Social Model (the UK signed in 1997). The main focus of this has been issues of employment and social policy. The context for its emergence in the 1990s was the challenge presented to Europe by globalization (Delanty and Rumford 2005: 107–13). A clarification of a European social model was supposed to be a basis for a European social identity.

The European Social Model has generally been seen as weak. National societies with their own traditions of solidarity have stronger social models. The European Social Model has not been successful in any terms in reversing the subordination of society to markets. The last 20 years have seen a Europe-wide shift from protective and redistributive forms of solidarity to competitive and market oriented ones. There is in effect no functionally effective model of society in the European project. As a policy area it is limited in scope and little more than rhetoric. The EU needs a new debate on its social model. It has the potential to place a concern with the social at the centre of Europeanization. However the problem is that the social model is generally interpreted as a means by which society can be organized by the state rather than seeing it as having potential to drive European transformation (Delanty and Rumford 2005: 106–7).

The limits of the idea of a European Social Model can be partly explained by contrasting it with the quite different notion of a European Model of Society, an idea with which it is often confused. While the idea of a European Social Model was primarily based on state policy towards society, the latter notion – popular for a time with the Delors Commission in the 1980s – suggested a wider vision of society and one that did not subordinate society to the market. So social cohesion and harmonization could be achieved by a mix of market and social policies. But at the end it is market regulation that has been dominant. The result has been the decline of solidarity on the European level.

There is an urgent need to revive this notion of a European Model of Society in different terms than the relatively narrow terms of a

social model. It is necessary in order to resist social and cultural fragmentation. The declining significance of the nation is only one aspect of
the consequences of the transnationalization of national societies. The
other side of the coin is the declining significance of class as a focus of
consciousness and political identification.

Many theorists – Claus Offe and Pierre Manent, for instance – who
are sceptical of the capacity of the EU to create forms of solidarity,
tend to look to the national state (Manent 2006). These criticisms are
justified and there is no doubt that national models are more effective,
but the critical point here is that this concerns only national social
models. While it is unlikely that the EU will succeed in creating a viable
social model in the sense of a welfare state, there is a chance that a
wider model of society can be initiated. This can only be possible on a
European level since the issues relevant to its creation require a wider
conception of the social than the national level is capable of articulating, even if in the final analysis it will be implanted by national
societies. In this context issues related to migration are highly pertinent. To articulate such a vision of society a debate on social values is
needed. This is why a perspective on rights alone is insufficient, however important rights are. Rights do not offer a vision for a society but
a means to enable liberty and justice.

When one looks at European society from the outside as opposed to
a view from a national standpoint, what is striking is the presence of
core values that have defined social and political struggles in the
modern era and which have been reflected in the modern national
state. Solidarity as associated with social justice is one of the most
characteristic features of European society and a stark contrast to
other parts of the world. It is in this context that the question can be
asked whether there are core European values that could be the basis
of a new European Model of Society. Despite the apparent absence of a
transnational European identity that unites all Europeans, there is
more commonality than is often thought. Of what does it consist?

One of the core European values is that of solidarity and a concern
with social justice. This is often overlooked in accounts of European
identity where the emphasis is on cultural differences as linked to
national and ethnically specific concepts of culture. This perspective
can be overlooked in views of cultural diversity that stress the sepa-
rateness of groups. The result is a neglect of the role of social values in
European modernity. Such values have a greater salience today as the

European project enters a new phase in which social issues have moved to the fore.

The tradition of social solidarity has been reflected in trade union-ism, social Catholicism, charity, trade unionism and many civil society movements. The very notion of solidarity derives from medieval Christian notions of a harmonic order. The later tradition of Christian charity and modern Christian social thought have promulgated social values. Early twentieth-century Catholic corporatism promoted the related notion of subsidiary, which was later to enter into the political vocabulary of European integration. In addition to the religious origins of subsidiarity the European political traditions of radical liberalism and socialism were critical in the development of a social agenda in modern politics. From its origins in socialism and the trade union movement, the modern welfare state emerged along with the rise of social democratic parties with their policies of redistributive justice.

A broad view of this would suggest that modernity was heavily influenced by the value of social justice. It is possible to see modernity as a process that has been shaped by the specific ways in which the state, market and civil society have interacted. A feature of the European political heritage is that this triple interaction did not allow for the rule of the market or the domination of the state over society. Due to social movements, class conflict and traditions of civic autonomy, European modernity was never entirely a product of the state tradition. The result of this has been a relatively strong concern with social justice and which can be related to resistance to both capitalism and the state. The specific form the state took in Europe was influenced by civil society and processes of democratization of which the most significant was the labour movement. The welfare state and the institutionalization of redistributive justice in the post-1945 period was in many ways a uniquely European achievement. Although criticized by the left for diffusing social content of its radical edge and in institutionalizing the class conflict, the inescapable fact is that the welfare state was the model by which European societies reduced social inequalities. The welfare state too was the model in which multiculturalism developed. Despite the trend towards economic lib-eralism and Third Way politics, the welfare state is far from in demise and it is arguably stronger than ever despite greater demands placed on it. But what has changed is that the social and economic founda-tions on which it was created have been eroded. The post-Second

World War project of creating full employment – which was not only a project of the social democratic left – has become obsolete and there have been major changes to the class structure, the nature of work as well as to capitalism. Full employment based on industrial manufacture is no longer a likely prospect and not a viable basis for social integration. Trade unions are no longer the principal actors in the public sphere and the traditional political cleavages of right and left have lost their capacity to shape politics, opening the political domain to many new actors.

The obsolescence of the older social democratic project does not mean the end of the welfare state and the project of bringing about a more inclusive kind of society. Pierre Bourdieu (2001, 2003) argued for the recreation of a radical project of the left on a European level and a new debate on capitalism. The chances that this might happen are slim and while there is no movement in the direction of a European welfare state for the reasons discussed earlier, it is not untimely for a debate to commence on the creation of a European Model of Society. The terms of such a debate will have to include the experiences of minorities, for migration has brought about a new context for issues of social justice. That is why the older social democratic project, which developed within exclusively national contexts, is ill-equipped for this purpose, but for the present there is no other viable model that could be the basis of an inclusive model of society. However there is room for some hope. Solidarity has been given specific mention in the EU's Charter of Fundamental Rights, which was adopted in Nice 2000 and incorporated into the Constitutional Treaty in 2004 (Ross 2007). The preamble states that the Union 'is founded on the indivisible, universal values of human dignity, freedom, equality and solidarity'. This is becoming more significant but still remains an elusive concept. However the basis exists for solidarity to be developed into something more substantial such as a European commonwealth.

My argument, in sum, is that solidarity needs to be linked to a cosmopolitan conception of political community. Already there is not an insignificant sense of an emerging European political community based on citizenship. However this is at best confined largely to rights and has not been connected with the long established tradition of solidarity and social justice that has been integral to national traditions of citizenship. The creation of a deeper kind of European political community will be an important challenge for the future of the European project.

The cosmopolitan implications of Europeanization

Modernity gave rise to the ideas of national sovereignty and national identity which today are being reshaped in an age of post-sovereign politics, capitalist crisis and multiple identities. The implications of this for political community are not altogether clear. The obstacles to a post-national European political community are certainly not insignificant and cannot be underestimated. The sovereign state was able to provide a basis for social solidarity, but nothing like this exists on a European level, despite the attempt of the EC to insert a commitment to solidarity in the new constitutional treaty. Such forms of national solidarity have been connected with historical legacies which often were formed out of revolution or an act of national liberation against foreign tyranny. For Europe as a whole there is nothing comparable to national myths of emancipation against occupation or tyranny. No nation-state was founded solely on a constitutional treaty and those whose national heritage did place a central value on the constitution – England in the seventeenth century, France and the United States in the eighteenth – had a prior history of struggle against tyranny.

What Europe lacks is an enemy against whom it can forge the kind of solidarity that has been the chief mark of the success of the nation-state. Another shortcoming is a common language. Unlike the nation-state which, with few exceptions (notably Belgium and Switzerland), was based on a common language, there is no common European language. It is not possible to speak of a European people in a way comparable, despite widespread pluralization, to national expressions of collective identity. As an institution created to facilitate the movement of goods, labour, capital and services, the EU does not invite strong forms of identity or a foundation for belonging. Mobility is not in itself a basis for the creation of identity or ties of belonging. The result is that a European identity does not exist in a sense comparable to national forms of identity. Instead we have the paradox of the attempt to create a European identity through the policy mechanisms of European integration, which must create what it believes it needs (Antonsich 2008).

The scenario sketched here is not particularly cosmopolitan, but it would be a hasty conclusion to assume the continued and unchallenged existence of national forms of political community. An argument can be made to avoid looking at Europeanization through the lens of the nation-state, which has not survived unscathed from more than five decades of European integration and the wider consequences of globalization. But more than this, Europeanization is not simply a project of the transnationalization of the nation-state leading towards the creation of a suprastate. Despite considerable differences of views, there is some agreement that whatever political form the EU is taking, it is a multi-levelled polity that does not supersede the nation-state but exists alongside it in constantly changing relations. Positions on this vary from Milward's argument that the EU rescued the nation-state by disburdening it of those functions it was ill-equipped for to the thesis of the EU as a regulatory form of statehood (Majone 1996; Milward 1993). An argument gaining increased support is a view of the EU as a largely problem-solving organization in which different levels of governance interact in a complex field involving many different political actors. This would suggest that neither the neo-federalist vision of a supranational federal Europe nor the traditional realist vision of a Europe of sovereign states capture the emerging reality of what Castells has aptly termed a network state (Castells 1998, 2000). For Castells the societal form of Europeanization is that of a horizontally connected network. Networks establish themselves in societies that have informational economies based on knowledge. In the network the local and the global are connected horizontally as opposed to vertically as in the nation-state. In this tendentially more open social order of the network, nation-states are less central since economic, cultural and political flows are multidirectional: space has been replaced by flows. This notion of a network captures some aspects of the dynamics of Europeanization as a multi-dimensional process in which different levels are connected horizontally. In these terms, then, Europeanization is more than a matter of different levels of governance as is suggested by the notions of subsidiarity and multi-levelled governance; it is also not merely a matter of cross-cutting horizontal links between different European societies, as Castells claims, but includes in addition to horizontal links between European societies, vertical links, and transversal links between European societies, the EU and the wider global context.

The EU is not simply eroding the nation-state, but is bringing about a transformation of statehood in Europe leading to new expressions of political community and the very idea of a polity that is neither exclusively national nor transnational. It is more accurate to see in the logic of Europeanization a process of societal transformation rather than the erosion of the nation-state, in other words the nation-state is not disappearing or becoming less important, as theorists such as Castells argue, but is being reshaped. One only has to consider the ways in which many of the Central and Eastern European member states who joined the EU in 2004 found in the EU a means of exercising national autonomy: the 'return to Europe' was a 'return to nationhood'. This example shows that participation in the European polity is not contrary to the national perspective. Nations are adjusting to Europeanization rather than being rendered obsolete.

The example of European citizenship illustrates this very well. EU citizenship was codified by the Maastricht Treaty in 1993 and has been the subject of a considerable amount of studies (see, for example, Eder and Giesen 2001; Hansen and Weil 2001; Lehning and Weale 1997; Weiner 1998). This was a significant departure from the model of European integration established by the founding Treaty of Rome in that for the first time it defined the EU in terms of a relation to the individual citizen. Although generally regarded as only a token citizenship and part of the EU's attempt at identity building, it put the EU on the road to a constitutional polity as opposed to an intergovernmental organization based on states and market-based mobility. No longer exclusively defined in terms of a relation of the state to the transnational or European level of governance, the EU became increasingly implicated in citizenship. The key point is that the creation of EU citizenship did not result in the demise of national citizenship but existed alongside it and indeed was predicated on the prior existence of national regimes of citizenship. But the national tradition did not go unchanged as a result of Europeanization. One of the most important aspects of the relation between Europeanization and citizenship and which arguably was the real legacy of the EU to citizenship was the capacity of the EU to bring about change on the national level. The EU has been an important agent in enhancing the social rights of workers. A significant legacy too has been in bringing about equality for women and more recently anti-discrimination for minorities (Meehan 1993). The Europeanization of citizenship has been achieved through legal implementation whereby national states change their legislation as a result of EU directives. Compared with the symbolic EU passport, it is this dimension of citizenship that accords with the republican tradition of a polity based on rights and has a certain resonance in the cosmopolitan tradition of equality based on personhood rather than peoplehood. This dimension of European citizenship is often ignored in discussions of European citizenship where the assumption is that citizenship must be defined in terms of a passport or a clearly codified bundle of rights underpinned by a clear set of values. The Europeanization of citizenship can be seen as a gradual process of convergence, although it is unlikely to lead to a situation of total uniformity due to the continued diversity of national traditions. All the indications point to the pluralism of legal regimes.

The Europeanization of the nation-state is not then leading towards the creation of a bigger version of the nation-state. The EU is not a suprastate for it is a post-sovereign power, a power whose sovereignty is shared. Neither the nation-state nor the EU are homogeneous, autonomous and sovereign entities. Most states have to reconcile their provider role with a regulatory role within not just a European environment but also a global one. Europeanization cannot be viewed as a simple defensive response to globalization, defending European nation-states against global forces. While there is no doubt that the EU has been very successful in constituting Europe as a powerful world trading region, it cannot be viewed as distinct from globalization (Rumford 2002). Globalization does not simply stop at the ever-changing borders of Europe, but exists within Europeanization. Indeed, Europeanization can be seen as a form of globalization in the sense of an enhanced connectivity between countries. Also as Kriesi *et al.* (2006) show, political reactions to economic and cultural globalization are increasingly becoming a significant feature of conflict in European countries and there are new groups of winners and losers as a result of cleavages arising out of the impact of globalization. They argue that it is in fact national government responses to these challenges that is the decisive feature of the changing political landscape.

Whatever Europeanization is, it is not a straightforward process of integration, and for this reason the term Europeanization is preferable to the notion of European integration. The term integration covers both social integration and system integration and, moreover, exists alongside a process of differentiation. To follow a well-known sociological argument, integration can be achieved through social and cultural processes (social institutions, education, values) and it can also be achieved through systemic processes (e.g. market, law, the state) (Habermas 1984; Lockwood 1964). Until now European integration has generally operated on the second level, with social integration relatively neglected but becoming more and more an issue today. However, the emphasis on social integration should not neglect the fact that, especially on a cross-national level, processes of integration do not simply produce a unified framework such as a new kind of society, for integration takes place alongside differentiation. This makes difficult any assumption about overall integration leading to convergence, as the logic of differentiation tends towards pluralization. There is of course considerable evidence that European societies are converging more and more in areas ranging from education, cost of living, family patterns, work etc. The point is that Europeanization cannot be understood in terms of a state- or EU-led project of 'integrating' society into a systemic framework. Many other forms of integration and differentiation are also unfolding, making Europeanization a multidimensional process.

Viewed in these terms a cosmopolitan approach is all the more timely to understand the emerging shape of Europe in which anti-systemic forces are also increasingly playing a role. European societies are linked in many ways to each other and to societies that lie beyond the European context. European societies are themselves internally diverse, as argued in Chapter 5. Indeed the very notion of society is problematical as John Urry and others have argued (Gane 2004; Urry 2000). All of this makes the notion of Europeanization highly complicated and one which cannot be understood in the functionalist logic of 'ever-closer union' or an entity that can be embodied in a constitutional form or a set of treaties. It is not implausible to assert that Europe is a social reality *sui generis* and exists in different forms. In a certain sense this requires 'abductive' reasoning rather than deductive or inductive reasoning (Bertillson 2004).[23] The cosmopolitan perspective aims to capture some of these levels of Europe as a new reality. Europe has a discursive existence in that one of the most significant expressions of Europeanization is in discourses about Europe. This points to a view of Europe as an emergent kind of reality based on repertoires of evaluation, modes of communication, imaginaries and cultural models. An interesting example of this was the debate over the proposed European Constitution from 2004 to 2008, a debate that entailed the articulation of new discourses of Europe and ones which have not yet reached a conclusion.

---

[23] Abduction refers to the epistemological approach of making sense of emerging patterns of social reality and can be contrasted to deduction and induction.

In many ways Europe has been symbolically constituted as an imaginary. Although this does not constitute a cultural community as such,
the symbolic form of Europe is growing, as is reflected in a proliferation
of EU cultural symbols and the beginnings of a political community
based on citizenship and rights, albeit one, as argued earlier, that is
emerging through the transformation of national societies. Symbolic
forms on their own are insignificant unless they are accompanied by
wider socio-cognitive structures, for people must be able to cognitively
imagine a social world for it to exist in a meaningful way. While many
critics – Cris Shore (2000, 2004) and Anthony Smith (1992) – claim this
is not possible for Europe, there is enough to suggest that Europe does
have less a cultural existence than a political one. Shore is undoubtedly
correct in arguing that the creation of awareness of cultural diversity
will not lead to the various identities fitting together harmoniously
simply because of the inevitable politicization that results when the
various tiers of loyalty become enmeshed in issues of power and sovereignty. The problem with Shore's critique is that it is based on a limited
view of cultural identity as a community of fate. Culture viewed as a
dynamic and creative process of imaginary signification suggests a very
different perspective. In this alternative and more communicative
understanding of culture the emphasis is on the construction of cultural
models in which, as Touraine (1977) has argued, a society creates itself
in battles over its 'historicity', that is struggles over how the social world
is to be organized. Europeanization has now reached the critical threshold of constituting itself through the articulation of a cultural model.
This cultural model is not manifest as a community of fate or an ethnos
in a sense comparable to the national community of the nation-state,
but it has become an increasing force in defining Europe.

One way to look at the cultural constitution of Europe, or cultural
Europeanization, is to see it in terms of a notion of public culture, as
opposed to being an ethnos, and having an essentially communicative
nature. The notion of public culture avoids the dualism of a cultural
versus a political conception of community. European public culture is
not prior to the political but is expressed in debates and has a discursive,
argumentative nature. The loss of markers of certainty in recent years
has led to an emphasis on a more communicative notion of culture. In
these terms it is possible to speak of European public culture reflecting
the beginnings of a European cultural model, in the sense of a shift in
cognition whereby Europe becomes a frame of reference that exists

alongside and often in tension with national frames of reference. This way of looking at the cultural question also avoids another dilemma, the 'thick' versus 'thin' conception of culture. Thus to an extent a European political community is discursively created in discourses about Europe. The notion of culture that underpins this is less a shared common culture than an interactive or discursive one. In the terms of the theory of cosmopolitanism proposed in this book we can say that the European and the national are not two separate domains of culture, with the latter 'thick' and the former 'thin'. The strengthening of the European as a cultural and political reference point is not at the cost of national identification since what is occurring is a transformation of the national by the European rather than the overcoming of the national. Europeanization can be found in a variety of developments which go beyond a narrowly defined model of transnationalization in the direction of a supranational level that exists above the national level with which it is in tension. It is possible to speak of the emergence of a European cultural model that shapes or structures new discursive frameworks. In these frameworks an emergent reality takes shape under conditions which are radically indeterminate. Europeanization is not then exclusively a state-led project, but a key feature is the transformative relation between the different aspects of the configuration of identities and actors which act on each other. The relation of the national to the transnational is more than one of co-existence. For as the various levels co-evolve as they do, something new, an emergent reality, is produced. So against the notion of European as a transnationalization of the nation based on a logic of integration, an alternative view is that the cultural significance of Europeanization rather consists in the creation of a cultural model that can be characterized in terms of cosmopolitanism. A cosmopolitan Europe is one in which the national and the global levels are mediated in a transformative way.

Cosmopolitan tendencies can also be demonstrated in changing identity patterns. There is now adequate empirical evidence of European identity as an identity that is not necessarily in competition with national or regional or ethnic identities, but an identity that can co-exist with other kinds of identity and with which it may have a reflexive relation (Herrmann *et al.* 2004). This is an important indicator of cosmopolitanism in so far as it suggests a reflexive relation between different identities with the national and the European existing in a relation of complementarity. The movement towards multiple and overlapping identities which includes a European level is, in principle, cosmopolitan in the additional sense of having an expanding horizon. An interesting example of this is the Europeanization of Turkish Islam, that is the tendency by which Islam in Turkey has become an agent of democratization as a result of its willingness to undergo change.

The cosmopolitan interpretation proposed in this chapter differs from both the post-national position, e.g. Habermas and the Euro-sceptical position that political community requires a solid foundation in traditions of nationhood. The objection against the post-national constitutional argument is that it demands too strong a test for post-national community to overcome the nation-state. Moreover, its assumption of an underlying 'European humanity' is not a basis for identification. In contrast, the cosmopolitan position put forward in this book would see European post-nationalism in more interactive terms as formed out of the interaction of multiple publics. Habermas's approach does not recognize the cosmopolitan currents within national cultures with the result that post-nationalism must form itself from outside the national in the renunciation of the nation-state. On the other side, the rejection of a post-national conception of a European political community on the grounds that it cannot compete with national traditions of identification leads to two unsatisfactory outcomes: either a techno-cratic vision of Europe as a matter of efficiency or an unrealistic retreat into a purely values-based notion of peoplehood. The cosmopolitan alternative is one that emphasizes public culture and the interaction of multiple publics rather than an exclusive focus on the Europeanization of the nation-state. This is not merely a normative vision of an alter-native course for the European project, but one that is reflected in current societal trends wherein immanent possibilities of transcendence can be discerned.

It has been increasingly recognized that there has been a major cultural reorientation of Europeanization in the direction less of a state or market than of a post-national political community (Balibar 2004; Beck and Grande 2007; Berezin and Schain 2003; Delanty and Rumford 2005; Eder and Giesen 2001; Soysal 1994). Beck and Grande (2007) specifically highlight the cosmopolitanism of Europeanization. This is a not a clearly defined project but one marked by contradictions, ambivalences and paradoxes. Unlike the purely Habermasian constitutional conception of cosmopolitanism, Beck and Grande emphasize a rooted cosmopolitanism that does not seek to polarize the national and the European. This is based on two principles: a principle of the recognition of diversity and a commitment to procedural norms. In their view the strengthening of democracy alone will not create cosmopolitanism; instead what is needed is cosmopolitan integration, which has both internal and external dimensions, but with the internal being the most important for the moment (on the external dimension see Chapter 9).

The kind of cosmopolitan that is suggested by Beck and Grande is more than the simple co-existence of difference, in the sense of multiculturalism. The relation is not one of co-existence because the various levels co-evolve leading to the creation of an emergent reality. For this reason a cosmopolitan perspective entails the recognition of the transformative dimension of societal encounters. The cross-fertilization that occurs when societies come into contact leads an intensification of pluralization as well as convergence. This is more than what is indicated by the term unity in diversity, since this slogan refers to a supposed co-existence of nation-states and regions within the broader arena of the EU. The point is rather that the integration of societies also entails processes of differentiation, which is not a contrary logic but is more than a situation in which different cultural traditions simple achieve a balance. This corresponds closely to Beck and Grande's notion of cosmopolitan integration. The convergence of European societies does not mean uniformity, but it could signal greater pluralization. This is one reason Europeanization is a process that is not easy to democratize, since it tends to produce difference and with this comes more points of view and contentious demands (see Trenz and Eder 2004).

This situation of polyvocality accords with the present situation of questioning certainty and taken-for-granted assumptions that is more generally a feature of the present era. This cultural shift has now become apparent in a questioning of the foundations of the EU polity and the values that define the European heritage. The nation-state is no longer the unquestioned bedrock of the EU even though it is far from being renounced. It is possible to see the current situation as one of a reflexive integration, as Eriksen (2005) argues. This accords with the cosmopolitan perspective, but does not fully capture the implications of European transformation in the wider global context, since the national, the European and the global levels interact with each other. Europeanization resembles more closely the model of cosmopolitanism: a multi-levelled and uni-linear process by which nation-states and societal systems are themselves transformed by a movement that is not entirely to be explained by an EU masterplan.

Rather than looking at conflicts between primordial national cultures and a supranational European order of governance, a more differentiated analysis is required. This must include the recognition of increased societal interpenetration, the Europeanization of the state and legal transformation, the rise of a European public space, socio-cognitive and cultural change. European societies are now more and more interconnected due to factors that are not explained by Europeanization but by global processes such as global markets, Americanization, developments in popular culture such as sport, travel and communications. Aside from transversal societal interpenetration, there is no denying the tremendous impact of the EU on the state and above all on national law. As a result of the superiority of EU law over national law, no national society can claim to be autonomous. This is what is meant by the notion of the post-sovereign state. The European space has become a part of political communication in most European states. This is the informal space of the public sphere that is becoming one of the most important expressions of the public. Where the two previously mentioned expressions of Europeanization take effect on the macro level of societal change, this occurs on the *meso* level of social movements and of various organizations based on interests ranging from economic to cultural to political. It is the polyvocal and polycentric space of civil society and political communication and is a constitutive element of the public sphere, the Europeanness of which has been recently the subject of much discussion (Fossum and Schlesinger 2007). A European public sphere exists in two senses. There are Europeanized public spheres, in the sense of a Europanization of nationally based public spheres, as is reflected for instance in greater awareness of other countries. However it is also possible to speak of a European public space in the strong sense of cross-connecting public spheres. This is expressed in common debates arising out of the cross-fertilization of discourses. Though there is not a common European public sphere, there are Europe-wide discourses which are more than reporting and awareness of issues in other countries.

Europeanization entails new forms of self-understanding that are not measurable by opinions or approval rates. Although such surveys do provide indicative information on societal trends, they do not measure longitudinal change and above all do not measure changes in socio-cognitive and cultural models, that is, the emergence of new frames by which social reality is constructed. Such framing processes are not reducible to individual identities. There is no denying the emergence of a European master frame. Although, it is unlikely that this will replace national frames, it is becoming increasingly more and more articulated. Such a master frame could be seen as expressed in terms of a growing consciousness of what European cultures have in common as opposed to a frame that transcends these national cultures. We can term this cosmopolitan to the degree to which it is expressed in debates and disputes, for instance, over the meaning and direction of European integration.

Conclusion

Major challenges to Europeanization remain despite the great deal of change that has already taken place on the cultural as well as on the institutional level. The EU needs to articulate the core values of the European democratic heritage in a more explicit way. Central to this heritage is the concern with social justice and solidarity. Rather than compete with the nation-state in a fruitless search for a new supranational identity that will transcend and negate national identities, the only alternative for the EU is to give substance to what can be termed cosmopolitan commonwealth based on solidarities. The current danger is that xenophobic currents will capture the social space. Already there is much to suggest that the rise in right-wing populist parties with xenophobic programmes lies in the ability of these parties to gain significant electoral support on the basis of social concerns. However, xenophobic parties are not themselves the problem – instead, they are the result of a problem, namely the relative failure of European democracy to address social issues.

9 | Europe as a borderland

Introduction

Chapter 8 looked at the internal transformation of the European political community with a view to establishing the limits and possibilities for cosmopolitanism. My concern in this chapter is to look beyond the internal dynamics of change to consider the implications of the enlargement of the EU, especially since the fifth enlargement in 2004, for cosmopolitanism. The chapter is chiefly concerned with the changing relation of centres and peripheries and the wider geopolitical shape of Europe. This will be explored largely around the question of the kinds of borders that are being created in the periphery as a result of Europeanization. My argument is that there is now a changed relation between the periphery and the core, with the periphery emerging from marginalization to become a site of cosmopolitan re-bordering. However, the true significance of the relation of core to periphery is more inter-civilizational than a matter of the transnationalization of the nation-state. Europe is not simply a product of Western civilization, but is an inter-civilizational constellation in which many civilizational heritages interact. This suggests a post-Western conception of Europe as a field of interacting cultures, rather than a unity or an integrated geopolitical entity that can be understood along the lines of nation-state formation or by reference to a primary origin.

In the terms of critical cosmopolitanism developed in this book, the most important aspect here is the interactive dimension as opposed to the logic of integration. This is not to suggest that integration is not important, but that other logics of development are also taking place. Europeanization can be looked at in terms of three logics of development: as a process of integration, as a process of polarization and as a process of pluralization. By integration is generally understood a movement towards greater unity and homogenization, a transcendence of the particular. In the case of the enlargement process, this is reflected in a

Westernization of Central and Eastern Europe, suggesting reduced agency in the Central and Eastern countries where there has been, allegedly, the imposition of a Western model. Such a view would see the fifth enlargement as simply the continuation of earlier ones and the EU, as a result, is more integrated without significant cultural issues being produced. Europeanization is often seen in quite different terms as involving less integration than polarization, in particular a polarization of West and East, which are allegedly culturally different and based on different cultural mentalities. This suggests a fragile and divided Europe in which EU-led systemic forms of integration collide with nationally based traditions of social integration. It signals resistance from the periphery to the core.

Now, while evidence for both of these perspectives can be found, an alternative and more cosmopolitan view is that the cultural logic of Europeanization results in pluralization. In this chapter, I argue that the enlargement process on the whole confirms this view of the opening up of new and varied worlds. By cultural pluralization is meant: hybridization (the mixing of different cultures, hyphenated identities, cultural borrowing, appropriation and adaptation but without an overall unity, cosmopolitanism in the sense of limited cultural unity through diversity and post-national identifications), differentiation (less polarization than societal variation and cultural diversity) and cosmopolitanism (the reshaping of identities around normative concepts of justice and rights). A perspective that emphasizes pluralization as opposed to homogenization or polarization suggests that the enlargement of the EU has resulted in an internal transformation of both West and East as opposed to one that is externally determined. I argue that the enlargement process has affirmed a sense of Europe as diverse – a borderland – rather than a single entity, and that such pluralization does not only produce polarization but immanent possibilities of transformation. In addition to internal transformation, there has also been an external transformation in the relation of the EU to the rest of the world. This position avoids an emphasis on either consensus or conflict, opening up possibilities for immanent transcendence through the interaction of different cultural and political traditions in light of the consciousness of global ethics. The cosmopolitan perspective suggests, too, that there is likely to be greater uncertainty as to what the cultural identity of Europe is: European identity is more diluted but also open to more interpretations. For this reason, I dispute the view that Europe is becoming a new fortress formed in opposed to another an external Other and propose instead the notion of a borderland as a more appropriate evocation of a geopolitical system in which openness and closure, inclusion and exclusion, are mutually implicated processes.

The first section of the chapter looks at how the question of borders should be conceptualized under the conditions of globalization and the argument is made that borders, both internal and external, are becoming more and more networked systems rather than fixed lines that separate an inside from an outside. In the second section this is applied to Europe's ever-changing external border. Here it is argued that the external border of Europe should be understood in terms of re-territorialization and this border, which is closer to a borderland, challenges conventional understandings of the border as a fixed line of demarcation between an inside and an outside. The third section develops the argument that Europe is best understood as a borderland and one that is today taking an increasingly post-Western form.[24] In the final section, the implications of this are discussed with regard to the significance of the periphery and the wider context of the enlargement of the EU.

Theorizing borders

Borders are not natural but products of human agency.[25] Although many borders appear natural where geographical criteria are invoked, few borders are determined by geography alone. As a political design, borders are like society itself; they are human artefacts. As societies change, so too does the border. Borders are reflections of the cultural life of a society as much of the territorial boundaries of the society. Definitions of insiders and outsiders are often related to the border, which is also the site of memories and collective identities (Meinhof 2002; Wilson and Donnan 1998). Both memories and identities, themselves related, require boundaries, and borders are one such system of

---

[24] The notion of a Europe as a borderland can be attributed to Balibar (2004). The notion of a post-Western Europe was originally formulated in Delanty, G. 2003. 'The Making of a Post-Western Europe: A Civilizational Analysis', *Thesis Eleven* 72: 8–24.

[25] Some of the following is based on ideas originally published Delanty, G. 2006. 'Borders in a Changing Europe: An Analysis of Recent Trends', *Comparative European Politics* 4 (2): 183–202.

classification and with symbolic and cognitive implications. Different kinds of societies have different conceptions of their borders, some viewing it as open and expanding and others as historically determined by geography. A border is a line of demarcation and as such it creates a distinction between an inside and an outside. But borders are also institutions. Geography, politics and culture are combined in different ways in elaborating and sustaining the lines of the distinction (Coakley 1982; Paasi 1996). Borders are social, political and cultural; they are social in that they are a way of organizing societies, political in that they are sites of conflicts, and cultural in the way they embody memories and symbolic representations.

Borders have been seen as military and physical frontiers and as symbolic boundaries. Anthropological studies on borders have noted the role of the boundary as a marker of the collective identity of social groups (Barth 1969; Cohen 1985; Paasi 1996). Boundaries provide identities with the basic forms of classification in order to distinguish Self and Other (see Newman and Paasi 1998). Borders thus have a symbolic role in marking the boundaries of the 'we group'. As a mechanism for establishing difference, the border functions to express the identity of the group rather than being a structure that inheres in geography. In such cases, the physical nature of the border is relatively unimportant. But borders also serve military and economic functions. They serve as buffer zones, lines of demarcation between centres and peripheries. Borders became more and more central to societal organization with modernity. In earlier ages, the borders of empires were relatively open and were fixed only at those points where they were weak, as in the case of Hadrian's Wall or the Great Wall of China. Although the Roman Empire is often portrayed as having rigid borders, it was not based on a geographically defined area and the imperial *limes* were a line of declining control rather than a frontier (Whittaker 2000).

While the distinction between border and frontier is at best fuzzy, there is a general tendency to view the border between states as a frontier, a fixed line of demarcation. Borders refer to the outer part or an edge of a territory, while frontiers refer to the border between two countries (see Newman 2004). In EU law the concept of frontier tends to be the term used to refer to the borders between states, while the external borders are simply called borders (Müller-Graff 1998: 15). Frontiers in Europe thus suggest limits of zones, the end of a territory rather than points of transition. The term was originally a military zone where the enemy was engaged (Anderson 1996: 9). This does not mean that frontiers cannot expand. A famous example of an expanding frontier is the notion of the 'limitless western frontier' of the United States. Frederick Turner, in a classic work on the American western frontier, noted how the American national character was shaped in the nineteenth century with the expanding western frontier extending the American nation (Turner 1921). The frontier mentality was one of an open horizon of limitless opportunities that was conducive to a liberal national character. In this case the western frontier was an example of an open border, until the threshold of closure was finally reached in the twentieth century. This sense of the frontier is closer to the idea of the border as zone of potential expansion for a territory that lacks closure.

John Ruggie (1995), in an influential article, has argued that with modernity a territorial politics arose in which sovereignty was invested in a single political authority, the sovereign state. This led to borders having an added significance in maintaining the new territoriality. Ruggie draws attention to the cognitive function of space in shaping modern politics. He argues modern territoriality was characterized by a politics of perspectivism by which a single spatial perspective was established and centred on the state which possessed this single perspective. Ruggie's point is that this has now been replaced by a 'multi-perspectival polity', of which in his estimation the EU is the best example.

Borders can be usefully conceptualized in terms of two sets of distinctions: hard or soft and open versus closed borders. Hard borders generally are military or political borders that separate states or state systems. The Iron Curtain – while also having powerful symbolic resonances – is an example of a hard border in which political and military functions combined to create a border that was impermeable and rigid in separating two global blocs for forty years. An example of a soft border would be symbolic borders, such as those that often mark the boundaries between ethnic groups. The notion of a 'clash of civilizations', which is often held to replace Cold War hard borders, is also a pertinent example – even if it is more a product of ideology than of political analysis – of a soft border defined in cultural terms. Hard borders are thus closer to frontiers. This leads to the second point. Borders can be open or closed. Hard borders such as the borders of states will tend to be on the whole closed, although this will vary depending on the various aspects of the border. In terms of immigration policy this may vary from openness to closure, but in terms of territory on the whole this will be relatively closed. As nation-states consolidated in the late nineteenth century, hard borders became more central to the codification of citizenship. Passports were introduced to regulate the movement of populations across borders (Torpey 2000). The passport is an example of a hard border, which distinguishes citizens from non-citizens.

The relation between open and closed borders is particularly relevant to the EU and to the general context of Europeanization. The EU itself is an example of a state system that while having relatively hard borders does not have fixed borders that are closed – they have been opened on four occasions in recent times. The political borders of the EU are not final frontiers, but open to new states. The EU member states themselves have more open borders than non-EU states and within the category of EU member states, the Schengen countries have more open borders than those that are not within this agreement. Examples of open borders pertaining to culturally defined groups might be the Council of Europe, which is more open than the EU and which has what can be called a soft definition of Europe as a cultural and geographical area that includes more than forty countries. While there are many examples of soft cultural categories that are open, examples of soft borders that are closed to outsiders are some kinds of ethnic groups and religious orders (not everyone can become Japanese or Jewish while it is possible to become French and British by naturalization and, by conversion, Islamic and Catholic).

The distinctions indicated by the polarities of hard/soft and open/ closed should not be seen in normative terms, as 'good' in the sense of more inclusive versus 'bad' in the sense of more exclusive borders. War zones, for instance, are often defined by soft criteria with relatively open borders. Detention camps and refugee camps are clearly hard as opposed to culturally defined, but increasingly they are more likely to be open than territorially closed in the sense that they are mobile and thus flexible with respect to territory. Another example of hard but open borders are so-called 'smart borders', open points of access within closed and hard borders. On the other hand, the collapse of states and their borders leads to the proliferation of ethnic enclaves, often with violent results as the examples of the collapse of the Yugoslavian Federation and Iraq illustrate. As David Newman has argued, borders are becoming more and more permeable than in the past, but they remain the hard lines which determine the territorial limits of the state and the citizenship of those included within it (Newman 2004). New and less visible borders are emerging in the changing landscape of post-territorial space and in these often liminal spaces new kinds of exclusion are emerging. For instance in the UK, as in many countries, the declining significance of the traditional borders between states has been met with a move to create high-tech identity cards involving biometric data and the increased use of profiling. Such new technologies of identification and surveillance can be as an alternative to the passport, and will entail less closed – and also less visible – i.e. 'smart borders' for the global elite. But for many people these will be more regulated and controlled borders. There is clearly an increase in hard borders that take open forms, in the sense of structures and regimes that are not constrained by territory. The rise in disciplinary zones, such as detention camps for refugees, for instance, is an example of more open/ hard zones. Guantanamo Bay is the paradigmatic instance of such developments. The scale of such developments cannot be easily assessed in quantitative terms and the observations made here are intended to draw attention to the global increase in non-territorial forms of hard borders. The changing logic of openness/closure is vividly reflected in developments related to soft borders.

With regard to Europe and the process of Europeanization the question of borders clearly concerns changing relations between, on the one side, the internal borders of Europe and, on the other side, the external borders of Europe. With regard to internal borders the assumption can be made that there is a movement towards more open borders within the countries of the EU and its associated states, such as Norway – a member of the Schengen group of states but not an EU member state – and Switzerland. The argument can furthermore be made that in the past Europe's internal borders between states were largely hard and relatively closed borders and that – with the exception of the Iron Curtain – Europe's external borders were soft and relatively open to changing circumstances. Notwithstanding this hard frontier, even within the EU the outer border was fairly open to expansion, as the various enlargements of the EU illustrate. Today, in contrast, the internal borders of Europe are becoming more open and in some cases there is an indication of a move towards soft borders. Some dramatic examples of this are the opening of the border between North and South Cyprus and the easing of security on the border between the

Republic of Ireland and Northern Ireland. The point can also be illustrated by reference to the borders between France and Germany, which today have ceased to be war zones. The borders that demarcate European countries are now mostly devoid of any military significance and have also lost their function as trading zones; to varying degrees they are now reduced to policing functions.

While this movement is clearly occurring, there is another, but less clear-cut development in the direction of a hardening of the external border. It would be tempting to argue that the former hard/closed border that separated the nation-states of Europe is being transferred to the outer border of the EU and that Europe is becoming, like the United States, a fortress. There is a general change in the nature and function of borders in Europe. Europe's external borders are not simply replicating national borders, despite the obvious fact that the EU is spending more and more money on border controls. One of the major impacts on it – as well as on internal borders – is the global context. Moreover, internal borders are not simply becoming more open in the sense of becoming more inclusive. What is occurring is re-territorialization whereby old borders overlap with new and less visible ones, such as increased policing and security checks, leading to a networked border system in which inside and outside are less clear-cut.

Europe and its borders

For several centuries now the question has been asked where the borders of Europe lie. This question was once posed in terms of a civilizational notion of the unity of European civilization and concerned the relationship between culture and geography. Cultural concepts of Europe as Christian or as a civilization based on Rome and Athens were thus translated into geographical terms, such as the notion of a continent or a western landmass separated from Asia by territorial markers, ranging from rivers, mountains to seas. Depending on the purpose for which it was intended, and this of course was determined by political motives on the part of various groups, the definition oscillated from the cultural to the geographical. Imperial notions were thus used to define Europe. What differed only was the empire in question. The Romanovs invoked a territorial concept of Europe that included Russia, while the Catholic Church and the Christian states of the Middle Ages and

Renaissance era invoked a cultural concept of Europe to underline the political distinction between a westward expanding Islamic East and a belligerent Christian West. For Napoleon, Europe was a limitless frontier that could be shaped in the image of the French Empire and which could push back the frontiers of the Ottoman Empire. But the idea of Europe always remained primarily a cultural concept to describe a civilization that could never be reduced to territory and rarely coincided for long with political designs (Delanty 1995). In the age of the Great Powers, but going back to the early inter-state system since it emerged after 1648, the reality of this European civilization was not Christendom or the vaguely and ever-shifting geographical limits of whatever was termed Europe: it was a Europe of (largely imperial) states. The idea of Europe was merely a residual category that served as a cultural reference point, but had little geopolitical weight.

In the twentieth century, especially since 1945, purely cultural definitions of Europe gave way to stronger political definitions. First, there was the Cold War, which defined Europe in geopolitical terms as the eastern frontier of the United States and a very much truncated Western Europe emerged, bereft of much of the historical centre of what had been European civilization. In this redefinition and reconfiguration of the borders of Europe, Europe was subordinated to the West and to American leadership. Second, the rise of the European Union since the Treaty of Rome (1957) led slowly to an economic and political conception of Europe that was no longer defined in terms of nations. It was only with the consolidation of the European Union as a transnational polity in the last two decades since the Maastricht Treaty (1993) that the political definition of Europe took predominance over other definitions. Until then it appeared to be the case that the cultural and the geographical dimensions had faded into the background. This was because in the age of the nation-state that was the basis of the European Union in its formative period, from the 1950s to the mid 1980s, geographical borders were largely a matter of national borders and the Cold War set the wider geopolitical limits of Europe. Partly discredited as a result of the totalitarianism of the first half of the twentieth century and partly because of the overwhelming appeal of American popular culture, questions of European cultural identity were not centre stage (De Grazia 2005). Of course the relative weakness of a cultural idea of Europe did not mean that the border did not have a cultural dimension; it meant that the cultural presuppositions of the border reflected wider geopolitical considerations.

This has changed today for several reasons. There is some evidence that American social and cultural influence in Europe has waned and there is a growing confidence in certain aspects of what can be called European society in terms of a way of life and a distinctive social model. Most importantly because with the end of the Cold War, the hard border that separated Europe from the East has disappeared and the EU has expanded into potentially open, though not limitless, territory. In addition to these reasons, there is the wider global context of post-territorial globalization and developments in the direction of re-territorialization. In sum, the political, social and cultural presuppositions of the twentieth century are no longer valid when it comes to an analysis of the border in Europe today. The result of this is that the border takes on a new significance.

So the current situation is marked by the return of the border on a European scale at precisely the same time as the borders of the nation-state are being challenged by global processes. With the return of the cultural question of the meaning of Europe, inevitably the border too takes on a cultural dimension. It is obvious that today Europe cannot be defined by settled political criteria anymore than it can be defined by traditional cultural or geographical aspects. Since the enlargement process and the constitutional debate on the ongoing transnationalization of the state, the EU is no longer a clearly defined economic and administrative organization and nor has it become a state contained by settled territorial limits. The EU's constitutive units, its member states, too have been transformed both by the progressive movement towards the transnationalization of the state and by wider processes of globalization. In this situation then the question of borders takes on a new significance. Of the many aspects of borders in Europe today is the centrality of the cultural dimension, which can be viewed, like Europeanization itself, as an open process characterized by moments of closure.

My argument is that the border is becoming increasingly shaped by the global context and that it is characterized by alternating hard and soft forms. It is not possible to define the border in Europe as a hard border, as reflected in the notion of a Fortress Europe whereby hard national borders are simply transferred to the European level, but it is also not possible to define it as soft border, as in the notion of Europe as a culturally defined area that is essentially open. The border is a process rather than a fixed line and is constituted in new and changing relations between cores and peripheries and is the site of political contestations where power and culture interact. With the growing importance of the global context, Europe's external border takes on a post-imperial form whereby inside and outside are not clearly delineated.

The border has long marked the rise of modernity and the geopolitical system of nation-states that it brought into existence. Although these units are still with us, they have been considerably diminished, at least within Europe, insofar as they are defined with respect to their borders. Borders are no longer dividing lines akin to the traditional frontier in the sense of a line demarcating one state from another; they have become considerably weakened and are more diffuse, often sites of overlapping communities and regions. This is also the case with respect to the external relation of Europe to the wider world. The border is a networked and fluid process rather than a fixed line and is constituted in new and changing relations between cores and peripheries. Europeanization has neither eliminated borders nor created a new external frontier. New kinds of borders are taking shape in the European space.

Borders in Europe can be seen as influenced by three major forces: internal developments relating to national borders, the rise of a European transnational state system in which an external European border has been created, and the wider global context. The global context is becoming more and more important in the shaping of borders today. The tendency until now is to concentrate on the national and EU borders, but these borders do not take shape independently of global developments such as the new kinds of borders produced by global markets and transnational movements of various kinds such as mobile borders, networks, liminal zones and invisible borders.

Following Urry (2002: 40–9) and Mol and Law (1994), global space can be seen in terms of regions, networks and flows. Regions refer to the space of bounded societies; networks refer to relational constancy between components; and flows refer neither to boundaries nor networks but movement and process. Much of global space can be conceptualized as flows and thus suggests a notion of territory as fluid rather than spatially fixed. But networks, too, are central to global space, as Castells (2000) and Urry (2000, 2002) have claimed. As Walters (2006) has argued, there is a new system of borders taking shape in Europe around transport networks whereby 'the entire road transportation system becomes a kind of networked border. The border transforms into a mobile, non-contiguous zone materializing at the very surface of the truck and every place it stops' (Walters 2006: 196). Clearly these notions have implications for Europeanization as a process that entails major re-scaling of borders. Conventional conceptions of the internal and external borders of Europe tend to remain on the level of a notion of regional space, neglecting these new kinds of space, which should be seen as a re-territorialization of space in which policing is often central. Thus Canada and the US are moving customs and immigration inspections away from the borders and the USA Patriot Act has created a category of 'trusted travellers' who through electronic identification can quickly get through security checks. The resulting 'smart borders' occur within layered levels of policing at land, sea and air ports of entry (Andreas 2003: 98).

   In addition to these new borders, which are generally products of re-territorialization, there is also the increasing salience of the 'imperial' *limes*, the border as a diminishing zone of control over which the centre loses control of the periphery. This border is less a new European version of what Webb (1952) called the 'Great Frontier'; rather it is the zone of semi-peripheries, which in earlier times were buffer zones but today are borderlands. In the terms of Hardt and Negri (2000), this aspect of 'Empire' is a feature of states in the present day: 'In contrast to imperialism, Empire establishes no territorial centre of power and does not rely on fixed boundaries or barriers. It is a decentred and deterritorialized apparatus of rule that progressively incorporates the entire global realm within its open, expanding frontier' (Hardt and Negri 2000: xii). It designates a territorial situation in which there is a general weakening of the border beyond the areas directly controlled by the centre, where the periphery fades into an outer borderland. Although developed with reference to globalization and US hegemony, the point has more applications and, with some qualifications, is relevant to Europeanization, which due to its expanding logic has brought into play a range of forces operating within and alongside its outer border.[26] The logic of territory that is characteristic of the global context can be summed up as one that entails changing relations of interiority and exteriority beyond modern territoriality. In these new borders it is more difficult to conceptualize borders as an edge or frontier

---

[26] For a critique of the notion of empire see Rumford (2008: Chapter 6).

separating one region from another – exterior space for the outside is often within the inside. Instead it is more helpful to see the border in terms of networks of cross-cutting lines on inclusion and exclusion. For example, the Central and Eastern European countries who have recently joined the EU provide a policing role to the rest of the EU, which provides subsidies for such policing controls. However, the border that they establish is not a straightforward frontier but a more complicated mechanism of control involving policing, economic and military functions. In general the emphasis is less on the military and more on the policing (Andreas 2003). It needs also to be considered that the EU is not a state as such and does not have the traditional monopoly over the means of violence that Max Weber believed to be the defining feature of the state. Another example of the changing relation of the centre to the periphery in Europe is the emerging of a new kind of governance whereby the EU expands its governance beyond the member states to neighbouring regions. Such regions, while being formally excluded from legal membership, are also not excluded but are part of a networked political system in which 'fuzzy borders' come into play (Lavenex 2004: 681). Examples of this are accession association (for potential members), neighbourhood association (Mediterranean and Near Eastern countries), development co-operation (Africa and wider Asian countries) and various kinds of co-operation (see Lawson 2003). In this context it makes little sense to speak of borders exclusively in terms of the legal boundaries of a given territory. Stein Rokkan referred to these relations of cores and peripheries as a European system of cleavages (Rokkan 1999, cited in Eder 2006).

The emerging European border is not taking the shape of a frontier in a sense comparable to the frontiers of the nation-state. The European external border, despite the context of securitization, is not a clear-cut line of demarcation that is capable of dividing an inside from an outside. The East–West axis – roughly from the Baltic to the Adriatic – which is one of the main contours of the external border, has often been called a faultline to indicate the reality of a complicated borderland that has been the site of many conflicts (Delanty 1996; Dingsdale 2000; Meinhof 2002). It is not a settled 'Great Frontier', but has shifted many times in history. From the inter-war period to the post-Cold War period to the present enlargement, this axis witnessed continuous repositioning (Delanty and Rumford 2005: 33). The present contours of the EU do not amount to a final frontier.

There is no point at which an Iron Curtain is reached. The southern frontier – the North–South border – has become more salient (Suarez-Navaz 2004), but it is not a straightforward replacement of the East–West axis. As noted above, the EU's system of governance now extends beyond EU space to the wider south and entails relations that are neither exclusively open nor closed. Despite an increased budget for such purposes, the EU does not possess a security and defence policy comparable to nation-states and cannot therefore maintain closed and hard borders. The capacity of nation-states to do this is greater, but as argued earlier is also not unlimited. The EU's external border and its internal national borders are inter-locking and multi-perspectival. Some borders have disappeared altogether, such as the border between East and West Germany, while others have become relaxed, such as the Greek–Turkish border between North and South Cyprus, and alongside these developments new borders have arisen, such as the border between the Czech Republic and Slovakia, and the now more rigid border between Hungary and Romania. In this latter case a fairly flexible border, in effect a borderland, has now become the site of the external border of the EU. The incorporation of the Baltic countries into the EU has led to the isolation of Kalingrad, which has become a Russian enclave not directly connected to the Russian Federation, the result of this being the creation of a corridor connecting the two territories through Lithuania and Belarus. Enclaves of a different nature are protectorates, such as Kosovo, which has become a new kind of European space. And of course many EU member states are colonial powers with borders extending far beyond Europe into the wider world (see Böröcz and Sarkar 2005).

So it can be established that the EU's external border is a complicated mosaic of borders, including changing national borders, but it is also inter-continental. There are also the prospects of further enlargement with the result that the borders of Europe will be extended further eastwards and will, with the eventual though as yet uncertain incorporation of Turkey, include parts of Asia. Where then does Europe end? It is evident from this that the outer border of Europe is an expanding one, that is in principle limitless. In the event of the eventual incorporation of Turkey the spatial distinction of Europe and Asia will be further diluted. The evidence of history – the ever-shifting North–South axis that has defined the East–West border – is that Europe's borders, especially its Eastern ones, are mobile and not written in geography. There is nothing guaranteed by either geography or culture that the

Bosporus will be a closed frontier. Europe's borders not only lack permanency, but are also porous. It was the very permeability of the Austro-Hungarian border in the summer of 1989 that eventually led to the break-up of the communist state system. In this case the border marked the site of an opening in Europe out of which a new European spatial configuration emerged in the following years. It is therefore difficult to see how the notion of bounded Europe can be meaningfully related to the current situation of constant re-bordering, expanding lines and changing relations of interiority and exteriority. This situation underlines the notion of the border as a networked process rather than a fixed structure.

The previous discussion has presupposed a modality of space as regional, with the emphasis being on territoriality. But as noted above, space is also organized as networks and as flows. Such forms of space are present within European space and have implications for the European border. Before considering these expressions of space on the European level, a few more remarks can be made on regional space. Schengen is an example of a regional bloc operating within the EU and associated countries in which internal borders have been largely abolished. It is too an example of an internal division within Europe in that the bloc of member states constitutes a border with the rest of the EU. Europe's borders are differentiated and variable and, as the case of Schengen illustrates, designed to encourage mobility (see Hassner 2002; Rumford 2006b). It is possible to see the field of Europe as made up of different 'Europes'. In addition to the previously discussed Old Europe (the major Western nation-states) versus a New Europe (largely post-communist countries) – with a Core Europe emerging within Old Europe – there are the older geopolitical spatial configurations, such as Central Europe and East Central Europe. Other relevant examples are mega-regional blocs, such as Nordic Europe, Iberia and the TransAlpine region (Keating 1998). Europe is not then spatially or territorially unified as the notion of Fortress Europe suggests, but is a field of differences in which symbolic battles continue to be fought on the multiple sites of the numerous borders that constitute it. Borders exist not on the edge of the territory of the state, but in numerous points within and beyond it.

This has led many critics to comment on Europe as a mosaic of differences which are not bounded. Massimo Cacciari thus describes Europe as an archipelago of spaces connected by various links (Cacciari 1997). He argues Europe is a network of differences, a mosaic of overlapping and connecting diversities. There is no overarching or underlying unity, only connections. This notion of Europe is clearly different from the vision of a fortress in which space is bounded by an outer frontier. More systematic applications of the notion of a network are to be found in the work of Castells and Sassen. Castells sees Europeanization as organized along the lines of a network with multiple connections between different spatial points (Castells 1998). In this view, cities, regions and states are connected vertically and horizontally in new kinds of governance. While Castells stresses the political opportunities networks offer for the mobilization of democratic projects, Sassen is more conscious of the wider global context of global markets whose expansion creates new kinds of space and movements (Sassen 1996, 2001).

It is for this reason that the global context must be considered in any discussion of European borders. The European context cannot be disconnected from the wider global context, as is the case in most discussions of Europeanization. This is particularly pertinent with respect to networks, which are not contained within Europe but interconnect with the wider world (Delanty and Rumford 2005: 132–3). The relation between Europe and the world is blurred when it comes to networked space since it is the nature of the kinds of borders related to networks that they do not take the same form as regional space. This is not to suggest that networks are open structures and that the global world is radically borderless, as is often suggested by the so-called hyperglobalist position. Global networks and flows produce borders and also produce new kinds of closed systems as well as new kinds of hierarchies (Preyer and Bos 2001; Sassen 2001). For example, networks produce lines of demarcation between different networks and also between the spaces that are not networked, spaces in which exclusion is more likely to be high. It is a striking feature of current patterns of territorialization that these spaces can be found in national space, within cities, in abandoned territories, in rural hinterlands. In other words, networks and flows produces less visible borders and ones that are manifest in social fragmentation.

The relevant point is that globalization operates within Europeanization as much as outside it. Globalization does not stop at the frontiers of the EU, where a different logic commences on which an integrated Europe is built. The argument advanced here is that the external context of globalization has a major influence on borders in

Europe, on both national and European space. In this view the internal and external must be seen as connected in multiple ways. A single example of this is the importance of cross-border co-operation, both within EU countries and between EU and non-European partnerships. As O'Dowd has argued, such examples illustrate the ambiguous and contradictory nature of borders in Europe (Anderson *et al.* 2003; O'Dowd 2002).

One way in which to conceptualize the European border in a manner that is more in tune with the different modalities of space and discontinuous relations of territory and borders is the notion of a borderland (see Delanty and Rumford 2005: 131–4). This is a new spatiality in which discontinuities are more significant than a simple dividing line, as in a frontier defining the edge of a given territory. The significance of the notion of the borderland is that it captures much of the reality of European space on borders, where inside and outside are not easily separated. According to Balibar (2004: 219) Europe is itself a borderland. This may be taking the notion too far, for the networked space and the space of flows does not eliminate closed borders and hard frontiers, which continue to operate. What the notion of borderlands calls into question, however, is the notion of Europeanization as a project that is comparable to nation-state formation in which territorial closure is the basis of the identity of the polity. This is not compatible with the consolidation of multiple centres and geopolitical spatial patterns within Europe and multidirectional movements. In sum, any clear-cut separation of the European and non-European must be questioned as a result of the various dynamics of openness and closure identified in the foregoing.

The idea of a post-Western Europe

Europe is increasingly taking a post-Western shape. Until now, as discussed in Chapter 8, one of the cosmopolitan features of the European project was the steady development of a post-national/post-sovereign polity whereby the sovereign national state had to share its sovereignty with other levels of governance, which included regions and the EU itself. While this remains a feature of contemporary Europe, there is a more far-reaching cosmopolitan development apparent here that goes beyond issues of governance. The reshaping of Europe since the end of communism and the enlargement of the EU, the prospect of the inclusion of much of the former Yugoslavia and possibly Turkey's eventual membership, suggests a change in the identity of Europe in the direction of a multiple constellation of regions. This is more than a geopolitical shift; it is also a shift in cultural self-understanding. Europe today is no longer a Western enclave centred around the core founding states. The earlier EU was largely determined by the circumstances of its birth in the reconciliation of France and Germany. It was a Europe centred on the Rhine and the historical territory of the Carolingian Empire with the Elbe and Danube marking its outer eastern limits. As noted earlier, the addition of other countries to this did not change the basic shape of this civilizational current; it was a Europe based on the Western heritage of Latin Christendom, the Enlightenment, democracy and the free-market economy. The exception was Greece, whose claim to the European heritage was not based on Christianity but classical antiquity. The Western nature of post-war Europe was consolidated in the twentieth century with the rise of the United States.

What we are witnessing today is the emergence of different civilizational heritages. These do not so much make redundant or challenge the Western heritage but add to it. Europe's cosmopolitanism derives from the richness of its civilizational heritages. Until now the dominant approach has been to emphasize the diversity of Europe in terms of its nations. Indeed, this is the main meaning of the term 'unity in diversity', which has come to be the principal statement of its cultural and political identity. This is a unity defined in terms of the diversity of national cultural and political traditions. A broader and more cosmopolitan view of the transformation of Europe suggests an inter-civilizational perspective since the shape Europe is now assuming is one that is determined by both its civilizational context and, related to this, different routes to modernity. An inter-civilizational perspective, as opposed to a state-centric approach, is suggested by the enlargement of the EU into areas of the continent that have had different experiences of modernity. The case of Central Europe is one such example of an inter-civilizational heritage, which while being part of the Western European heritage has also been shaped by its proximity to Eastern and Western Europe. In the case of Eastern Central Europe – where the emphasis shifts to the Eastern orientation – this inter-civilizational dimension is much more significant, for the region has been considerably influenced by Russia and by the wider Euro-Asian borderland. The notion of borderlands is relevant here in the context of inter-civilizational zones of overlapping identities, heritages and experiences of modernity. Of relevance, too, is the emerging identity of what is increasingly being termed the Euro-Balkan region. While the recent enlargement of the EU has tended to emphasize Central and Eastern Europe, the South-eastern region is another part of the European civilizational constellation. Much of this region has been influenced by the Ottoman tradition and thus suggests the relevance of the inter-civilizational dimension, which in this case is less 'Eastern' than 'Southern'. At the present, only Slovenia is a member of the EU, but this is a complicated case since arguably Slovenia belongs more to *Mitteleuropa* than to the Euro-Balkan region (see Vidar and Delanty 2008).

While Slovenia might be considered to be somewhere 'in-between' *Mitteleuropa* and the Balkans, the case of Romania and Bulgaria are particularly interesting examples of the inter-civilizational nature of Europe. Unlike the countries that make up Central Europe, in the stricter sense of the term, Romania and Bulgaria were products of the Eastern Roman Empire. Especially in Romania, the culture of the Byzantine Empire made its impact, as did the Ottoman tradition and, of course, these countries later fell within the orbit of Russia. The cultural specificity of these countries is not one that can be accounted for exclusively in terms of national trajectories. As discussed in Chapter 7, the civilizational shaping of the modern nation-state is much in evidence in terms of the model of modernity adopted and in societal structures and identities (Arnason 2003).

From a historical sociological perspective, the emerging shape of Europe is perhaps understood as deriving from three basic configurations, which constitute 'three Europes': a Western Europe, a Central Eastern Europe, and a South-eastern Europe. Of these, the latter is the most problematic. In a classic essay, Scüzs (1988) argued that Europe consists of three geopolitical units, which were formed out of the East–West divide: a Western 'Carolingian' Europe, a Central Eastern Europe, and an Eastern Europe, which has been closely linked with Russia and has no clear-cut eastern frontier. The fate of Europe was determined by these three historic regions. There can be little doubt that it was the first one that was decisive in shaping the European legacy, which Scüzs claimed was characterized by a synthesis of diverse elements that were assembled out of the prior disintegration of the older imperial structures. With the partial incorporation of some of the eastern region into what might now be called Central Eastern Europe, the notion of an

Eastern Europe might be redefined to include the southern sphere of Europe. In any case, it seems incontrovertible that the old East versus West division of European history must now be modified to one that is more sensitive to the diversity of the Central and Eastern regions (see also Delanty 1995; Halecki 1962). The notion of 'three historical' Europes needs to be redefined to take into account the fact that all three variants included relations to a wider civilizational area: Western Europe includes the wider colonial context; Central Eastern Europe includes the engagement with Russia and the wider Slavic dimension; and South-eastern Europe includes within it the Ottoman, Byzantine and Slavic heritages. All three were shaped by many common strands – the Roman Empire, Judeo-Christianity in both its Latin and Greek forms – suggesting a hyphenated notion of civilization as a plural phenomenon.

In emphasizing the civilizational sources of contemporary Europe, my aim is neither to exaggerate these differences nor to suggest that what we have is some kind of a clash of civilizations. In this respect, I refute the Huntington thesis that the eastern borders of Europe are zones of civilizational clashes. The seductiveness of the thesis is in part due to a core of truth in the argument: the post-1989 world is not exclusively determined by the older political ideologies, and civilizational factors are playing themselves out in different ways. The error of the argument is to see civilizational differences only in terms of conflicts. My argument is rather to see the civilizational background to contemporary Europe as a source of its diversity where, rather than clashes, we can see signs of mutual cooperation. Moreover, Huntington's thesis is false in that there is no evidence of civilizational clashes or conflicts of a cultural nature as far as the enlargement of the EU is concerned. With the single exception of the Balkans, the integration of post-1989 Europe – from German unification to post-communist transition, to the enlargement of the EU – has been remarkably peaceful. The case of ethnic cleansing in the Balkans can be seen as a product of the collapse of the state rather than as resulting from a primordial cultural conflict.

Looking at Europe as a whole, it may be suggested that Europe is steadily moving eastwards towards the Black Sea. The new axis is less that of the Baltic and Adriatic than the Baltic and the Black Sea. The notion of a post-Western Europe is intended to capture the spirit of this movement. Indicated by the term is a multiple kind of Europe, consisting of many heritages and experiences with modernity. Some of these are older than the Western tradition and are coming to play a role in the making of Europe today in ways that cannot be reduced to a simple notion of a clash of cultures. The notion of a post-Western Europe is also intended to indicate a reflexive relation in the identity of Europe as no longer exclusively determined by the relation with the United States. This does not mean anti-Americanism, for on the contrary many Central and Eastern European countries – notably Poland and the Czech Republic – are strongly pro-US; rather it points to a more self-problematized identity and one that does not have the same kind of self-assurance that it had until about ten years ago.

The periphery considered

On the basis of the foregoing argument concerning the emergence of a post-Western Europe in which the inter-civilizational dynamic is an important but neglected dimension, I would like to clarify the question of the periphery and its relation to the core. Obviously a periphery can be understood only in relation to a core. In the case of the European core and peripheries, I am arguing that the relation of the core to the periphery is multidimensional and evolving, and that it cannot therefore be easily reduced to a one-dimensional notion of the domination of the periphery by the core. My second thesis is that there is a general shift to the periphery, largely as a result of Europeanization, but partly as a consequence of globalization. Clearly the core still dominates, if not the periphery, at least the EU as a whole. The core Western countries – Germany, France, the UK – are the largest and most powerful economies in Europe and among the most powerful in the world, and the terms of EU membership were not open to much negotiation. Notwithstanding these obvious objections, the point is not that the periphery is not disadvantaged or that it now stands in a relation of equality, but that a more complex relationship has emerged as far as power and marginality are concerned.

A feature of the eastern enlargement of the EU is the incorporation of countries that were once on the margins of Europe and many of which had been in a subordinate status with respect to the major European powers. It is also noteworthy that many of these are small countries – the Baltic states, Slovenia, the Czech Republic, Slovakia, Hungary, Cyprus, Malta – and those that are territorially relatively large, such as Bulgaria, are demographically small and traditionally peripheral. Poland, with a population of *c.*30 million, is an exception, as is possibly Romania, with a not insignificant population of 22 million, but both have traditionally been peripheral. Aside from the question of Turkey, the next wave of accession countries will be those in the Balkans: Serbia, Croatia, Bosnia Herzegovina. Constituting what German historians once called an 'in-between Europe' (*Zwischeneuropa*), these countries experienced marginalization for much of the modern history of Europe and in many cases were subjugated by the totalitarian states, East and West. Emerging out of this background, participation in the EU offers many advantages. A longer view of history will place the current transformation of Central and Eastern Europe in the context of the re-invention of political modernity.

It is arguably the case that the smaller European countries have benefited from EU membership. That is certainly the case in Ireland. Since joining in 1973, it has been a major beneficiary. While the rapid economic growth that Ireland has experienced since the early 1990s has been due to many factors, EU membership has played a major role in economic recovery. Greece and Portugal, although not experiencing the same economic take-off, have benefited too. It is far too soon to assess the implications for the recently joined countries, but there is enough evidence to suggest that the triple transition to democracy, market society and national autonomy has been relatively successful. In the case of German–Polish relations, while some of the old asymmetries have reappeared, Spohn (2003: 137) has commented that these have crystallized in new forms: the Europeanization of the German economy and Polish economic growth have weakened the older core–periphery dynamic and the nationalistic forces have lost their power. Furthermore, the EU itself has been an important lever of democratization in applicant countries, as is evidenced by the example of the rapid democratization of Turkey and, in recent years, Bulgaria and Romania.

In political terms, the EU is now significantly different in that the large number of small countries have changed the balance of power. This inevitably leads to a different kind of relation between the core and periphery. The pre-1989 EU did not experience any challenges from the small countries of the periphery, represented by Ireland, Greece and Portugal. The smaller founding countries – Belgium, Luxembourg and the Netherlands – were relatively prosperous and part of the core. This was also true of Denmark and later the Nordic countries. Until the 1990s, the EU was largely shaped by the dynamic of the core countries while today an entirely different dynamic is emerging. The crisis of the constitutional treaty in 2005 and the current hiatus is an indication of a growing uncertainty in the political identity of a union of 27 members with the prospect of more to come. The project of deepening European integration socio-economically and politically was premised on a smaller group of countries with similar levels of socio-economic development. The societies of Central and Eastern Europe have put the brakes on deepening, but have not arrested the further development of, Europeanization, which is currently re-adjusting to what can be viewed as the encounter with different models of modernity, some of which, as argued above, are related to civilizational contexts.

For the first time, the core countries have found themselves challenged by the encroachment of the periphery. Fears of increased immigration from Central and Eastern Europe have been at the forefront of most countries' politics and in several cases have led to a reorientation in political support for the mainstream parties, often benefiting the extreme right. But in many cases large-scale migration, where it has occurred, has not resulted in significant challenges. In Ireland, for instance, the 2006 census reports that there are over 400,000 non-nationals resident in the country, making migrants about 10 per cent of the population. Polish immigration is a major part of this. It has been estimated that up to one million migrants from the newly joined EU countries, the vast majority being Poles, migrated to the UK since 2004. What is particularly significant is that about half this number have already left the UK, suggesting that post-enlargement migration is multidirectional and non-permanent (Pollard *et al.* 2008). A pattern is emerging by which European migration is multidirectional, with migrants moving from east to west on a non-permanent basis. Europe is moving towards a situation in which the periphery is already located within the core and where there is no hard, fast distinction between core and periphery.

With the gradual incorporation of the periphery into the core, the periphery does not disappear. Rather new peripheries emerge. This is already the case with regard to the division that is now becoming evident between the countries that have joined the EU and those that remain outside. Although the older term 'Eastern Europe' is now losing its meaning in that it does not refer to a specific regional entity, the functional equivalent is taking shape with countries further to the east – such as Moldova, Belarus and Ukraine – and to the south-east – such as the Balkan countries. Relations between cores and peripheries are also being redefined based on new kinds of power relations around energy supplies, as the example of gas pipelines illustrates. Another example is the recent case of the alignment of Poland and the Czech Republic with the United States in allowing the construction of missile defence installations directed at Russia.

What this suggests is that the core–periphery distinction is no longer the only model available for understanding marginality and patterns of growth and change in Europe today. Europeanization and globalization have, to an extent, eroded the core–periphery distinction insofar as this was a simple polarity. Rumford has argued that globalization reshapes the hierarchal framework within which the core–periphery relation has been constituted (Rumford 2002). What has emerged instead is a more complicated spatial structure which could be understood in terms of the notion of a network; a structure that is more polycentric and which entails a basic pluralization of the core–periphery relation. In this sense, then, the older core–periphery relation is one that was more a feature of the pre-1989 model of Western Europe, while the advent of a post-Western Europe signals a different spatial dynamic in which cosmopolitan orientations are present.

Conclusion

The enhanced momentum of Europeanization has neither eliminated borders nor created a new external frontier. It would be tempting to suggest that the appropriate metaphor for the European border, and of Europe itself, is not the fortress, but the Deleuzean notion of a post-imperial 'Empire' as theorized by Hardt and Negri (2000): the lack of frontiers and a movement that has no territorial limits and which is not spearheaded by a state-led project. While this concept can only be applied to Europe with some qualifications, it captures something close to an open conception of space that has multiple dimensions and, in addition, has resonances in European history in the Roman *limes*, that is, the expanding borders of the empire. However, caution must be exercised in such notions of a tendentially open Europe. The emphasis on mobility that has been a feature of recent social theory has led to an over-emphasis on the disappearance of borders. Borders are not disappearing, but taking new forms and as they do so new kinds of exclusion are generated (Paasi 2005; Rumford 2006b, 2008).

I have emphasized the wider global context for an understanding of the new kinds of borders that are taking shape in European space.

The global, the national and the European dimensions interact to produce a complex field of borders and re-bordering out of which emerges hard and soft borders, open and closed ones and with different degrees of spatial intensity by which regions, networks and flows operate. The changing nature of the border has implications for identity, since the system of classifications the border establishes provides identities with means of distinguishing insiders from outsiders. The emerging networked border challenges existing notions of a European identity built upon foundational assumptions about territory and culture. Inside/outside relations are not easily distinguished either in the domains of space or identity/culture. The borders that constitute the basic structures of space and culture are shaped in dynamics of openness and closure which are particularly evident in the current phase of Europeanization. Only by recognizing the global context in which this unfolds can such dynamics be linked to a project of identity building that does not make the error of trying to reproduce on the European level the logic of nation-state building. As argued throughout this book, political community has both a particularistic dimension, which is reflected in nation-states and the republican political heritage, and an open and more cosmopolitan dimension. Most forms of political community embody both of these dimensions, with the national community being more inclined in the direction of particularity. Transnational entities such as the EU, while reflecting particularity, are more open to cosmopolitan inclusion. However, this does not occur without conflict and without a constant reinterpretation of the particularity.

While it cannot be said that the European periphery is now on an equal footing with the core, the relation has changed to the advantage of the periphery. In this respect, one can be reminded of James Joyce's cosmopolitan intention to 'Europeanize Hibernia and Hibernicize Europe'. Taking Ireland as a metaphor for the periphery, the task has contemporary relevance in drawing attention to the need for Europe to find a mutually positive relationship between the core and the periphery. The next and final chapter will look at cosmopolitan orientations in the wider global context of a post-Western world.

10 | *Conclusion: inter-cultural dialogue in a post-Western world*

One of the main aims of this book has been to argue for the contemporary relevance of cosmopolitanism as a normative critique of globalization. This is not to set up a basic dichotomy of cosmopolitanism and globalization, since globalization is multi-faceted and cosmopolitanism, too, is highly varied. Some of the most important expressions of cosmopolitanism emerged in the context of major social transformations of an epochal and global nature: the eastward expansion of the Hellenistic Empire of Alexander the Great; the rise Confucian cosmopolitanism in the fifth to second centuries BCE during the period of the Warring States; the revival of the cosmopolitan idea in Europe in the seventeenth and eighteenth centuries as a result of the crisis of European absolutism; the re-emergence of cosmopolitanism in the aftermath of the Second World War; and, in the present day, the resurgence of cosmopolitanism with the post-sovereign state, the worldwide transformation of political community and the global crisis of capitalism. Rather than view cosmopolitanism as an alternative to globalization or to the nation-state – as some kind of utopian ideal of an alternative social and political order – the approach set out in this book has been to stress the embedded nature of cosmopolitanism in current societal developments. Globalization creates a world of enhanced connections, but does not itself constitute the cosmopolitan condition; instead it establishes preconditions for its emergence. Its capacity for transcendence is immanent rather than external. Chris Rumford has put the cosmopolitan challenge succinctly: 'Cosmopolitanism requires us to recognise that we are all positioned simultaneously as outsiders and insiders, as individuals and group members, as Self and Other, as local and global. Cosmopolitanism is about relativizing our place within the global frame, positioning ourselves in relation to multiple communities, crossing and re-crossing territorial and community borders' (Rumford 2008: 14).

I have attempted to place at the core of cosmopolitan analysis the concept of immanent transcendence. The idea of immanent transcendence, which derives from the Hegelian Marxism legacy and is integral to the tradition of critical theory, entails self-transformation as the source of social and political change. The critical normative critique of the present must be grounded in the analysis of concretely existing phenomena, which provide the immanent terms of social transformation. Thus where globalization generally invokes an externally induced notion of social change, such as the global market, cosmopolitanism understood in terms of immanent transcendence refers to an internally induced social change whereby societies and social agents undergo transformation in their moral and political self-understanding as they respond to global challenges. In this view, then, globalization rather provides the external preconditions for the emergence of cosmopolitanism. Nowhere is this more apparent than today with the crisis of the moral and political order of capitalism. This is a crisis that extends beyond capitalism to a crisis in social values. Although it would be premature to claim cosmopolitanism is likely to be the result of what is now finally the end of the ideology of the free market, the essential preconditions for cosmopolitanism to become a 'thick' as opposed to a 'thin' consciousness are in evidence: demands for the transnational regulation of capitalism in the name of justice and responsibility complement calls for global approaches to environmental destruction and the recognition of human rights. Underlying these new demands is an assertion of the priority of social considerations of solidarity. As argued in Chapter 3, these concerns are not abstract invocations of universalistic principles and nor do they require the surpassing of the state, but are concrete expressions of everyday experiences and are not nationally specific.

In addition to the internal or immanent dimension, I have also stressed the interactive dimension of cosmopolitanism. It is here that the critical thrust of cosmopolitanism can be linked to a dialogic or communicative understanding of critique.[27] Cosmopolitanism implied in this approach refers to a condition in which cultures undergo

---

[27] For a similar approach see Kurasawa (2004) who also writes of dialogical cosmopolitanism. However I have stressed to a greater extent a notion of critique based on immanent transcendence and which extends beyond the self-critique of Western modernity.

transformation in light of the encounter with the Other. This can take different forms, ranging from the soft forms of multiculturalism to major reorientations in self-understanding in light of global principles or re-evaluations of cultural heritage and identity as a result of inter-cultural communication. But what is noteworthy here is the interactive dimension to the fusion of horizons, which is not a condition of external agency or a self-transcending subjectivity, but an orientation that develops out of the interplay of Self, Other and World relations. In this context it is worth recalling that G. H. Mead, who provided the basis of the sociological theory of symbolic interactionism, argued that the nature of human interaction leads to an 'international mindedness' that results from the globally connected society of the day (Mead 1934: 270–1).

For this reason, the conception of cosmopolitanism developed in this book has avoided the reduction of cosmopolitanism to either diversity or to transnationalism since neither diversity itself nor globality guarantee a critical reorientation in values. As argued in Chapter 2, this essentially transformative condition is best seen as a process rather than a zero-sum condition in which cosmopolitanism is either present or absent. It is a process in which interactive dynamics are particularly important, whether the interaction of whole societies, ethnic or culturally defined groups or civilizations. But more than this, it is also necessary to demonstrate that, arising out of the encounter or interaction with the Other, moral and political evaluation occurs. Without this reflective and critical moment, cosmopolitanism is not a relevant category. So cosmopolitanism is ultimately more than a condi-tion of connectivity requiring a balancing of differences or an accom-modation of difference; it is a constructive process of creating new ways of thinking and acting. The implication of this for cosmopolitan analysis is that cosmopolitanism is expressed less in particular indivi-duals – cosmopolitans as opposed to locals – than in collective identity processes, such as debates, narratives, forms of cognition, networks of communication, ethical and political principles. Viewed in such terms, cosmopolitanism is thus not a 'thin' identity than can be compared against a strong and more rooted 'thick' national identity, and nor is it a belief; it is rather an orientation that emerges out of social relations and discursive transformation.

To sum up the central argument, cosmopolitan orientations take at least four main forms. They can simply take the form of a limited capacity for the relativization of one's own culture or identity in light of the encounter with the Other, but they can also take a stronger form in the positive recognition of the Other. An example of the first is the soft cosmopolitanism of consumer-driven cultural appropriation or the example discussed in Chapter 1 of the Enlightenment's self-critique through the engagement with the East, while the second is illustrated in programmes of cultural awareness and liberal multiculturalism with its typical emphasis on tolerance and rights. The motto of the 2008 Olympics in Beijing, 'One World, One Dream', reflected this dimension of the cosmopolitan spirit as the recognition of unity without a corresponding fusion of horizons. A yet stronger form of cosmopolitanism is to be found in a mutual critical evaluation whereby the interacting cultures undergo transformation and approach a fusion of horizons. In this case, it is not a matter of a native or main culture accommodating another one, as in the previous instance, or recognizing that we all live in one world, but a case of mutual learning and recognition of diversity whereby no one culture is prioritized. This can be regarded as an intensified form of cosmopolitan self-awareness in that the moment of transcendence occurs in the immanent self-transformation of cultural standpoints arising out of the encounter with the Other. Finally, cosmopolitanism can be expressed in the movement beyond diversity to a common normative world. In this instance, cosmopolitanism can be related to the emergence of new norms and to new worldviews. This goes beyond the Gadamerian 'fusion of horizons' to a new kind of political practice in which interpretation and political change merge, for to interpret is to change (see Tong 2009). The first two forms of cosmopolitanism are conventional in that they do not entail significant change. The encounter of Self and Other is largely superficial. The second two entail stronger degrees of transformation. In these cases there is the possibility of inter-cultural dialogue. Without this dimension of dialogue cosmopolitanism lacks significant normative force.

My argument is that one of the striking features of cosmopolitanism as a process of self-transformation is the communicative dimension. As a dialogic condition cosmopolitanism can be understood in terms of a notion of critical dialogue or deliberation. A deliberative conception of culture and politics contains within it the essential cosmopolitan spirit of engaging with the perspective of the Other as opposed to rejecting it. It is in this respect that cosmopolitanism can be linked to critical theory for the mutual advancement of both. In recent years critical theory has moved beyond the critique of domination and the critique of ideology that was a feature of the older critical theory of the Frankfurt School to a communicative theory of social action. Replacing the notion of false consciousness with a theory of distorted communication, Habermas reoriented critical theory in a direction that has been advanced, on the one side, by his later concern with a discursive theory of democracy, and, on the other side, by Honneth's concern with recognition as expressed in social contexts of struggle. These developments have important implications for cosmopolitanism but have not been properly explored. Indeed, it would appear critical theory, like much of social theory, has remained trapped within the paradigm of late Western modernity.

Deliberative or discursive democracy can be seen as a post-universalistic cosmopolitanism that is open to a diversity of interpretations and applications. This does not require reaching a consensus in every case but it goes beyond liberal conceptions of compromise and accommodation to a position whereby the actors are forced to re-evaluate their positions in light of the perspective of the Other. The cosmopolitan dimension of deliberative democracy has not been widely commented on. With some exceptions, notably James Bohnan's work on cosmopolitan democratic theory and the public sphere, there has been only limited discussion on critical theory and cosmopolitanism.[28] The major proponents of deliberative democracy have mostly operated within the context of national societies or, in the case of Habermas, a republican conception of political community where the kinds of cultural challenges that are normally associated with cosmopolitanism are kept out of the deliberative situation, which, in Habermas's terms, is a culturally neutral territory. The cultural dimensions of discursive democracy and its relation to political struggles beyond the Western world have not been addressed. There is no reason why deliberative democracy cannot be extended into a wider sphere of application. I have tried to show in this book how a communicative conception of cosmopolitanism is highly relevant to many aspects of political community and to culture more generally, including to knowledge and education. Cosmopolitanism concerns the broadening of horizons when one culture meets another or when

---

[28] See Bohman (2007). Mention too should be made of Benhabib's recent work on cosmopolitanism (Benhabib 2008).

one point of view is forced to re-evaluate its claims in light of the perspective of an Other. The cognitive logic at work in this is essentially a communicative relation and unfolds in diverse ways through processes of immanent transcendence.

It is also for this reason that cosmopolitanism takes a variety of forms. That is why I have referred to contemporary cosmopolitanism as post-universal and post-Western, for Western expressions of cosmopolitanism are but one form, and within these there are different versions. The American debate on cosmopolitanism, with some notable exceptions such as James Bohman's contributions, has been predominantly confined to the politics of identity and multiculturalism. The new European debate on the other hand has been more focused on societal transformation, as reflected in some recent contributions, such as the work of Beck and Balibar. Where the American debate has stressed cosmopolitanism as transnationalism – emphasizing hybridity and disaporic identities, the European debate has been largely confined to a conception of cosmopolitanism as post-nationalism, whereby the national culture has been transformed by Europeanization. The main alternative to these positions is a notion of cosmopolitanism as a global normative culture that transcends all rooted cultures, whether ethnic, local or national. This is reflected in Archibugi's recent work on a global commonwealth (Archibugi 2008) and in mainstream normative political philosophy.

A challenge for the future is the investigation of alternative expressions of cosmopolitanism throughout the world. Cheah has made a strong case for a reorientation of cosmopolitan theory around the kinds of struggles taking place in the South (Cheah 2006). This is an important corrective of the conventional association of cosmopolitanism with the concerns of the North. The following remarks are designed to make the case for a wider inter-cultural conception of cosmopolitanism with specific reference to Asia and China in particular.

Asian cosmopolitanism is particularly important due not least to the historical legacy of cosmopolitan cultures and an emerging political culture of cosmopolitanism.[29] Limiting cosmopolitanism to European specificity results not only in the neglect of Asian variants

---

[29] See Pollock's major work on Sanskrit and cosmopolitanism in early modern India (Pollock 2006).

of cosmopolitanism, but also limits the true significance of a cosmopolitan approach, which we argue resides in learning from the Other in the context of global concerns (Delanty and He 2008). In line with the argument developed in Chapter 7 regarding multiple modernities and inter-civilizational encounters, we can see how the civilizations of Asia have been products of cross-cultural fertilization as opposed to separate and autonomous civilizations; they have borrowed from each other as well as having borrowed from European civilization. European liberalism, nationalism and Marxism have all been absorbed by Asian civilizations to the extent that these European ideologies have become internalized as an essential component of Asian cultures. Hinduism, Islam, Buddhism and Confucianism established the basic preconditions and orientations for Asian cultures to create dynamic and hybrid societies in which cosmopolitanism has been as much a popular phenomenon as an elite project. Many political, economic and cultural reforms or the transformation of Asian societies have been taken in the light of the perspectives from Europe and America. In contrast, the same cannot be so easily said of borrowing and hybridity in the opposite direction. In Europe borrowings have been more selective and so far no European country has internalized aspects of Asian culture in the way Marxism, Confucianism and Buddhism have been formed in a long engagement with the civilizations of Asia. It is certainly difficult to claim that European society has transformed itself in the light of the perspective of Asia. Thus it could be argued that there is a stronger 'external' dimension to Asia than is the case in Europe.[30]

The case of China is particularly illuminating. In China a major experiment with modernity has been taking place over the past three decades and there are signs of cosmopolitanism emerging as a new model of modernity emerges. The concept of modernity, I have argued – to simplify a complex debate – refers to the interaction of state, market and civil society in ways that make possible the self-transformative capacity of society leading to the emergence of cultural models that affirm human autonomy and freedom. Now, this has taken a huge variety of forms, as has been increasingly recognized in recent scholarship (and of course there is a great variety of forms of state formation,

---

[30] I am grateful to Baogang He for this point. See our joint article (Delanty and He 2008).

capitalist accumulation and democratization and of cultural models of autonomy). There is no one model of modernity, which is not Western and nor is it universal. Its singularity, to follow Jameson (2002), at most consists of its capacity to open up the immanent possibilities for self-transcedence. It is only in this sense that modernity can be considered as singular. The European experience – itself diverse – has been different from the American route. One main difference has been in the European case the relative containment of capitalism by the state and civil society, where in the American case a weaker state was the basis of both the development of a dynamic civil society and an expansive market-based society. But both were influenced by each other and, in the European case, by non-Western civilization, share comparable cultural models of autonomy and freedom. The Chinese route to modernity, as in Europe and Russia, has been largely shaped by revolution and reform of the state but, unlike the European experience, the interaction with civil society and the market has been less significant. Today the market under the conditions of capitalist accumulation has of course become pivotal to a new and dynamic expression of modernity, which obviously differs remarkably from other routes through modernity, such as those of Japan and Russia. While the place and role of civil society in this remains undeveloped – though there are interesting expressions of village democracy – a model of modernity is taking shape that emerged directly through the reform of a model of modernity that failed elsewhere and which, in its current Chinese form, can no longer be understood as an alternative modernity formed in opposition to the West. It is simply a different version of modernity and one that has signalled a major societal transformation. Part of this includes the emergence of a cultural model that offers something like the equivalent of a new project of modernity based on neo-Confucianism. Neo-Confucianism has become an important substitute for the communist ideology, making possible a different moral and political order in which social values can be given a firmer foundation.[31] There is no doubt that the Chinese combination of capitalist development and a single-party state along with the revitalized neo-Confucianist value system is a new model of modernity and one that has emerged out of the reform of communism, which elsewhere failed to sustain a viable model of modernity.

---

[31] For a detailed and nuanced account of neo-Confucianism, see Bell (2007).

However, this view of the multiple nature of modernity does not imply a vision of different models of modernity developing in isolation from each other. The emergence of modernity has always been part of a global network of connections. This is where the relevance of a cosmopolitan perspective can be demonstrated. It is through interaction in a global context that modernity takes shape. An interactionist account of the rise of modernity would place the emphasis on the dynamics and modes of interaction whereby different parts of the world become linked through the expansion and diffusion of systems of exchange, networks of communication, and various forms of cosmopolitan third culture. Thus it was not the case that modernity was European per se or that different models of modernity emerged spontaneously there, but the rise of modernity was determined by the extent to which in a given part of the world the capacity existed for the expansion of local cultures into a globally oriented third culture. It was consequential that this happened in Europe and – only in certain parts of Europe – but this does not mean that modernity was European or Western per se. So in China we are witnessing the combination of two antagonistic models of modernity, which divided the West – if we can include Russia within this category – for much of the previous century. Whether China will succeed in this experiment and create something quite new and cosmopolitan remains one of the great questions which only the future can answer. In view of the increasing sense of a global dimension to social and economic problems, the possibility of a cosmopolitan turn in China will be an essential precondition for a global cosmopolitan order. The neo-Confucianist value system, as it is currently articulated by the intellectual and political elites in China, is embedded in the cosmopolitan heritage of Mencius and is reflected in, for example, the notion of China as a 'soft power' and in an approach to the world that emphasizes the priority of securing the conditions of social existence.[32]

Approaching the problem of modernity from the cosmopolitan perspective of global history, which is what I am defending, offers, then, a corrective to the received view of modernity as a Western condition that was transported to the rest of the world, which either accepted or rejected it. Moreover, it also avoids some of the problems of an appeal to a non-Western modernity or some kind of indigenous modernity.

---

[32] Since 2008, the notion of soft power has become the official policy of the Chinese Communist Party.

The notion of modernity, divested of its Eurocentric assumptions, has a direct relevance to cosmopolitan analysis if it is accepted that it is a transformative condition that arises out of multiplicity and interaction. It is a concept that cannot be confined to national patterns of development, but has a wider application including, importantly, civilizational influences and interactions.

I want to suggest, then, that the significance of the past three decades in China lies in the emergence of a new kind of modernity, the implications of which go beyond China. The implications are cosmopolitan. Since Deng Xiaoping opened China to the wider world in 1978, China has become increasingly part of the global system. With the end of the Cold War and the consolidation and expansion of the European Union as a post-sovereign and post-national state, a post-Western world has come about in which China is a crucial player. In this the relation with Europe is particularly important, as is the increasingly significant Sino-African relationship. The full significance of the transformation of China for cosmopolitanism is at best unclear. China can play a major role in bringing about a more cosmopolitan future than has been the case in the previous century when the West was dominant and challenged only by a modernity that failed. The critical task is the struggle for social justice and solidarity. For the EU – where the transnationalization of the nation-state has now finally reached its limits – the challenge will be to create stronger forms of social solidarity. But in a globally connected world this is also a cosmopolitan challenge. This, too, is a challenge for China, where market forces are not just transforming the face of China but have wider global consequences. For Europe, where the tradition of social justice remains strong, globalization means more or less Asian capitalism provoking a defensive nationalism as a response. The EU is China's largest trading partner and China is the EU's second largest trading partner, after the United States. The danger is that this will be a relation defined exclusively by market forces. Yet, the basis of a genuine co-operation has only recently been established. While Europe has succeeded over the past five decades in diminishing nationalism in the creation of a post-sovereign polity, this has yet to be established in the international context where, on the one side, national interests dominate and, on the other side, chaotic global markets rule. Against both nationalism and market-driven globalization, the only viable future is a cosmopolitan one in which the national interest is diluted and global capitalism constrained by a commitment to social justice.

In emphasizing the varieties of cosmopolitan experience the global context cannot be neglected as some of the most important expressions of cosmopolitanism are those related to normative transnationalism in which global ethics and principles of justice play a central role. In the terms of the four-fold model of cosmopolitanism, the fourth dimension has particular relevance in this regard, for a major challenge today is for positive political forms of transnational co-operation to develop. I have argued that this will require a cosmopolitan imagination in so far as it will require going beyond narrow economic and security concerns to address problems of global justice and cultural equality. This is a cosmopolitan challenge in a deeper cognitive sense in that it concerns the capacities of major powers to transform themselves in light of the perspective of the Other.

The notion of a post-universalistic cosmopolitanism is particularly appropriate to current times, which can be characterized as a post-Western world. In Chapter 9 I commented on the emergence of a post-Western Europe. With the enlargement of the European Union in recent years to include most of Central and Eastern Europe, the exclusively Western nature of Europe has been diluted with the inclusion of societies that have had quite different historical experiences. The recognition that the logic of Europeanization leads to greater diversification suggests a cosmopolitan perspective. A cosmopolitan project of Europe clearly transcends a conventional reading of liberal democratic politics centred on the nation-state and explicitly points to the need for a European democratic order that not only recognizes, but explicitly engages with, the multiple cultural and civilizational background of Europe. In this regard, it can be argued that 1989 has fundamentally altered the stakes of European integration (Blokker 2009a, 2009b). This tendency towards post-Westernization is enhanced by Europe's growing importance as a global actor. It is noteworthy that as Europe undergoes internal transformation in the direction of a post-Western order, it does so in the context of an increasingly post-Western world. It is not only Europe that is post-Western but the global context is one in which the West has lost its cultural and political unity. The EU along with the United States and China are now the major powers, perhaps with the continued significance of Russia. This is a multipolar world that is no longer united by a Western alliance, which since the Iraq War has been fraught with problems. A major challenge for the future will be the creation of cosmopolitan forms of interaction in which the national interest will not be the only one.

Inter-cultural communication is now more important than ever. But it needs to be given a more substantial basis than the conventional approach, which tends to separate cultural understanding from political action. It is not merely a question of dialogue or understanding, but also requires deliberative reasoning and the critical scrutiny of cultural and political standpoints. Inter-cultural communication conceived of in cosmopolitan terms has five main characteristics. First, it is a mode of communication that is deliberative. Second, it is reflective. Third, it is critical in its orientation. Fourth, it entails societal learning. Fifth, it concerns political practice that has a global relevance. The purpose of inter-cultural communication is not simply communication for its own sake but has the deliberative objective of settling disagreements through consensual communication rather than through force or manipulation. This does not necessarily require consensus as the final outcome. It does however require the acceptance of discursive procedures and the inclusion of as many people as possible in the discursive process. Inter-cultural dialogue is also reflective in that it forces the social actors to reflect on their assumptions and their standpoints. In this sense it is Self- as well as Other-directed. Conventional inter-cultural dialogue seeks only the understanding of the perspective of the Other without further reflection on the implications of the dialogue for one's own position. Critical cosmopolitanism challenges the notion of an Other who must be understood, for in the process of interpretation and dialogue differences become diminished. Following from the reflective moment is a stronger critical orientation. Cosmopolitan inter-cultural dialogue has a critical trust in that it does not simply take for granted the normative claims of the cultures that are involved in the communicative process but requires a re-evaluation of positions. Leading from the reflective and critical are processes of collective or societal learning leading to new kinds of political practice. The point of inter-cultural dialogue is lost if learning does not result and new horizons are opened up.

Cosmopolitan inter-cultural dialogue is not an impossible goal. Within the European context more than five decades of political, economic and cultural integration have provided some of the preconditions for cosmopolitanism. The transnationalization of the European nation-state and with it the relaxing of borders and economic integration has offered opportunities for cosmopolitanism to become a significant factor. Europeanization until now was predominantly shaped by internal factors relating to the transnationalization of the nation-state, but today the external is coming increasingly to the fore, central to which is the relation to Asia. In the global context, normative transnationalism as represented by transnational organizations such as the EU, the UN, ASEAN, global civil society and international law offers opportunities for cosmopolitanism to develop transnationally. While economic and security concerns dominate the international context relationship between Asia and Europe and there is a long way to go in furthering cosmopolitan relations between East and West, there are some signs of cosmopolitanism becoming a compelling force and constituting a new kind of imagination. This book has provided some arguments as to why the cosmopolitan imagination has become a challenge to the national imagination as well as to the belief in the market.

Bibliography

Aijmer, G. and Abbink, J. (eds.) 2000. *Meanings of Violence: Cross-Cultural Perspective*. Oxford: Berg.

Al-Azmeh, A. 1993. *Islam and Modernity*. London: Verso.

Al Sayyad, N. and Castells, M. (eds.) 2002. *Muslim Europe or Euro-Islam*. Lanham: Lexington Books.

Amin, S. 1989. *Eurocentrism*. London: Zed Books.

Amit, V. and Rapport, N. (eds.) 2003. *The Trouble with Community*. Oxford: Blackwell.

Anderson, B. 1983. *Imaginary Communities: Reflections on the Origin and Spread of Nationalism*. London: Verso.

Anderson, J., O'Dowd, L. and Wilson, T. M. (eds.) 2003. *New Borders for a Changing Europe: Cross-border Cooperation and Governance*. London: Frank Cass.

Anderson, M. 1996. *Frontiers: Territory and State Formation in the Modern World*. Cambridge: Polity Press.

Anderson, M. and Bort, E. (eds.) 1999. *The Frontiers of Europe*. London: Pinter.

Andreas, P. 2003. 'Redrawing the Line: Borders and Security in the Twenty-First Century', *International Security* 28 (2): 78–111.

Ang, I. 2003. 'Cultural Translation in a Globalized World', in Paperstergiadis, N. (ed.) *Complex Entanglements: Art, Globalization and Cultural Difference*. Sydney: Rivers Oran Press.

Anthias, F. and Yuval-Davis, N. (eds.) 1989. *Women-Nation-State*. London: Macmillan.

Antonsich, M. 2008. 'Europe between "National" and "Postnational" Views', *European Journal of Social Theory* 11 (4).

Apel, K.-O. 1978. 'The Conflicts of Our Time and the Problem of Political Ethics', in Dallmayr, F. (ed.) *From Contract to Community: Political Theory at the Cross Roads*. New York: Dekkar.

Apel, K.-O. 1987. 'The Problem of a Macroethic of Responsibility to the Future in the Crisis of Technological Civilization', *Man and World* 20: 3–40.

Apel, K.-O. 1988. *Diskurs und Verantwortung: Das Problem des Übergangs zur postkonventionellen Moral*. Frankfurt: Suhrkamp.

Apel, K.-O. 1990. 'The Problem of a Universalistic Macroethics of Co-Responsibility', in Griffioen, S. (ed.) *What Right Does Ethics Have?* Amsterdam: VU University Press.

Apel, K.-O. 1992. 'The Ecological Crisis as a Problem for Discourse Ethics', in Ofsti, A. (ed.) *Ecology and Ethics*. Trondheim: Nordland Akademi for Kunst og Vitenskap.

Apel, K.-O. 1993. 'How to Ground a Universalistic Ethics of Co-Responsibility for the Effects of Collective Actions and Activities', *Philosophica* 52 (2): 9–29.

Apel, K.-O. 1996. 'A Planetary Macroethics for Humankind: The Need, the Apparent Difficulty and the Eventual Possibility', in *Karl-Otto Apel: Selected Essays*. Vol. 2. New Jersey: Humanities Press.

Apel, K.-O. 2000. 'Globalization and the Need for Universal Ethics: the Problem in Light of Discourse Ethics', *European Journal of Social Theory* 3 (2): 137–55.

Apel, K.-O. 2001. 'On The Relation Between Ethics, International Law and Politico-Military Strategy in Our Time: A Philosophical Retrospective on the Kosovo Conflict', *European Journal of Social Theory* 4 (1): 29–39.

Appadurai, R. 1996. *Modernity at Large: Cultural Dimension of Globalization*. Minneapolis: University of Minnesota Press.

Appiah, K. 1998. 'Cosmopolitan Patriots', in Cheah, P. and Robbins, B. (eds.) *Cosmopolitics: Thinking and Feeling Beyond the Nation*. Minneapolis: University of Minnesota Press.

Appiah, K. 2004. *Ethics of Identity*. Princeton: Princeton University Press.

Appiah, K. 2006. *Cosmopolitanism: Ethics in a World of Strangers*. New York: Norton.

Archibugi, D. 1995. *Cosmopolitan Democracy: An Agenda for a New World Order*. Cambridge: Polity Press.

Archibugi, D. 2003. 'A Critical Analysis of the Self-Determination of Peoples: A Cosmopolitan Perspective', *Constellations* 10 (4): 488–505.

Archibugi, D. 2008. *The Global Commonwealth of Citizens*. Princeton: Princeton University Press.

Archibugi, D., Held, D. and Kögler, M. (eds.) 1999. *Reimagining Political Community*. Cambridge: Polity Press.

Arjomand, S. and Tiryakian, E. (eds.) 2004. *Rethinking Civilizational Analysis*. London: Sage.

Arnason, J. 1991. 'Modernity as a Project and a Field of Tensions', in Honneth, A. and Joas, H. (eds.) *Communicative Action*. Cambridge: Polity Press.

Arnason, J. 1993. *The Future that Failed: Origins and Destinies of the Soviet Model*. London: Routledge.

Arnason, J. 2003. *Civilizations in Dispute: Historical Questions and Theoretical Traditions*. Leiden: Brill.

Arnason, J. 2006. 'Contested Divergence: Rethinking the "Rise of the West"', in Delanty, G. (ed.) *Europe and Asia Beyond East and West*. London: Routledge.

Asad, T. 1986. 'The Concept of Cultural Translation in British Social Anthropology' in Clifford, J. and Marcus, G. (eds.) *Writing Culture: The Poetics and Politics of Ethnography*. Berkeley: University of California Press.

Asad, T. 2003. *Formations of the Secular: Christianity, Islam, Modernity*. Stanford University Press.

Assmann, J. 1997. *Moses the Egyptian: The Memory of Egypt in Western Monotheism*. Cambridge, MA: Harvard University Press.

Badiou, A. 2003. *Saint Paul: The Foundation of Universalism*. Stanford University Press.

Baldry, H. C. 1965. *The Unity of Mankind in Greek Thought*. Cambridge University Press.

Balibar, E. 2004. *We the People of Europe: Reflections on Transnational Citizenship*. Princeton University Press.

Barnett, R. 1999. *Realizing the University in an Age of Supercomplexity*. Buckingham: Open University Press.

Barry, B. 2002. *Culture and Equality: An Egalitarian Critique of Multiculturalism*. Cambridge, MA: Harvard University Press.

Barth, F. (ed.) 1969. *Ethnic Groups and Boundaries: The Social Organization of Cultural Difference*. London: Allen and Unwin.

Bartky, L. 2002. *Sympathy and Solidarity and Other Essays*. Lanham: Rowman & Littlefield.

Bassnett, S. and Lefevere, A. (eds.) 1990. *Translation, History and Culture*. London: Pinter.

Baudelaire, C. 1964. 'The Painter of Modern Life', in Baudelaire, C. *The Painter of Modern Life and Other Essays*. London: Pluto Press.

Bauer, J. and Bell, D. (eds.) 1999. *The East Asian Challenge for Human Rights*. Cambridge University Press.

Bauman, Z. 2000. 'Wars of the Globalization Era', *European Journal of Social Theory* 4 (1): 11–28.

Bauman, Z. 2001. *Liquid Modernity*. Cambridge: Polity Press.

Bayly, C. 2004. *The Birth of the Modern World, 1780–1814: Global Connections and Comparisons*. Oxford: Blackwell.

Beck, U. 2000. 'The Cosmopolitan Perspective: Sociology of the Second Age of Modernity', *British Journal of Sociology* 51 (1): 79–105.

Beck, U. 2002. 'The Cosmopolitan Society and its Enemies', *Theory, Culture and Society* 19 (1–2): 17–44.

Beck, U. 2006. *The Cosmopolitan Outlook*. Cambridge: Polity Press.

Beck, U. and Grande, E. 2007. *Cosmopolitan Europe*. Cambridge: Polity Press.

Beck, U. and Sznaider, N. 2006. 'Unpacking Cosmopolitanism for the Social Sciences: a Research Agenda', *British Journal of Sociology* 57 (1): 1–23.

Beck, U., Sznaider, N. and Winter, R. (eds.) 2000. *Global America: The Cultural Consequences of Americanization*. Liverpool University Press.

Beitz, C. 1999. *Political Theory and International Relations*. Princeton University Press.

Bell, D. 2000. *East Meets West: Human Rights and Democracy in East Asia*. Princeton University Press.

Bell, D. 2007. *China's New Confucianism: Politics and Everyday Life in a Changing Society*. Princeton University Press.

Bellamy, R., Castiglione, D. and Santoro, E. (eds.) 2004. *Lineages of European Citizenship: Rights, Belonging and Participation in Eleven Nation-States*. London: Palgrave.

Benedict, R. 1935. *Patterns of Culture*. London: Routledge and Kegan Paul.

Benhabib, S. 2002. *The Claims of Culture: Equality and Diversity in the Global Era*. Princeton University Press.

Benhabib, S. 2004. *The Rights of Cultures: Aliens, Residents and Citizens*. Cambridge University Press.

Benhabib, S. 2008. *Another Cosmopolitanism*. Oxford University Press.

Benjamin, A. 1989. *Translation and the Nature of Philosophy*. London: Routledge.

Benjamin, W. 1982. 'The Task of the Translator', *Illuminations*. London: Routledge.

Bennett, T. 2001. *Differing Diversities: Cultural Policy and Cultural Diversity*. Strasbourg: Council of Europe.

Ben-Rafael, E. and Sternberg, Y. (eds.) 2005. *Comparing Modern Civilizations: Pluralism versus Homogeneity*. Leiden: Brill.

Bentley, J. 1993. *Old World Encounters: Cross-Cultural Contacts and Exchanges in Premodern Times*. New York: Oxford University Press.

Bentley, J. 2002. 'The New World History', in Kramer, L. and Maza, S. (eds.) *A Companion to Western Historical Thought*. Oxford: Blackwell.

Berezin, M. and Schain, M. (eds.) 2003. *Europe without Borders: Remapping Territory, Citizenship and Identity in a Transnational Age*. London: Palgrave.

Berges, S. 2005. 'Loneliness and Belonging: Is Stoic Cosmopolitanism still Defensible?', *Res Publica* 11: 3–25.

Bertillson, M. 2004. 'The Elementary Forms of Pragmatism', *European Journal of Social Theory* 7 (3): 371–89.

Bhabha, H. 1990. *Nation and Narration*. London: Routledge.

Bhabha, H. 1994. *The Location of Culture*. London: Routledge.

Bhambra, G. 2007. *Rethinking Modernity: Postcolonialism and the Sociological Imagination*. London: Palgrave.

Biedenkopf, K., Geremek, B. and Michalski, K. 2004. '*The Spiritual and Cultural Dimension of Europe*'. Vienna: Institute for the Human Sciences.

Binnie, J., Holloway, J., Millington, S. and Young, C. (eds.) 2006. *Cosmopolitan Urbanism*. London: Routledge

Blaut, J. D. 1993. *The Coloniser's Model of the World: Geographical Diffuionism and Eurocentric Theory*. London: Guilford Press.

Blok, A. 1998. 'The Narcissism of Minor Differences', *European Journal of Social Theory* 1 (1): 33–56.

Blokker, P. 2005. 'Post-Communist Modernization, Transition Studies, and Diversity in Europe', *European Journal of Social Theory* 8 (4): 503–25.

Blokker, P. (ed.) 2009a. Special Issue of *European Journal of Social Theory* 12 (3).

Blokker, P. 2009b. *Multiple Democracies in Europe: Political Culture in New Member State*. London: Routledge.

Blum, H. 2002. 'The Republican Mirror: The Dutch Idea of Europe', in Pagden, A. (ed.) *The Idea of Europe: From Antiquity to the European Union*. Cambridge University Press.

Blumenberg, H. 1983. *The Legitimacy of the Modern Age*. Cambridge, MA: MIT Press.

Bohman, J. 1998. 'The Globalization of the Public Sphere', *Philosophy and Social Crititicism* 24 (2/3): 199–216.

Bohman, J. 2007. *Democracy and Across Borders: From Demos to Demoi*. Cambridge, MA: MIT Press.

Bohman, J. and Lutz-Bachmann, M. (eds.) 1997. *Perpetual Peace: Essays on Kant's Cosmopolitan Ideal*. Cambridge, MA: MIT Press.

Bok, S. 1995. *Common Values*. Missouri: University of Missouri Press.

Boli, J. and Thomas, G. (eds.) 1999. *Constructing World Culture: International Non-Governmental Organizations since 1875*. Stanford University Press.

Boltanski, L. 1999. *Distant Suffering*. Cambridge: University Press.

Bontempi, M. 2005. 'Religious Pluralism and the Public Sphere', in Lattes, G. B. and Recchi, E. (eds.) *Comparing European Societies*. Bologna: Monduzzi Editore.

Böröcz, J. and Sarkar, M. 2005. 'What is the EU?', *International Sociology* 20 (2): 153–73.

Bourdieu, P. 2001. *Acts of Resistance: Against the Myth of Our Time*. Cambridge: Polity Press.

Bourdieu, P. 2003. *Fighting Back*. Cambridge: Polity Press.

Bowan, J. 2005. 'Normative Pluralism in Asia: Regions, Religions, and Ethnicities', in Kymlicka, W. and He, B. (eds.) *Multiculturalism in Asia*. Oxford University Press.

Bowden, B. 2003. 'Nationalism and Cosmopolitanism. Irreconcilable Differences or Possible Bedfellows?', *National Identities* 5 (3): 235–49.

Brague, R. 2002. *Eccentric Culture: A Theory of Western Civilization*. South Bend: St. Augustine's Press

Braudel, F. 1972/3. *The Mediterranean and the Mediterranean World in the Age of Philip II*. London: Fontana.

Breckenridge, C. A., Bhabha, H., Pollock, S. and Chakrabarty, D. (eds.) 2002. *Cosmopolitanism*. Durham, NC: Duke University Press.

Brenan, T. 1997. *At Home in the World: Cosmopolitanism Now*. Cambridge, MA: Harvard University Press.

Brock, G. and Brighouse, H. (eds.) 2005. *The Political Philosophy of Cosmopolitanism*. Cambridge University Press.

Brown, G. W. 2005. 'State Sovereignty, Federation and Kantian Cosmopolitanism', *European Journal of International Relations* 11: 495–522.

Brubaker, R. and Cooper, F. 2000. 'Beyond "Identity"', *Theory, Culture and Society* 29: 1–47.

Bruce, S. 1996. *Religion in the Modern World: From Cathedrals to Cults*. Oxford University Press.

Brunkhorst, H. 2005. *Solidarity: From Civic Friendship to a Global Legal Community*. Cambridge, MA: MIT Press.

Brunkhorst, H. 2007. 'Globalizing Solidarity: The Destiny of Democratic Solidarity in Times of Global Capitalism, Global Religion, and the Global Public', *Journal of Social Philosophy* 38 (1): 93–111.

Burkert, W. 1992. *The Orientalizing Revolution: Near Eastern Influence on Greek Culture in the Early Archaic Age*. Cambridge, MA: Harvard University Press.

Budick, S. and Iser, W. (eds.) 1996. *The Translatability of Cultures*. Stanford University Press.

Buruma, I. and Marglit, A. 2004. *Occidentalism: the West in the Eyes of its Enemies*. London: Penguin Press.

Butler, J. 2004. *Precarious Life: The Powers of Mourning and Violence*. London: Verso.

Buultjens, R. and Mazlish, B. (eds.) 1993. *Conceptualizing Global History*. Boulder: Westview Press.

Cacciari, M. 1997. *L'Arcipelago*. Milan: Adephi.

Calhoun, C. (ed.) 1992. *Habermas and the Public Sphere*. Cambridge, MA: MIT Press.

Calhoun, C. 2003a. 'The Class Consciousness of the Frequent Travelers: Towards a Critique of Actually Existing Cosmopolitanism', in Archibugi, D. (ed.) *Debating Cosmopolitics*. London: Verso.

Calhoun, C. 2003b. '"Belonging" in the Cosmopolitan Imaginary', *Ethnicities* 3 (4): 531–68.

Callon, M., Law, J. and Ripp, A. 1986. *Mapping the Dynamics of Science and Technology*. London: Macmillan.

Carens, J. 1995. 'Aliens and Citizens: The Case for Open Borders', in Beiner, R. (ed.) *Theorizing Citizenship*. New York: State University of New York Press.

Casanova, J. 1994. *Public Religions in the Modern World*. University of Chicago Press.

Casanova, J. 2001. 'Civil Society and Religion', *Social Research* 68 (4): 1041–80.

Castells, M. 1996. *The Rise of the Network State. Vol. 1. The Information Age*. Oxford: Blackwell.

Castells, M. 1997. *The Power of Identity. Vol. 2. The Information Age*. Oxford: Blackwell.

Castells, M. 1998. *The End of the Millennium. Vol. 3. The Information Age*. Oxford: Blackwell.

Castells, M. 2000. 'Materials for an Exploratory Theory of the Network Society', *British Journal of Sociology* 51 (1): 5–24.

Castoriadis, C. 1987. *The Imaginary Institution of Society*. Cambridge: Polity Press.

Chakrabarty, D. 2000. *Provencializing Europe: Postcolonial Thought and Historical Difference*. Princeton University Press.

Chambers, S. and Kymlicka, W. (eds.) 2002. *Alternative Conceptions of Civil Society*. Princeton University Press.

Chaney, D. 2002. 'Cosmopolitan Art and Cultural Citizenship', *Theory, Culture and Society* 19 (1–2): 157–74.

Cheah, P. 1998. 'Rethinking Cosmopolitical Freedom in Transnationalism', in Cheah, P. and Robbins, B. (eds.) *Cosmopolitics: Thinking and Feeling Beyond the Nation*. Minneapolis: University of Minnesota Press.

Cheah, P. 2006. *Inhuman Conditions: On Cosmopolitanism and Human Rights*. Cambridge, MA: Harvard University Press.

Cheah, P. and Robbins, B. (eds.) 1998. *Cosmopolitics: Thinking and Feeling Beyond the Nation*. Minneapolis: Minnesota University Press.

Chernilo, D. 2006a. 'Social Theory: Methodological Nationalism and Critique', in Delanty, G. and Kumar, K. (eds.) *Handbook of Nations and Nationalism*. London: Sage.

Chernilo, D. 2006b. 'Social Theory's Methodological Nationalism: Myth and Reality', *European Journal of Social Theory* 9 (1): 5–22.

Chernilo, D. 2007. 'A Quest for Universalism: Re-assessing the Nature of Classical Social Theory's Cosmopolitanism', *European Journal of Social Theory* 10 (1): 17–35.

Cheyette, B. and Marcus, L. (eds.) 1998. *Modernity, Culture and 'The Jew'*. Cambridge University Press.

Clarke, J. J. 1997. *Oriental Enlightenment: The Encounter between Asian and European Thought*. London: Routledge.

Clifford, J. 1992. 'Traveling Cultures', in Grossberg, L., Nelson, C. and Treichler, P. (eds.) *Cultural Studies*. New York: Routledge.

Clifford, J. 1997. *Routes: Travel and Translation in the Late Twentieth Century*. Cambridge, MA: Harvard University Press.

Clough, P. and O'Malley, J. (eds.) 2007. *The Affective Turn: Theorizing the Social*. Durham, NC: Duke University Press.

Coakley, J. 1982. 'Political Territories and Cultural Frontiers: Conflicts of Principle in the Formation of States in Europe', *West European Politics* 5 (4): 34–49.

Cohen, A. 1985. *The Symbolic Construction of Community*. London: Routledge.

Cohen, J. (ed.) 1996. *For Love of Country: Debating the Limits of Patriotism*. University of Chicago Press.

Connolly, W. 1995. *The Ethos of Pluralization*. Minneapolis: University of Minnesota Press.

Connolly, W. 1999. *Why I am not a Secularist?* Minneapolis: University of Minnesota Press.

Connolly, W. 2002. *Neuropolitics: Thinking, Culture, Speed*. Minneapolis: University of Minnesota Press.

Coser, L. 1956. *The Function of Social Conflict*. New York: The Free Press.

Cowan, J. K., Dembour, M. and Wilson, R. (eds.) 2001. *Culture and Rights: Anthropological Perspective*. Cambridge University Press.

Cronin, M. 1998. *Unity in Diversity: Current Trends in Translation Studies*. Manchester: St Jerome Press.

Crossley, N. 2000. 'Citizenship, Intersubjectivity and the Lifeworld', in Stevenson, N. (ed.) *Culture and Citizenship*. London: Sage.

Crossley, N. and Roberts, J. (eds.) 2004. *After Habermas: New Perspectives on the Public Sphere*. Oxford: Blackwell.

Crouch, C. 2000. 'The Quiet Continent: Religion and Politics in Europe', *The Political Quarterly* 71 (1): 90–103.

Curtin, P. 1984. *Cross-Cultural Trade in World History*. Cambridge University Press.

Dallmayr, F. 1996. *Beyond Orientalism: Essays on Cross-Cultural Encounter*. New York: State University of New York Press.

Davis, G. 2000. *Religion in Modern Europe: A Memory Mutates.* Oxford University Press.

Davis, M. (ed.) 1995. *Human Rights and Chinese Values.* Oxford University Press.

de Barry, T. 1998. *Asian Values and Human Rights: A Confucian Communitarian Perspective.* Cambridge University Press.

De Grazia, V. 2005. *Irresistible Empire: America's Advance Through 20th Century Europe.* Cambridge, MA: Harvard University Press.

De Greiff, P. and Cronin, C. 2002. *Global Justice and Transnationalism.* Cambridge, MA: MIT Press.

Dean, J. 1996. *Solidarity of Strangers.* Berkeley: University of California Press.

Delanty, G. 1995. *Inventing Europe: Idea, Identity, Reality.* London: Macmillan.

Delanty, G. 1996. 'The Frontier and Identities of Exclusion in European History', *History of European Ideas* 22 (2): 93–103.

Delanty, G. 1997. 'Habermas and Occidental Rationalism: The Politics of Identity, Social Learning and the Cultural Limits of Moral Universalism', *Sociological Theory* 15 (3): 30–59.

Delanty, G. 1999. *Social Theory in a Changing World.* Cambridge: Polity Press.

Delanty, G. 2000. *Citizenship in the Global Age: Culture, Society and Politics.* Buckingham: Open University Press.

Delanty, G. 2001. *Challenging Knowledge: The University in the Knowledge Society.* Buckingham: Open University Press.

Delanty, G. 2003. 'The Making of a Post-Western Europe: A Civilizational Analysis', *Thesis Eleven* 72: 8–24.

Delanty, G. (ed.) 2006. *Europe and Asia Beyond East and West.* London: Routledge.

Delanty, G. and He, B. 2008. 'Comparative Perspectives on Cosmopolitanism: Assessing European and Asia Perspectives', *International Sociology* 23 (3): 323–44.

Delanty, G. and Rumford, C. 2005. *Rethinking Europe: Social Theory and the Implications of Europeanization.* London: Routledge.

Delanty, G., Wodak, R. and Jones, P. (eds.) 2008. *Migration, Belonging and Exclusion in Europe.* Liverpool University Press.

Derrida, J. 2001. *On Cosmopolitanism and Forgiveness.* London: Routledge.

Dingsdale, A. 2000. *Mapping Modernities: Geographies of Central and Eastern Europe, 1920–2000.* London: Routledge.

Dirlik, A. 2003. 'Global Modernity? Modernity in an Age of Global Capitalism', *European Journal of Social Theory* 7 (3): 275–92.

Dobson, A. 2006. 'Thick Cosmopolitanism', *Political Studies* 54 (1): 165–84.

Durkheim, E. (2001/1912) *The Elementary Forms of Religious Life*, trans. C. Gosman. Oxford University Press.

Eckersley, R. 2007. 'From Cosmopolitan Nationalism to Cosmopolitan Democracy', *Review of International Studies* 33: 675–92.

Eder, K. 1985. *Geschichte als Lernprozess? Zur Pathogenese politischer Modernität in Deutschland*. Frankfurt: Suhrkamp.

Eder, K. 1999. 'Societies Learn and Yet the World is Hard to Change', *European Journal of Social Theory* 2 (2): 195–215.

Eder, K. 2002. 'Europäische Säkularisierung– ein Sonderweg in die postsäkulare Gesellschaft? Eine theoretische Anmerkung', *Berliner Journal für Soziologie* 12: 331–44.

Eder, K. 2005. 'Making Sense of the Public Sphere', in Delanty, G. (ed.) *Handbook of Contemporary European Social Theory*. London: Routledge.

Eder, K. 2006. 'Europe's Borders', *European Journal of Social Theory* 9 (2): 255–71.

Eder, K. and Giesen, B. (eds.) 2001. *European Citizenship: National Legacies and Transnational Projects*. Oxford University Press.

Eikelman, D. and Salvatore, A. 2002. 'The Public Sphere and Muslim Societies', *European Journal of Sociology* XLIII (1): 92–115.

Eisenstadt, S. N. (ed.) 1986. *The Origins and Diversity of the Axial Civilizations*. New York: SUNY Press.

Eisenstadt, S. N. 2001. 'The Civilizational Dimension of Modernity', *International Sociology* 16 (3): 320–40.

Eisenstadt, S. N. 2003. *Comparative Civilizations and Multiple Modernities*, Vols. 1 and 2. Leiden: Brill.

Elliott, A. 2000. 'The Reinvention of Citizenship', in Stevenson, N. (ed.) *Culture and Citizenship*. London: Sage.

Ellmeier, A. and Radsky, B. 2006. *Differing Diversities: Eastern European Perspectives*. Strasbourg: Council of Europe.

Eriksen, E. (ed.) 2005. *Making the Euro-Polity: Reflexive Integration in Europe*. London: Routledge.

Eriksen, T. H. 2001. 'Between Universalism and Relativism: A Critique of the UNESCO Concept of Culture', in Cowan, J., Dembour, M. and Wilson, R. (eds.) *Culture and Rights: Anthropological Perspective*. Cambridge University Press.

Esposito, J. and Burgat, F. (eds.) 2003. *Modernizing Islam: Religion in the Public Sphere in Europe and the Middle East*. London: Hurst.

Favell, A. 2008. *Eurostars and Eurocities: Free Movement and Mobility in an Integrating Europe*. Oxford: Blackwell.

Fawaz, L. T. and Bayly, C. A. (eds.) 2002. *Modernity and Culture: From the Mediterranean to the Indian Ocean*. New York: Columbia University Press.

Featherstone, M. 2002. 'Cosmopolis: An Introduction', *Theory, Culture and Society* 19: 1–16.

Ferrara, A. 2007. 'Political Cosmopolitanism and Judgement', *European Journal of Social Theory* 10 (1): 53–66.

Fine, R. 2000. 'Crimes Against Humanity: Hannah Arendt and the Nuremberg Debates', *European Journal of Social Theory* 3 (3): 293–311.

Fine, R. 2003. 'Taking the "Ism" out of Cosmopolitanism', *European Journal of Social Theory* 6 (4): 451–70.

Fine, R. 2006. 'Cosmopolitanism and Violence: Difficulties of Judgement', *British Journal of Sociology* 57 (1): 50–67.

Fine, R. 2007. *Cosmopolitanism*. London: Routledge.

Fisher, C. 1999. 'Uncommon Values, Diversity and Conflict in City Life', in Smelser, N. and Alexander, J. (eds.) *Diversity and its Discontents: Cultural Conflict and Common Ground in Contemporary American Society*. New Haven: Princeton University Press.

Fojas, C. 2005. *Cosmopolitanism in the Americas*. West Lafayette: Purdue University Press.

Fossum, J. and Schlesinger, P. (eds.) 2007. *The European Union and the Public Sphere*. London: Routledge.

Foucher, M. 1998. 'The Geopolitics of European Frontiers', in Anderson, M. and Bort, E. (eds.) *The Frontiers of Europe*. London: Pinter.

Frank, A. G. 1998. *Re-Orient: Global Economy in the Asian Age*. Berkeley: University of California Press.

Frankenfeld, P. 1992. 'Technological Citizenship: A Normative Framework for Risk Studies', *Science and Technology and Human Values* 17 (4).

Freundlieb, D. 2000. 'Rethinking Critical Theory: Weaknesses and New Directions', *Constellations* 7 (1): 88–99.

Frosh, S. 2000. 'Psychoanalysis, Identity and Citizenship', in Stevenson, N. (ed.) *Culture and Citizenship*. London: Sage.

Fuller, S. 2000. *The Governance of Science*. Buckingham: Open University Press.

Furet, F. 1999. *The Passing of an Illusion: The Idea of Communism in the Twentieth Century*. University of Chicago Press.

Gadamer, H.-G. 1975. *Truth and Method*. London: Sheed and Ward.

Gane, N. (ed.) 2004. *The Future of Social Theory*. New York: Continuum.

Gaonkar, D. P. (ed.) 2001. *Alternative Modernities*. Durham, NC: Duke University Press.

Gellner, E. 1998. *Language and Solitude: Wittgenstein, Malinowski and the Habsburg Dilemma*. Cambridge University Press.

Giddens, A. 1984. *The Constitution of Society*. Cambridge: Polity Press.

Giddens, A. 1991. *Modernity and Self-Identity*. Cambridge: Polity Press.

Gilroy, P. 1993. *Black Atlantic: Modernity and Double Consciousness.* London: Verso.

Gilroy, P. 2004. *After Empire: Melancholia or Convival Culture?* London: Routledge.

Girard, R. 1981. *Violence and the Sacred.* Baltimore: Johns Hopkins University Press.

Goody, J. 2004. *Islam in Europe.* Cambridge: Polity Press.

Gould, C. 2007. 'Transnational Solidarities', *Journal of Social Philosophy* 38 (1): 148–64.

Grande, E. 2006. 'Cosmopolitan Political Science', *British Journal of Sociology* 57 (1): 87–111.

Greenfeld, L. 1992. *Nationalism: Five Roads to Modernity.* Cambridge, MA: Harvard University Press.

Gutmann, A. 2003. *Identity in Democracy.* Princeton University Press.

Habermas, J. 1984. *Theory of Communicative Action*, Vol. 1. Cambridge: Polity Press.

Habermas, J. 1986. *Autonomy and Solidarity.* London: Verso.

Habermas, J. 1987a. *Theory of Communicative Action*, Vol. 2. Cambridge: Polity Press.

Habermas, J. 1987b. *The Philosophical Discourse of Modernity.* Cambridge: Polity Press.

Habermas, J. 1989. *The Structural Transformation of the Public Sphere.* Cambridge: Polity Press.

Habermas, J. 1992. 'Citizenship and National Identity: Some Reflections on the Future of Europe', *Praxis International* 12 (1): 1–19.

Habermas, J. 1994. 'Struggles for Recognition in the Democratic Constitutional State', in Gutmann, A. (ed.) *Multiculturalism: Examining the Politics of Recognition.* Princeton University Press.

Habermas, J. 1996. *Between Facts and Norms: Contributions to a Discourse Theory of Law and Democracy.* Cambridge: Polity Press.

Habermas, J. 1997. 'Kant's Idea of Perpetual Peace, with the Benefit of Two Hundred Years' Hindsight', in Bohman, J. and Lutz-Bachmann, M. (eds.) *Perpetual Peace: Essays on Kant's Cosmopolitan Ideal.* Cambridge, MA: MIT Press.

Habermas, J. 1998. *The Inclusion of the Other: Studies in Political Theory.* Cambridge, MA: MIT Press.

Habermas, J. 1999. 'The War in Kosovo: Bestiality and Humanity: A War on Border between Legality and Morality', *Constellations* 6 (3): 263–72.

Habermas, J. 2001a. 'Why Europe Needs a Constitution?', *New Left Review* 11 (Sept.–Oct.).

Habermas, J. 2001b. *The Postnational Constellation.* Cambridge: Polity Press.

Habermas, J. 2003. 'Towards a Cosmopolitan Europe', *Journal of Democracy* 14 (4): 86–100.

Habermas, J. 2005. 'Equal Treatment of Cultures and the Limits of Postmodern Liberalism', *The Journal of Political Philosophy* 13 (1): 1–28.

Habermas, J. 2006. 'Religion in the Public Sphere', *European Journal of Philosophy* 14 (1): 1–25.

Habermas, J. and Ratzinger, J. 2005. *Dialektik der Säkularisierung. Über Vernunft und Religion*. Frieburg: Verlag Herder.

Halbfass, W. 1988. *India and Europe: An Essay in Understanding*. Albany: State University of New York Press.

Halecki, O. 1962. *The Limits and Divisions of European History*. Notre Dame University Press.

Halman, L. and Draulans, V. 2006. 'How Secular is Europe?' *British Journal of Sociology* 57: 263–88.

Hann, C. and Dunn, E. 1996. *Civil Society: Changing Western Models*. London: Routledge.

Hannerz, U. 1990. 'Cosmopolitanism and Locals in World Culture', *Theory, Culture and Society* 7: 237–51.

Hannerz, U. 1996. *Transnational Connections: Culture, People, Places*. London: Routledge.

Hansen, R. and Weil, P. 2001. *Towards a European Nationality: Citizenship, Immigration, and Nationality Law in the EU*. Basingstoke: Palgrave Macmillan.

Hardt, M. and Negri, A. 2000. *Empire*. Cambridge, MA: Harvard University Press.

Harrington, A. 2004. 'Ernst Troeltsch's Concept of Europe', *European Journal of Social Theory* 7: 479–98.

Harris, J. 2004. 'Nationality, Rights and Virtue: Some Approaches to Citizenship in Great Britain', in Bellamy, R., Castiglione, D. and Santoro, E. (eds.) *Lineages of European Citizenship*. London: Palgrave.

Harvey, J. 2007. 'Moral Solidarity and Empathetic Understanding: The Moral Value and Scope of the Relationship', *Journal of Social Philosophy* 38 (1): 22–37.

Hassner, P. 2002. 'Fixed Borders or Moving Borderlands?', in Zielonka, J. (ed.) *Europe Unbound: Enlarging and Reshaping the Boundaries of the European Union*. London: Routledge.

Hawley, J. (ed.) 2008. *India in Africa; Africa in India: Indian Ocean Cosmopolitanism*. Bloomington: Indiana University Press.

He, B. 2005. 'Minority Rights with Chinese Characteristics', in Kymlicka, W. and He, B. (eds.) *Multiculturalism in Asia*. Oxford University Press.

He, B. and Kymlicka, W. 2005. 'Introduction', in Kymlicka, W. and He, B. (eds.) *Multiculturalism in Asia*. Oxford University Press.

Heather, D. 1996. *World Citizenship and Government: Cosmopolitan Ideas in the History of Western Political Thought*. London: St Martin's Press.

Held, D. 1995. *Democracy and the Global Order*. Cambridge: Polity Press.

Held, D. 2002. 'Culture and Political Community: National, Global, and Cosmopolitan', in Vertovec, S. and Cohen, R. (eds.) *Conceiving Cosmopolitanism*. Oxford University Press.

Hellas, P. (ed.) 1998. *Religion, Modernity and Postmodernity*. Oxford: Blackwell.

Heller, A. 1999. *A Theory of History*. Oxford: Blackwell.

Herrman, R., Risse, T. and Breen, M. (eds.) 2004. *Transnational Identities: Becoming European in the EU*. New York: Rowman & Littlefield.

Hindess, B. 1998. 'Divide and Rule: The International Character of Modern Citizenship', *European Journal of Social Theory* 1 (1): 57–70.

Hobson, J. 2004. *The Eastern Origins of Western Civilization*. Cambridge University Press.

Hodgson, M. 1993. *Rethinking World History: Essays on Europe, Islam and World History*. Cambridge University Press.

Hoexter, M., Eisenstadt, S. N. and Levtzion, N. (eds.) 2002. *The Public Sphere in Muslim Societies*. New York: State University of New York.

Hollinger, D. 1995. *Postethnic America: Beyond Multiculuralism*. New York: Basic Books.

Holmes, D. 2000. *Integral Europe: Fast-Capitalism, Multiculturalism, Neofascism*. Princeton University Press.

Holmes, S. 2005. 'Nationalism in Europe', in Delanty, G. and Kumar, K. (eds.) *Handbook of Nations and Nationalism*. London: Sage.

Holton, R. 2002. 'Cosmopolitanism or Cosmpolitanisms? The Universal Races Congress of 1911', *Global Networks* 2 (2): 153–70.

Holton, D. 2009. *Cosmopolitanism: New Thinking and New Directions*. London: Palgrave Macmillan.

Honneth, A. 1996. *The Struggle for Recognition: The Moral Grammar of Social Conflicts*. Cambridge: Polity Press.

Hopkins, A. G. (ed.) 2002. *Globalization in World History*. London: Pimlico.

Husain, F. and O'Brien, M. 2000. 'Muslim Communities in Europe: Reconstruction and Transformation', *Current Sociology* 48 (4): 1–13.

Hutchings, K. and Dannreuther, R. (eds.) 1999. *Cosmopolitan Citizenship*. London: Macmillan.

Inglis, D. and Robertson, R. 2005. 'The Ecumenical Analytic: "Globalization", Reflexivity and the Revolution in Greek Historiography', *European Journal of Social Theory* 8 (2): 99–122.

Inglis, D. and Robertson, R. 2008. 'The Elementary Forms of Globality: Durkheim and the Emergence and Nature of Global Life', *Journal of Classical Sociology* 8 (1): 5–25.

Iriye, A. 1997. *Cultural Internationalism and World Order*. Baltimore: Johns Hopkins University Press.

Isin, E. 2002. *Being Political: Genealogies of Citizenship*. Minneapolis: University of Minnesota Press.

Isin, E. and Turner, B. (eds.) 2002. *Handbook of Citizenship Studies*. London: Sage.

Jabri, V. 2007. 'Solidarity and Spheres of Culture: The Cosmopolitan and the Postcolonial', *Review of International Studies* 33: 715–28.

Jacob, M. 2006. *Strangers Nowhere in the World: The Rise of Cosmopoltianism in Early Modern Europe*. Philadelphia: University of Pennsylvania Press.

Jacobsen, D. 1996 *Rights Across Borders: Immigration and the Decline of Citizenship*. Baltimore: Johns Hopkins University Press.

Jacoby, R. 1999. *The End of Utopia: Politics and Culture in an Age of Apathy*. New York: Basic Books.

James, W. (1977/1907) *A Pluralistic Universe*. Cambridge, MA: Harvard University Press.

Jameson, F. 2002. *A Singular Modernity*. London: Verso.

Jardine, L. and Brotton, J. (eds.) 2000. *Global Interests: Renaissance Art between East and West*. London: Reaktion Books.

Jaspers, K. 2001. *The Question of German Guilt*. New York: Fordham University Press.

Joas, H. 1999. 'The Modernity of Violence: Modernization Theory and the Problem of Violence', *International Sociology* 14 (4): 457–72.

Jonas, H. 1984. *The Imperative of Responsibility: In Search of an Ethics for the Technological Age*. University of Chicago Press.

Juergensmeyer, M. 2006. 'Nationalism and Religion', in Delanty, G. and Kumar, K. (eds.) *Handbook of Nations and Nationalism*. London: Sage.

Julien, F. 2008. *De l'universel*. Paris: Fayard.

Kaldor, M. 1996. 'Cosmopolitanism versus Nationalism: The New Divide', in Caplan, R. and Feffer, J. (eds.) *Europe's New Nationalism: States and Minorities in Conflict*. Oxford University Press.

Kamali, M. 2001. 'Civil Society and Islam: A Sociological Perspective', *European Journal of Sociology* XLII (3): 457–82.

Kamali, M. 2005. *Multiple Modernities, Civil Society and Islam: The Case of Iran and Turkey*. Liverpool University Press.

Kant, I. 1974. *Anthropology from a Pragmatic Point of View*. The Hague: Martinus Nijhoff.

Kant, I. 1991. 'Perpetual Peace'. Translated by H. B. Nisbet and edited by H. Reiss. *Kant: Political Writings*. Cambridge University Press.

Karagiannis, N. 2007a. 'Multiple Solidarities: Autonomy and Resistance', in Karagiannis, N. and Wagner, P. (eds.) *Varieties of World-making: Beyond Globalization*. Liverpool University Press.

Karagiannis, N. 2007b. 'Introduction: Solidarity in Europe – Politics, Religion, Knowledge', in Karagiannis, N. (ed.) *European Solidarity*. Liverpool University Press.

Kastoryano, R. 2002. *Negotiating Identity: States and Immigration in France and Germany*. Princeton University Press.

Kaya, I. 2003. *Social Theory and Later Modernities: The Turkish Experience*. Liverpool University Press.

Keane, J. 2000. 'Secularism?' *The Political Quarterly* 3 (5): 5–19.

Keating, M. 1998. *The New Regionalism in Western Europe*. Cheltenham: Edward Elgar.

Kelly, D. and Reid, A. (eds.) 1998. *Asian Freedoms: The Idea of Freedom in East and Southeast Asia*. Cambridge University Press.

Kendall, G., Woodward, I., and Skribis, Z. 2009. *The Sociology of Cosmopolitanism*. London: Palgrave Macmillan.

Kivisto, P. 2002. *Multiculturalism in a Global Society*. Oxford: Blackwell.

Kleingeld, P. 1999. 'Six Varieties of Cosmopolitanism', *Journal of the History of Ideas* 60 (3): 505–24.

Kofman, E. 2005. 'Figures of the Cosmopolitan: Privileged Nationals and National Outsiders', *Innovation: The European Journal of Social Research* 18 (1): 83–97.

Kögler, H.-H. 2005. 'Constructing a Cosmopolitan Public Sphere: Hermeneutic Capabilities and Universal Values', *European Journal of Social Theory* 8 (4): 297–320.

Koselleck, R. 1984. *Futures Past: On the Semantics of Historical Time*. Cambridge, MA: MIT Press.

Kriesi, H. P., Grande, E., Lachat, R., Dolezal, M., Bornschier, S. and Foley, T. 2006. 'Globalization and the Transformation of National Public Space: Six European Case Studies', *European Journal of Political Research* 45: 921–56.

Kristeva, J. 1991. *Strangers to Ourselves*. New York: Columbia University Press.

Kristeva, J. 1993 *Nations without Nationalism*. New York: Columbia University Press.

Kung, H. 1993. *Towards a Global Ethics: An Introductory Declaration*. Chicago: Parliament of the World's Religions.

Kurasawa, F. 2004. 'Cosmopolitanism from Below: Alternative Globalization and the Creation of a Solidarity without Bounds', *Arch. Europ. Social.* XLV (2): 233–55.

Kurasawa, F. 2004. *The Ethnological Imagination: A Crisis Cultural Critique of Modernity*. Minneapolis: University of Minnesota Press.

Kwok-bun, C. 2005. *Chinese Identities, Ethnicity and Cosmopolitanism*. London: Routledge.

Kymlicka, W. 1995. *Multicultural Citizenship: A Liberal Theory of Minority Rights*. Oxford University Press.

Kymlicka, W. 2005. 'Liberal Multiculturalism; Western Models, Global Trends, and Asia Debates', in Kymlicka, W. and He, B. (eds.) *Multiculturalism in Asia*. Oxford University Press.

Kymlicka, W. and He, B. (eds.) 2005. *Multiculturalism in Asia*. Oxford University Press.

Kymlicka, W. and Norman, W. (eds.) 2001. *Citizenship in Diverse Societies*. Oxford University Press.

Kymlicka, W. and Straehle, C. 1999. 'Cosmopolitanism, Nation-States, and Minority Nationalism: A Critical Review of Recent Literature', *European Journal of Philosophy* 7 (1): 65–88.

Laborde, C. 2002. 'From Constitutional to Civic Patriotism', *British Journal of Political Science* 32: 591–612.

Lach, D. F. 1970. *Asia in the Making of Europe*, Vol. 1. University of Chicago Press

Lach, D. F. 1977. *Asia in the Making of Europe*, Vol. 2. University of Chicago Press.

Lamont, M. and Aksartova, S. 2002. 'Ordinary Cosmopolitanisms: Strategies for Bridging Racial Boundaries among Working-class Men', *Theory, Culture & Society* 19 (4): 1–25.

Lash, S. 2002. *Critique of Information*. London: Sage.

Latouch, S. 1996. *The Westernization of the World*. Cambridge: Polity Press.

Latour, B. 1993. *We Have Never Been Modern*. Hemel Hempstead: Harvester Wheatsheaf.

Latour, B. 2004. 'Whose Cosmos, Which Cosmopolitics? Comments on the Peace Terms of Ulrich Beck', *Common Culture* 10 (3): 450–62.

Latour, B. 2005. *Reassembling the Social: An Introduction to Actor-Network Theory*. Oxford University Press.

Lavenex, S. 2004. 'EU External Governance in "Wider Europe"', *Journal of European Public Policy* 11 (4): 680–700.

Lawson, S. (ed.) 2003. *Europe and the Asia-Pacific*. London: RoutledgeCurzon.

Lechner, F. and Boli, J. 2005. *World Culture: Origins and Consequences*. Oxford: Blackwell.

Lefort, C. 1986. 'The Question of Democracy', in *Democracy and Political Theory*. Cambridge: Polity Press.

Lehning, P. and Weale, A. (eds.) 1997. *Citizenship, Democracy, and Justice in the New Europe*. London: Routledge.

Levenson, J. R. 1971. *Revolution and Cosmopolitanism: the Western Stage and the Chinese Stages*. Berkeley: University of California Press.

Levy, D. and Sznaider, N. 2002. 'Memory Unbound – The Holocaust and the Formation of Cosmopolitan Memory', *European Journal of Social Theory* 5 (1): 87–106.

Levy, D., Pensky, M., and Torpey, J. (eds.) 2005. *Old Europe, New Europe, Core Europe: Transatlanitic Relations after the Iraq War*. London: Verso.

Linklater, A. 1998. *The Transformation of Political Community*. Cambridge: Polity Press.

Lockwood, D. 1964. 'Social Integration and System Integration', in Zollschan, G. K. and Hirsch, W. (eds.) *Explorations in Social Change*. Boston: Houghton Mifflin.

Löwith, K. 1949. *Meaning in History: The Theological Presuppositions of the Philosophy of History*. University of Chicago Press.

Lu, C. 2000. 'The One and Many Faces of Cosmopolitanism', *The Journal of Political Philosophy* 8 (2): 244–67.

Luhmann, N. 1990. 'The World Society as a Social System', in *Essays in Self-reflexivity*. New York: Columbia University Press.

Lukes, S. 2003. *Liberals and Cannibals: The Implications of Diversity*. London: Verso.

Lyotard, J.-F. 1984. *The Postmodern Condition: A Report on Knowledge*. Manchester University Press.

McCarthy, T. 2001. 'On Reconcilling Cosmopolitan Unity and National Diversity', in Gaikar, D. P. (ed.) *Alternative Modernities*. Durham, NC: Duke University Press.

MacIntyre, A. 1984. 'Translation and Tradition', in *After Virtue: A Study in Moral Theory*. University of Notre Dame.

McNeil, W. 1963. *The Rise of the West: A History of Human Community*. University of Chicago Press.

McNeil, W. 1986. *Policy-Ethnicity and National Unity in World History*. Toronto University Press.

McRobbie, A. 2006. 'Vulnerability, Violence and (Cosmopolitan) Ethics: Butler's *Precarious Life*', *British Journal of Sociology* 57 (1): 69–86.

Madeley, J. 2003a. 'European Liberal Democracy and the Principle of State Religious Neutrality', *West European Politics* 26 (1): 1–24.

Madeley, J. 2003b. 'A Framework for the Comparative Analysis of Church-State Relations in Europe', *West European Politics* 26 (1): 23–50.

Madeley, J. and Enyedi, Z. (eds.) 2003. Special issue on Church and State in Contemporary Europe, *West European Politics* 26 (1).

Madsen, R. 2002. 'Confucian Conceptions of Civil Society', in Chambers, S. and Kymlicka, W. (eds.) *Alternative Conceptions of Civil Society*. Princeton University Press.

Madsen, R., Sullivan, W., Swidler, A. and Tipton, S. (eds.) 2002. *Meaning and Modernity: Religion, Polity, and the Self*. Berkeley: University of California Press.

Majone, G. 1996. *Regulating Europe*. London: Routledge.

Manent, P. 2006. *A World Beyond Politics? A Defence of the National State*. Princeton University Press.

Mann, M. 1987. 'Ruling Class Strategies and Citizenship', *Sociology* 21 (3): 339–54.

Marshall, T. H. 1992. *Citizenship and Social Class*. London: Pluto Press.

Marx, K. and Engels, F. 1967. *The Communist Manifesto*. London: Penguin.

Mau, S., Mewes, J. and Zimmerman, A. 2008. 'Cosmopolitan Attitudes Through Transnational Social Practices', *Global Networks* 8 (1): 1–24.

Mayhew, L. 1997. *The New Public: Professional Communication and the Means of Social Influence*. Cambridge University Press.

Mead, G. W. 1934. *Mind, Self and Society*. University of Chicago Press.

Meehan, E. 1993. *Citizenship and the European Community*. London: Sage.

Meinecke, F. 1970. *Cosmopolitanism and the National State*. Princeton University Press.

Meinhof, U. H. (ed.) 2002. *Living (with) Borders: Identity Discourses on East-West Borders in Europe*. Aldershot: Ashgate.

Mendieta, E. 2007. *Global Fragility: Globalization, Latin Americanization and Critical Theory*. New York: SUNY.

Menendez, A. J. 2004. 'A Pius Europe? Why Europe Should not Define itself as Christian', ARENA Working Paper no. 10/04.

Merton, R. 1968 [1947]. 'Patterns of Influence: Local and Cosmopolitan Influentials', in *Social Theory and Social Structure*. New York: Free Press.

Meyer, J. W., Boli, J., Thomas, G. M. and Ramirez, F. O. 1997. 'World Society and the Nation-state', *The American Journal of Sociology* 103 (1): 141–81.

Mignolo, W. 2000. *Local Histories/Global Designs: Coloniality, Subaltern Knowledge, and Border Thinking*. Princeton University Press.

Mignolo, W. and Tlostanova, A. 2006. 'Theorizing from the Borders: Shifting to Geo- and Body Politics of Knowledge', *European Journal of Social Theory* 9 (2): 205–11.

Milward, A. 1993. *The European Rescue of the Nation-State*. London: Routledge.

Mol, A. and Law, J. 1994. 'Regions, Networks and Fluids: Anaemia and Social Topology', *Social Studies of Science* 24: 641–71.

Mouzelis, N. 1999. 'Modernity: A Non-European Conceptualization', *British Journal of Sociology* 50 (1): 141–59.

Mozaffari, M. (ed.) 2002. *Globalization and Civilization*. London: Routledge.

Müller, J.-W. 2007. *Constitutional Patriotism*. Princeton University Press.

Müller-Graff, P.-C. (1998) 'Whose Responsibilities are Frontiers?', in Anderson, M. and Bort, E. (eds.) *The Frontiers of Europe*. London: Pinter.

Munck, R. and de Silva, P. (eds.) 2000. *Postmodern Insurgencies: Political Violence, Identity Formation, and Peacemaking in Contemporary Perspective*. London: Macmillan.

Nash, K. 2003. 'Cosmopolitan Political Community: Why Does it Feel so Right?', *Constellations* 10 (4): 506–18.

Nava, M. 2002. 'Cosmopolitan Modernity: Everyday Imaginaries and the Register of Difference', *Theory, Culture and Society* 19 (1–2): 81–99.

Nava, M. 2007. *Visceral Cosmopolitanism*. Oxford: Berg.

Nederveen Pieterse, J. 2004. *Globalization and Culture: Global Mélange*. New York: Rowman & Littlefield.

Nederveen Pieterse, J. 2006. 'Emancipatory Cosmopolitanism: Towards an Agenda', *Development and Change* 37 (6): 1247–57.

Negt, O. and Kluge, A. 2003. *Öfftlichkeit und Erfahrung. Zur Organisationsanalyse von bürgerlicher und proletarischer Öffentlichkeit*. Frankfurt: Suhrkamp.

Nelson, B. 1976. 'Orient and Occident in Max Weber', *Social Research* 43 (1): 114–29.

Nelson, B. 1981. *On the Roads to Modernity*. New York: Rowman & Littlefield.

Newman, D. 2003. 'On Borders and Power: A Theoretical Framework', *Journal of Borderlands Studies* 18 (1): 13–25.

Newman, D. 2004. 'Conflict at the Interface: The Impact of Boundaries and Borders on Contemporary Ethno-National Conflict', in Flint, C. (ed.) *The Impact of Boundaries and Borders on Contemporary Ethno-National Conflict*. Oxford University Press.

Newman, D. and Paasi, A. 1998. 'Fences and Neighbours in the Postmodern World: Boundary Narratives in Political Geography', *Progress in Human Geography* 22 (2): 186–207.

Norris, P. 1997. 'Towards a More Cosmopolitan Social Science?', *European Journal of Political Research* 30 (1): 17–34.

Norris, P. 2000. 'Global Governance and Cosmopolitan Citizens', in Nye, J. (ed.) *Governance in a Globalizing World*. Washington, DC: Brookings Institute Press.

Norris, P. and Inglehart, R. 2004. *Sacred and Secular: Religion and Politics Worldwide*. Cambridge University Press.

Nussbaum, M. 1996. 'Patriotism and Cosmopolitanism', in Cohen, J. (ed.) *For Love of Country: Debating the Limits of Patriotism*. University of Chicago Press.

Nussbaum, M. 1997. 'Kant and Cosmopolitanism', in Bohman, J. and Lutz-Bachmann, M. (eds.) *Perpetual Peace: Essays on Kant's Cosmopolitan Ideal*. Cambridge, MA: MIT Press.

Nussbaum, M. 2001. *The Fragility of Goodness: Luck and Ethics in Greek Tragedy and Philosophy*. Cambridge University Press.

O'Brien, K. (1997). *Narratives of Enlightenment: Cosmopolitan History from Voltaire to Gibbon*. Cambridge University Press.

O'Dowd, L. 2002. 'The Changing Significance of European Borders', *Regional and Federal Studies* 12 (4): 13–36.

Ohmae, K. 1996. *The End of the Nation-State: The Rise of Regional Economies*. London: HarperCollins.

Ong, A. 1999. *Flexible Citizenship: The Cultural Logics of Transnationality*. Durham, NC: Duke University Press.

Outhwaite, W. 2007. 'Who Needs Solidarity?', in Karagiannis, N. (ed.) *European Solidarity*. Liverpool University Press.

Özbudun, E. and Keyman, F. 2002. 'Cultural Globalization in Turkey', in Berger, P. and Huntington, S. (eds.) *Many Globalizations*. Oxford University Press.

Paasi, A. 1996. *Territory, Boundaries and Consciousness*. New York: John Wiley.

Paasi, A. 2005. 'The Changing Discourse on Political Boundaries', in Houtum, H., van Kramsch, O. and Zierhofer, W. (eds.) *B/Ordering Space*. Aldershot: Ashgate.

Papastergiadis, N. 2006. 'Glimpses of Cosmopolitanism in the Hospitality of Art', *European Journal of Social Theory* 10 (1): 139–52.

Parekh, B. 2000. *Rethinking Multiculturalism: Cultural Diversity and Political Theory*. London: Macmillan.

Pensky, M. 2007. 'Two Cheers for Cosmopolitanism: Cosmopolitan Solidarity as a Second-Order Inclusion', *Journal of Social Philosophy* 38 (1): 165–84.

Pettit, P. 1997. *Republicanism: A Theory of Freedom and Government*. Oxford University Press.

Phillips, T. 2002. 'Imagined Communities and Self-Identity: An Exploratory Quantitative Analysis', *Sociology* 36 (3): 597–617.

Pogge, T. 1992. 'Cosmopolitanism and Sovereignty', *Ethics* 103 (Oct.): 48–75.

Pogge, T. 2002. 'Moral Universalism and Global Economic Justice', *Politics, Philosophy and Economics* 1: 29–58.

Pollard, N., Latore, M. and Sriskandarajah, D. 2008. *Floodgates or Turnstiles? Post-EU Enlargement Migration Flows to (and from) the UK*. London: Institute of Public Policy Research (IPPR).

Pollis, A. 2005. 'Greece: A Problematic Secular State', in Safran, S. (ed.) *The Secular and the Sacred: Nation, Religion and Politics*. London: Frank Cass.

Pollock, S. 2002. 'Cosmopolitan and Vernacular in History', in Breckenridge, C. A., Bhabha, H., Pollock, S. and Chakrabarty, D. (eds.) *Cosmopolitanism*. Durham, NC: Duke University Press.

Pollock, S. 2006. *The Language of the Gods in the World of Men: Sanskrit, Culture, and Power in Premodern India*. Berkeley: University of California Press.

Popkewitz, T. 2008. *Cosmopolitanism and the Age of School Reform*. London: Routledge.

Povinelli, E. 2002. *The Cunning of Recognition: Indigenous Alterities and the Making of Australian Multiculturalism*. Durham, NC: Duke University Press.

Powell, J. L. 2005. *Social Theory and Aging*. Lanham: Rowman & Littlefield.

Preuss, U. 2004. 'Problems of a Concept of European Citizenship', in Bellamy, R., Castiglione, D. and Santoro, E. (eds.) *Lineages of European Citizenship*. London: Palgrave.

Preyer, G. and Bos, M. 2001. 'Introduction: Borderlines in Time of Globalization', *Protosociology* 15.

Putnam, R. 1999. *Bowling Alone*. New York: Simon & Schuster.

Rajan, G. and Sharma, S. (eds.) 2006. *New Cosmopolitanism: South-Asians in the US*. Stanford University Press.

Ramos, R. 2004. 'Portuguese, but not Citizens: Restricted Citizenship in Contemporary Portugal', in Bellamy, R., Castiglione, D. and Santoro, E. (eds) *Lineages of European Citizenship*. London: Palgrave.

Rapport, N. and Stade, R. 2007. 'A Cosmopolitan Turn – or Return? *Social Anthropology* 15 (2): 223–35.

Rawls, J. 1987. 'The Idea of an Overlapping Consensus', *Oxford Journal of Legal Studies* 7: 1–25.

Rawls, J. 1993. *Political Liberalism*. New York: Columbia University Press.

Rawls, J. 1999. *A Law of Peoples*. Cambridge, MA: Harvard University Press.

Remond, R. 1999. *Religion and Society in Modern Europe*. Oxford: Blackwell.

Renteln, A. 1990. *International Human Rights: Universalism versus Relativism*. London: Sage.

Restivo, S. 1991. *The Sociological Worldview*. Oxford: Blackwell.

Ricoeur, P. 1995. 'Reflections on a New Ethos for Europe', *Philosophy and Social Criticism* 21 (5/6): 3–13.

Ricoeur, P. 1996. *Oneself as Another*. University of Chicago Press.

Robbins, B. 1998. 'Comparative Cosmopolitanisms', in Cheah, P. and Robbins, B. (eds.) *Cosmopolitics: Thinking and Feeling Beyond the Nation*. Minneapolis: Minnesota University Press.

Robbins, K. 2006. *The Challenge of Transcultural Diversities: Cultural Policy and Cultural Diversity*. Strasbourg: Council of Europe.

Robertson, R. 1992. *Globalization: Social Theory and Global Culture*. London: Sage.

Robinson, W. 2001. 'Social Theory and Globalization: the Rise of a Transnational State', *Theory and Society* 30 (2): 157–200.

Rokkan, S. 1999. *State Formation, Nation Building, and Mass Politics. The Theory of Stein Rokkan*. Oxford University Press.

Romm, J. 1992. *The Edges of the Earth in Ancient Thought*. Princeton University Press.

Rorty, R. 1998. 'Justice as a Larger Loyalty', in Cheah, P. and Robbins, B. (eds.) *Cosmopolitics: Thinking and Feeling Beyond the Nation*. Minneapolis: Minnesota University Press.

Rosenfeld, S. 2002. 'Citizens of Nowhere in Particular: Cosmopolitanism, Writing, and Political Engagement in Eighteenth-Century Europe', *National Identities* 4 (1): 25–43.

Ross, M. 2007. 'Promoting Solidarity: From Public Services to a European Model of Competition?', *Common Market Law Review* 44: 1057–80.

Roudemetof, V. 2005. 'Transnationalism, Cosmopolitanism and Glocalization', *Current Sociology* 53 (1): 113–15.

Roudemetof, V. and Haller, W. 2007. 'Social Indicators of Cosmopolitanism and Localism in Eastern and Western Europe', in Rumford, C. (ed.) *Cosmopolitanism and Europe*. Liverpool University Press.

Rousseau, J. 1997. 'Of the Social Contract' (Geneva Manuscript) *Rousseau: The Social Contract and Other Later Political Writings*, edited and translated by V. Gourevitch. Cambridge University Press.

Ruggie, J. 1995. 'Territoriality and Beyond: Problematizing Modernity in International Relations', *International Organization* 47 (1): 139–74.

Rumford, C. 2002. *The European Union: A Political Sociology*. London: Routledge.

Rumford, C. (ed.) 2006a. *Cosmopolitanism and Europe*. Liverpool University Press.

Rumford, C. 2006b. 'Borders and ReBordering', in Delanty, G. (ed.) *Europe and Asia Beyond East and West*. London: Routledge.

Rumford, C. 2007. 'Does Europe have Cosmopolitan Borders?', *Globalizations* 4 (3): 1–13.

Rumford, C. 2008. *Cosmopolitan Spaces: Europe, Globalization, Theory*. London: Routledge.

Safran, W. 2003. 'Religion and *Laïcité* in a Jacobin Republic: The Case of France', in Safran, S. (ed.) *The Secular and the Sacred: Nation, Religion and Politics*. London: Frank Cass.

Said, E. 1978. *Orientalism*. London: Penguin.

Sassen, S. 1996. *Losing Control? Sovereignty in an Age of Globalization*. New York: Columbia University Press.

Sassen, S. 2001. 'Spatialities and Temporalities of the Global Economy: Elements for a Theorization', in Appadurai, A. (ed.) *Globalization*. Durham, NC: Duke University Press.

Sassen, S. 2002. *Global Networks/Linked Cities*. London: Routledge.

Sassen, S. 2007. *Territory, Authority, Rights*. New York: Norton.

Scott, D. and Hirschkind, C. (eds.) 2006. *Powers of the Secular Modern: Talal Asad and his Interlocutors*. Stanford University Press.

Schlereth, T. 1977. *The Cosmopolitan Ideal in Enlightenment Thought*. South Bend: University of Notre Dame University Press.

Schlesinger, P. and Foret, R. F. 2006. 'Political Roof and Sacred Canopy? Religion and the EU Constitution', *European Journal of Social Theory* 9 (1): 59–81.

Schwab, R. 1984. *The Oriental Renaissance: Europe's Re-Discovery of India and the East 1680–1880*. New York: Columbia University Press.

Schwartz, B. 1985. *The World of Thought in Ancient China*. Cambridge, MA: Harvard University Press.

Schwartz, J. 2007. 'From Domestic to Global Solidarity: The Dialectic of the Particular and Universal in the Building of Social Solidarity', *Journal of Social Philosophy* 38 (1): 131–47.

Scüzs, J. 1988. 'Three Historical Regions of Europe', in Keane, J. (ed.) *Civil Society and the State*. London: Verso.

Seidentop, L. 2000. *Democracy in Europe*. London: Penguin.

Seligman, A. 2000. *Modernity's Wager: Authority, the Self and Transcendence*. Princeton University Press.

Sellars, J. 2006. *Stoicism*. Berkeley: University of California Press.

Sennett, R. 1977. *The Fall of Public Man*. New York: Knoff.

Shabani, O. 2007. 'Cosmopolitan Justice and Immigration', *European Journal of Social Theory* 10 (1): 87–98.

Shaw, M. 1997. 'The State of Globalization: Towards a Theory of State Transformation', *Review of International Political Economy* 4 (3): 497–513.

Shore, C. 2000. *Building Europe: The Cultural Politics of European Integration*. London: Routledge.

Shore, C. 2004. 'Whither European Citizenship: Eros and Civilization Revisted', *European Journal of Social Theory* 7 (1): 27–44.

Siim, B. and Skjeie, H. 2004. 'The Scandinavian Model of Citizenship', in Bellamy, R., Castiglione, D. and Santoro, E. (eds.) *Lineages of European Citizenship*. London: Palgrave.

Singer, P. 2003. *One World: The Ethics of Globalization*. New Haven: Yale University Press.

Skribis, Z. and Woodward, I. 2008. 'The Ambivalence of Ordinary Cosmopolitanism: Investigating the Limits of Cosmopolitan Openness', *Sociological Review* 55 (4): 730–47.

Skribis, Z., Kendall, G. and Woodward, I. 2001. 'Locating Cosmopolitanism: Between Humanist Ideas and Grounded Social Category', *Theory, Culture and Society* 21 (6): 115–36.

Smelser, N. and Alexander, J. (eds.) 1999. *Diversity and its Discontents: Cultural Conflict and Common Ground in Contemporary American Society*. New Haven: Princeton University Press.

Smith, A. 1992. 'National Identity and the Idea of Europe', in *Nations and Nationalism in a Global Era*. Cambridge: Polity Press.

Smith, A. and Webster, F. (eds.) 1996. *The Postmodern University?* Buckingham: Open University Press.

Smith, W. 2007. 'Cosmopolitan Citizenship: Virtue, Irony and Worldliness', *European Journal of Social Theory* 10 (1): 37–52.

Sorensen, G. 2004. *The Transformation of the State*. London: Palgrave.

Soysal, Y. 1994. *The Limits of Citizenship*. University of Chicago Press.

Spohn, W. 2003. 'European East-West Integration, Nation-Building and National Identities: The Reconstruction of German-Polish Relations', in Spohn, W. and Triandafyllidou, A. (eds.) *Europeanization, National Identities and Migration*. London: Routledge.

Steinberg, S. 1989. *The Ethnic Myth*. New York: Beacon.

Stevenson, N. (ed.) 2000. *Culture and Citizenship*, London: Sage.

Stevenson, N. 2002. *Cultural Citizenship: Cosmopolitan Questions*. Buckingham: Open University Press.

Stevenson, N. 2006. 'European Cosmopolitan Solidarity', *European Journal of Social Theory* 9 (4): 485–500.

Strange, S. 1996. *The Retreat of the State. The Diffusion of Power in the World Economy*. Cambridge University Press.

Strydom, P. 1999a. 'Triple Contingency: The Theoretical Problem of the Pubic in Communication Societies', *Philosophy and Social Criticism* 25 (2): 1–25.

Strydom, P. 1999b. 'The Challenge of Collective Responsibility for Sociology', *Current Sociology* 47 (3): 65–82.

Strydom, P. 2002. *Risk, Environment and Society*. Buckingham: Open University Press.

Strydom, P. 2006. 'Contemporary European Cognitive Social Theory', in Delanty, G. (ed.) *Handbook of Contemporary European Social Theory*. London: Routledge.

Stuurman, S. 2004. 'Citizenship and Cultural Difference in France and the Netherlands', in Bellamy, R., Castiglione, D. and Santoro, E. (eds.) *Lineages of European Citizenship*. London: Palgrave.

Suarez-Navaz, L. 2004. *Rebordering the Mediterranean: Boundaries and Citizenship in Southern Europe*. New York: Berghahn Books.

Szersznski, B. and Urry, J. 2002. 'Cultures of Cosmopolitanism', *The Sociological Review* 50 (4): 461–81.

Szersznski, B. and Urry, J. 2006. 'Visuality, Mobility and Cosmopolitan: Inhabiting the World from Afar', *British Journal of Sociology* 57 (1): 113–31.

Tan, K.-C. 2004. *Justice without Borders: Cosmopolitanism, Nationalism and Patriotism*. Cambridge University Press.

Tarrow, S. 2005. *The New Transnational Activism*. Cambridge University Press.

Taylor, C. 1994. 'The Politics of Recognition', in Gutman, A. (ed.) *Multiculturalism: Examining the Politics of Recognition*. Princeton University Press.

Taylor, C. 1999. 'Conditions of an Unforced Consensus on Human Rights', in Bauer, J. and Bell, D. *The East Asian Challenge for Human Rights*. Cambridge University Press.

Taylor, C. 2007. *A Secular Age*. Cambridge, MA: Harvard University Press.

Taylor, P. 1999. *Modernities: A Geopolitical Interpretation*. Cambridge: Polity Press.

Therborn, G. 1994. *European Modernity and Beyond: the Trajectory of European Societies, 1945–2000*. London: Sage.

Therborn, G. 2003.'Entangled Modernities', *European Journal of Social Theory* 6 (3): 293–305.

Thompson, C.J. and Tambyah, S.K. 1999. 'Trying to be Cosmopolitan', *Journal of Consumer Research* 26: 214–41.

Tomlinson, J. 1999. *Globalization and Culture*. Cambridge: Polity Press.

Tong, S. 2009. 'Varieties of Universalism', *European Journal of Social Theory* 12 (4).

Torpey, J. 2000. *The Invention of the Passport: Surveillance, Citizenship, and the State*. Cambridge University Press.

Toulmin, S. 1992. *Cosmopolis: The Hidden Agenda of Modernity*. University of Chicago Press.

Touraine, A. 1977. *The Self-Production of Society*. University of Chicago Press.

Touraine, A. 1995. *Critique of Modernity*. Oxford: Blackwell.

Touraine, A. 1998. 'Sociology without Society', *Current Sociology* 16: 547–94.

Touraine, A. 2000. *Can we Live Together Equal and Different?* Cambridge: Polity Press.

Toyota, M. 2005. 'Subjects of the Nation without Citizenship: The Case of the "Hill Tribes"', in Kymlicka, W. and He, B. (eds.) *Multiculturalism in Asia*. Oxford University Press.

Trenz, H.-J. and Eder, K. 2004. 'The Democratizing Dynamics of a European Public Sphere', *European Journal of Social Theory* 7 (1): 5–25.

Troeltsch, E. 1931. *The Social Teachings of the Christian Churches*, Vols. 1 and 2. London: Allen and Unwin.

Tully, J. 1995. *Strange Multiplicities: Constitutionalism in an Age of Diversity*. Cambridge University Press.

Turner, B. S. (ed.) 1993. *Citizenship and Social Theory*. London: Sage.

Turner, B. S. 2001. 'Cosmopolitan Virtue: On Religion in a Global Age', *European Journal of Social Theory* 4 (2): 131–52.

Turner, B. S. 2002. 'Cosmopolitan Virtue: Globalization and Patriotism', *Theory, Culture & Society* 19 (1): 45–63.

Turner, B. S. 2005. 'The Sociology of Religion', in Calhoun, C., Rojek, C. and Turner, B. (eds.) *Handbook of Sociology*. London: Sage.

Turner, B. S. 2006. 'Classical Sociology and Cosmopolitanism: A Critical Defence of the Social', *British Journal of Sociology* 57 (1): 133–51.

Turner, B. S. and Rojek, C. 2001. *Society and Culture: Principles of Scarcity and Solidarity*. London: Sage.

Turner, C. 2004. 'Jürgen Habermas: European or German?', *European Journal of Political Theory* 3 (1): 293–314.

Turner, F. 1921. *The Frontier in American History*. New York: Holt.

Urry, J. 2000. *Sociology Beyond Societies: Mobilities for the Twenty-First Century*. London: Routledge.

Urry, J. 2002. *Global Complexity*. Cambridge: Polity Press.

Vertovec, S. and Cohen, R. (eds.) 2002. *Conceiving Cosmopolitanism*. Oxford University Press.

Vertovec, S. and Rogers, A. (eds.) 1998. *Muslim European Youth: Reproducing Ethnicity, Religion, Culture*. Aldershot: Ashgate.

Vidar, K. and Delanty, G. 2008. '*Mitteleuropa* and the European Heritage', *European Journal of Social Theory* 11 (2): 203–18.

Wagner, P. 1994. *A Sociology of Modernity: Liberty and Discipline*. London: Routledge.

Wagner, P. 2008. *Modernity as Experience and Interpretation: A New Sociology of Modernity*. Cambridge: Polity Press.

Wallerstein, I. 1996. 'Eurocentrism and its Avatars: The Dilemmas of Social Science', *New Left Review* 226: 93–108.

Walters, M. 2006. 'Border/Control', *European Journal of Social Theory* 9 (2): 187–203.

Walzer, M. 1983. *Thick and Thin: The Moral Argument at Home and Abroad*. New York: Basic Books.

Webb, W. P. 1952. *The Great Frontier*. Boston: Houghton Mifflin.

Weber, M. 1948. 'Religious Rejections of the World and Their Rejections', in Gerth, H. H. and Wright Mills, C. (eds.) *From Max Weber*. London: Routledge & Kegan Paul.

Weber, M. 1978. *The Protestant Ethic and the Spirit of Capitalism*. London: Allen & Unwin.

Weber, M. 1998. *Economy and Society*, Vol. 1. Berkeley: University of California Press.

Weber, M. 2007. 'The Concept of Solidarity in the Study of World Politics: Towards a Critical Theoretic Understanding', *Review of International Studies* 33: 693–713.

Weiler, J. 1999. *The Constitution of Europe*. Cambridge University Press.

Weiler, J. 2003. *Un' Europa cristianna*. Milan: Rizzoli.

Weiner, A. 1998. *European Citizenship Practice: Building Institutions of a Non-state*. Boulder: Westview Press.

Werbner, P. 1999. 'Global Pathways: Working Class Cosmopolitans and the Creation of Transnational Ethnic Worlds', *Social Anthropology* 7: 17–35.

Werbner, P. (ed.) 2008. *Anthropology and the New Cosmopolitanism*. Oxford: Berg.

Westwood, S. and Phizacklea, A. 2000. *Transnationalism and the Politics of Belonging*. London: Routledge.

Whittaker, C. 2000. 'Roman Frontiers and European Perceptions', *Journal of Historical Sociology* 13 (4): 462–82.

Williams, H. 2003. *Kant's Critique of Hobbes: Sovereignty and Cosmopolitanism*. London: Routledge.

Wilson, T. M. and Donnan, H. (eds.) 1998. *Border Identities: Nation and State at International Frontiers*. Cambridge University Press.

Wimmer, A. 2002. *Nationalist Exclusion and Ethnic Conflict: Shadows of Modernity*. Cambridge University Press.

Woodward, I., Skribis, Z. and Bean, C. 2008. 'Attitudes towards Globalization and Cosmopolitanism: Cultural Diversity, Personal Consumption and the National Economy', *British Journal of Sociology* 59 (2): 207–26.

Yegenoglu, M. 2005. 'Cosmopolitanism and Nationalism in a Globalising World', *Ethnic and Racial Studies* 28 (1): 103–32.

Yip, L. 2008. 'Sovereignty, Cosmopolitanism and the Ethics of European Foreign Policy', *European Journal of Political Theory* 7 (3).

Young, I. M. 1990. *Justice and the Politics of Difference*. Princeton University Press.

Young, I. M. 2000. *Inclusion and Democracy*. Oxford University Press.

Young, R. 1991. *White Mythologies: History Writing and the West*. London: Routledge.

Yuval-Davis, N. 1997. *Gender and Nation*. London: Sage.

Zimmerman, P. 1992. 'Technological Citizenship: A Normative Framework for Risk Studies', *Science, Technology and Human Values* 17 (4): 459–84.

Zolo, D. 1997. *Cosmopolis: Prospects for World Government*. Cambridge: Polity Press.

Zubaida, S. 1999. 'Cosmopolitanism and the Middle East', in Meijer, R. (ed.) *Cosmopolitanism, Identity and Authenticity in the Middle East*. Richmond: Curzon Press.

Index